THE
SACRED BOOKS OF THE EAST

Translated by
VARIOUS ORIENTAL SCHOLARS

Edited by
F. MAX MÜLLER

Vol. 6

SACRED BOOKS OF THE EAST

(50 VOLUMES)

Series Editor : *F. Max-Müller*

ISBN: 978-81-208-0101-1 (Set)

These volumes of the Sacred Books of the East series include translations of all the most important works of the seven non-Christian religions that have exercised a profound influence on the civilisations of the continent of Asia. The Vedic Brahmanic system claims 21 volumes, Buddhism 10, and Jainism 2; 8 volumes comprise Sacred Books of the Parsis; 2 volumes represent Islam; and 6 the two main indigenous systems of China. Translated by twenty leading authorities in their respective fields, the volumes have been edited by the late F. Max Müller. The inception, publication and the compilation of these books cover almost 34 years.

I. BUDDHISM

Vol. 49: Buddhist Mahayana Texts (2 Parts)
Vol. 11: Buddhist Suttas
Vol. 10: The Dhammapada and Sutta Nipata
Vols. 35 & 36: The Questions of King Milinda (2 Parts)
Vol. 21: The Saddharma Pundarika or the Lotus of the True Law
Vols. 13, 17 & 20: Vinaya Texts (3 Parts)

II. CHINESE

Vol. 19: The Fo-Sho-Hing-Tsan-King
Vols. 3, 16, 27, 28, 39 & 40: The Sacred Books of China (6 Parts)

III. A GENERAL INDEX

Vol. 50: A General Index to the Names and Subject-matter of the Sacred Books of the East

IV. ISLAM

Vols. 6 & 9: The Qur'an (2 Parts)

V. JAINISM

Vols. 22 & 45: The Jaina Sutras (2 Parts)

VI. PARSIS

Vols. 5, 18, 24, 37 & 47: Pahlavi Texts (5 Parts)
Vols. 4, 23 & 31: The Zend-Avesta (3 Parts)

VII. VEDIC-BRAHMANIC SYSTEM

Vol. 8: The Bhagavadgita with the Sanatsujatiya and the Anugita
Vols. 29 & 30: The Grihya-Sutras: Rules of Vedic Domestic Ceremonies (2 Parts)
Vol. 42: Hymns of the Atharva Veda together with Extracts from the Ritual Books and the Commentaries
Vol. 7: The Institutes of Vishnu
Vol. 25: The Laws of Manu
Vol. 33: The Minor Law Books
Vols. 2 & 14: The Sacred Laws of the Aryas as Taught in the Schools of Apastamba, Gautama, Vasishtha and Baudhayana (2 Parts)
Vols. 12, 26, 41, 43 & 44: The Satapatha Brahmana According to the Text of the Madhyandina School (5 Parts)
Vols. 1 & 15: The Upanishads (2 Parts)
Vols. 34 & 38: The Vedanta Sutras (2 Parts)
Vol. 48: The Vedanta-Sutras (with the commentary by Ramanuja)
Vols. 32 & 46: Vedic Hymns (2 Parts)

THE QUR'ĀN

PART I
CHAPTERS I TO XVI

Translated by
E.H. PALMER

MOTILAL BANARSIDASS PUBLISHERS
PRIVATE LIMITED • DELHI

*7th Reprint: Delhi, 2005, **2012***
First Published by the Oxford University Press, 1880

ISBN: 978-81-208-0107-3

MOTILAL BANARSIDASS
41 U.A. Bungalow Road, Jawahar Nagar, Delhi 110 007
8 Mahalaxmi Chamber, 22 Bhulabhai Desai Road, Mumbai 400 026
203 Royapettah High Road, Mylapore, Chennai 600 004
236, 9th Main III Block, Jayanagar, Bangalore 560 011
Sanas Plaza, 1302 Baji Rao Road, Pune 411 002
8 Camac Street, Kolkata 700 017
Ashok Rajpath, Patna 800 004
Chowk, Varanasi 221 001

UNESCO COLLECTION OF REPRESENTATIVE WORKS— Indian Series
This book has been accepted in the Indian Translation Series of the UNESCO Collection of Representative Works, jointly sponsored by the United Nations Educational Scientific and Cultural Organization (UNESCO) and the Government of India

Printed in India

By Jainendra Prakash Jain at Shri Jainendra Press,
A-45 Naraina, Phase-I, New Delhi 110 028
and Published by Narendra Prakash Jain for
Motilal Banarsidass Publishers Private Limited,
Bungalow Road, Delhi 110 007

RASHTRAPATI BHAVAN,
NEW DELHI-4
June 10, 1962

I am very glad to know that the Sacred Books of the East, published years ago by the Clarendon Press, Oxford, which have been out-of-print for a number of years, will now be available to all students of religion and philosophy. The enterprise of the publishers is commendable and I hope the books will be widely read.

S. RADHAKRISHNAN

PREFATORY NOTE TO THE NEW EDITION

Since 1948 the United Nations Educational, Scientific and Cultural Organization (UNESCO), upon the recommendation of the General Assembly of the United Nations, has been concerned with facilitating the translation of the works most representative of the culture of certain of its Member States, and, in particular, those of Asia.

One of the major difficulties confronting this programme is the lack of translators having both the qualifications and the time to undertake translations of the many outstanding books meriting publication. To help overcome this difficulty in part, UNESCO's advisers in this field (a panel of experts convened every other year by the International Council for Philosophy and Humanistic Studies), have recommended that many worthwhile translations published during the 19th century, and now impossible to find except in a limited number of libraries, should be brought back into print in low-priced editions, for the use of students and of the general public. The experts also pointed out that in certain cases, even though there might be in existence more recent and more accurate translations endowed with a more modern apparatus of scholarship, a number of pioneer works of the greatest value and interest to students of Eastern religions also merited republication.

This point of view was warmly endorsed by the Indian National Academy of Letters (Sahitya Akademi), and the Indian National Commission for UNESCO

It is in the spirit of these recommendations that this work from the famous series "Sacred Books of the East" is now once again being made available to the general public as part of the UNESCO Collection of Representative Works.

PUBLISHER'S NOTE

First, the man distinguished between eternal and perishable. Later he discovered within himself the germ of the Eternal. This discovery was an epoch in the history of the human mind and the *East was the first to discover it.*

To watch in the Sacred Books of the East the dawn of this religious consciousness of man, must always remain one of the most inspiring and hallowing sights in the whole history of the world. In order to have a solid foundation for a comparative study of the Religions of the East, we must have before all things, complete and thoroughly faithful translation of their Sacred Books in which some of the ancient sayings were preserved because they were so true and so striking that they could not be forgotten. They contained eternal truths, expressed for the first time in human language.

With profoundest reverence for Dr. S. Radhakrishnan, President of India, who inspired us for the task; our deep sense of gratitude for Dr. C. D. Deshmukh & Dr. D. S. Kothari, for encouraging assistance; esteemed appreciation of UNESCO for the warm endorsement of the cause ; and finally with indebtedness to Dr. H. Rau, Director, Max Müller Bhawan, New Delhi, in procuring us the texts of the Series for reprint, we humbly conclude.

CONTENTS.

INTRODUCTION.

BEFORE entering upon an intelligent study of the Qur'ân it is necessary to make oneself acquainted with the circumstances of the people in whose midst it was revealed, with the political and religious aspects of the period, and with the personal history of the prophet himself.

Arabia or *G*azîrat el 'Arab, 'the Arabian Peninsula,' as it is called by native writers, is bounded on the west by the Red Sea; on the east by the Persian Gulf and the Gulf of Oman; on the south by the Indian Ocean; and on the north it extends to the confines of Babylonia and Syria.

The Arabs were divided into those of the desert and those of the towns.

The first were settled in the sterile country of the Hi*g*âz, and the no less barren highlands of Ne*g*d.

The principalities bordering on Syria and Persia were vassals of the Roman and Persian empires; the kingdom of Himyar in Yemen, to the south of the Peninsula, was in free communication with the rest of the world; but the Hi*g*âz, 'the barrier,' had effectually resisted alike the curiosity and the attacks of the nations who fought around it for the empire of the world. Persia, Egypt, Rome, Byzantium had each unsuccessfully essayed to penetrate the country and conquer its hardy inhabitants.

The Hi*g*âz consists of the barren ranges of hills which lead up from the lowlands on the Eastern coast of the Red Sea to the highlands of Ne*g*d. In its valleys lie the holy cities of Mecca and Medînah, and here was the birthplace of el Islâm.

The Arabs of the desert preserved almost intact the manners, customs, and primeval simplicity of the early patriarchs.

They lived in tents made of hair or woollen cloth, and

their principal wealth consisted in their camels, horses, and male and female slaves.

They were a nomad race, changing their residence to the various places within their own territory, which afforded the best pasturage as the seasons came round.

Brave and chivalrous, the Arab was always ready to defend the stranger who claimed his protection, while he would stand by a member of his own clan and defend him with his life, whether he were right or wrong. This devotion to the tribe was one of the strongest characteristics of the Arabs, and must be borne in mind if we would understand aright the early history of Islâm.

They were generous and hospitable to a fault, and many a tale is told of a chief who gave away his last camel, or slew his favourite horse to feed a guest, while he and his family were well-nigh left to starve.

Pride of birth was their passion, and poetry their greatest delight; their bards recited the noble pedigrees and doughty deeds of their tribes,—as their own proverb has it, 'the registers of the Arabs are the verses of their bards,'—and in the numerous ancient poems still extant we have invaluable materials for the history of the race.

But their vices were as conspicuous as their virtues, and drunkenness, gambling, and the grossest immorality were very prevalent amongst them. Robbery and murder were their ordinary occupations, for an Arab looked on work or agriculture as beneath his dignity, and thought that he had a prescriptive right to the property of those who condescended to such mean offices. The death of an Arab, however, was revenged with such rigour and vindictiveness by the fierce laws of the blood feud, that a certain check was placed upon their bloodthirsty propensities even in their wars; and these were still further tempered by the institution of certain sacred months, during which it was unlawful to fight or pillage. Cruel, and superstitious too, they were, and amongst the inhuman customs which Mohammed swept away, none is more revolting than that, commonly practised by them, of burying their female children alive.

The position of women amongst them was not an elevated one, and although there are instances on record of heroines and poetesses who exalted or celebrated the honour of their clan, they were for the most part looked on with contempt. The marriage knot was tied in the simplest fashion and untied as easily, divorce depending only on the option and caprice of the husband.

As for government they had, virtually, none; the best born and bravest man was recognised as head of the tribe, and led them to battle; but he had no personal authority over them, and no superiority but that of the admiration which his bravery and generosity gained for him.

The religion of the Arabs was Sabæanism, or the worship of the hosts of heaven, Seth and Enoch being considered as the prophets of the faith.

This cult no doubt came from Chaldea, and the belief in the existence of angels, which they also professed, is traceable to the same source. Their practice of making the circuit of the holy shrines, still continued as part of the 'Ha*gg* ceremonies, probably also arose from this planetary worship.

The comparatively simple star-worship of the Sabæans was, however, greatly corrupted; and a number of fresh deities, superstitious practices, and meaningless rites had been introduced.

The strange sounds that often break the terrible stillness of the desert; the sudden storms of sand or rain that in a moment cover the surface of a plain, or change a dry valley into a roaring torrent; these and a thousand other such causes naturally produce a strong effect upon an imagination quickened by the keen air and the freedom of the desert.

The Arab, therefore, peopled the vast solitudes amidst which he dwelt with supernatural beings, and fancied that every rock, and tree, and cavern had its *g*inn or presiding genius. These beings were conceived to be both beneficent and malevolent, and were worshipped to propitiate their help or avert their harm. From the worship of these personifications of the powers of nature to that of the presiding genius of a tribe or of a place, is an easy transition, and we accordingly find that each tribe had its patron deity with the cult of which their interests were intimately bound up. The chief god of this vague national cult was Allâh, and most tribes set up a shrine for him as well as for their own particular deity. The offerings dedicated to the former were set apart for the advantage of the poor and of strangers, while those brought to the local idol were reserved for the use of the priests. If Allâh had by any chance anything better than the inferior deity, or a portion of his offerings fell into the lot of the local idol, the priests at once appropriated it; this practice is reprehended by Mohammed in the Qur'ân (VI, ver. 137).

The principal deities of the Arab pantheon were—

Allâh ta'âlah, the God most high.

Hubal, the chief of the minor deities; this was in the form of a man. It was brought from Syria, and was supposed to procure rain.

Wadd, said to have represented the heaven, and to have been worshipped under the form of a man.

Suwâ'h, an idol in the form of a woman, and believed to be a relic of antediluvian times.

Ya*gh*ûTH, an idol in the shape of a lion.

Ya'ûq, worshipped under the figure of a horse.

Nasr, which was, as the name implies, worshipped under the semblance of an eagle.

El 'Huzzâ, identified with Venus, but it appears to have been worshipped under the form of an acacia tree, cf. note 2, p. 132.

Allât, the chief idol of the tribe of THaqîf at *T*â'if, who endeavoured to make it a condition of surrender to Mohammed that he should not destroy it for three years, and that their territory should be considered sacred like that of Mecca, a condition which the prophet peremptorily refused. The name appears to be the feminine of Allâh.

Manât, worshipped in the form of a large sacrificial stone by several tribes, including that of HuDHeil.

Duwâr, a favourite idol with the young women, who used to go in procession round it, whence its name.

Isâf, an idol that stood on Mount Zafâ.

Naïla, an image on Mount Marwâ.

The last two were such favourite objects of worship that, although Mohammed ordered them to be destroyed, he was not able entirely to divert the popular regard from them, and the visitation of Zafâ and Marwâ are still an important part of the 'Ha*gg* rites.

'Hab'hab was a large stone upon which camels were slaughtered.

El 'Huzzâ, Allât, and Manât are mentioned by name in the Qur'ân, see Chapter LIII, vers. 19–20.

The Kaabah, or chief shrine of the faith, contained, besides these, images representing Abraham and Ishmael, each with divining arrows in his hand, and a statue or picture representing the virgin and child.

There were altogether 365 idols there in Mohammed's time.

Another object of worship then, and of the greatest veneration now, is the celebrated black stone which is inserted in the wall of the Kaabah, and is supposed to have been one of the stones of Paradise, originally white, though since blackened by the kisses of sinful but believing lips.

The worship of stones is a very old form of Semitic cult, and it is curious to note that Jacob 'took the stone that he had put for his pillow, and set it up for a pillar, and poured oil on the top of it; and he called the name of the place Bethel[1]:' and that at Mecca the principal object of sacred interest is a stone, and that the Kaabah has been known, from time immemorial, as Bâit allâh, 'the house of God.'

The *g*inn, like the angels, were held by the ancient Arabs to be the daughters of Allâh; they were supposed to be created out of fire instead of clay, but in all other respects to resemble mankind, and to be subject to the same laws of procreation and decease.

[1] Genesis xxviii. 18–19.

Mohammed believed that he was sent as an apostle to both men and *g*inns, and Sûrah LXXII contains an allusion to a vision in which he beheld a multitude of the *g*inns bowing in adoration and listening to the message which man had disdainfully refused.

Witches and wizards were also believed to exist, that is, persons who had contrived to subject one or more of these supernatural powers by spells, of which the holy name was the most powerful.

Two fallen angels, Hârût and Mârût, confined in a pit at Babylon, where they are hung by their heels in chains until the judgment day, are always ready to instruct men in the magical art.

The belief in Allâh himself was little more than a reminiscence, and as he had no priesthood, and was not the patron of any particular tribe, his supremacy was merely nominal.

The belief in a future life had not as yet taken a definite hold on the people, and the few who, following the old savage plan, buried a camel with its master or tied it up to die of hunger at his grave, so that he might not be obliged to enter the next world on foot, probably did it rather from custom than from a belief in its real significance.

In short, the Arab of Mohammed's time was what the Bedawi of to-day is, indifferent to religion itself, but using a few phrases and practising, in a merely perfunctory manner, a few observances which his forefathers had handed down to him.

Christianity had already established itself in Arabia. In Yemen, the city of Na*g*rân had become the seat of a Christian bishopric, and some of the more important tribes, like Kindeh and Ghassân, had embraced Christianity, which was also the religion of most of the Arabs of Syria.

But it had not penetrated deeply into their hearts, and its miracles, its doctrine of the Trinity, and the subtle disputes of monophysites and monothelites were absolutely incomprehensible to them.

Judaism was more in accordance with their habits and traditions: a number of Jews had found their way into the country after the repression of the revolt against the emperor Adrian, and had made numerous converts. Their creed, however, being based on the idea that they alone are the chosen people, was too exclusive for the majority of the Arabs, while the numerous and vexatious restrictions of its ritual and regulations for every-day life were but ill suited to the free and restless spirit of the sons of the desert.

At the time of Mohammed's appearance the national religion of the Arabs had so far degenerated as to have scarcely any believers. The primeval Sabæanism was all but lost, and even the worship of the powers of nature had become little more than a gross fetishism; as one of Mohammed's contemporaries said, when they found a fine stone they adored it, or, failing that, milked a camel over a heap of sand and worshipped that.

But by far the greater number had ceased to believe in anything at all; the pilgrimages, sacrifices, and worship of the tribal idols were still kept up, but rather for political and commercial reasons than as a matter of faith or conviction. Some, indeed, did consult the oracles, or vow an offering to their god in case of some desired event coming to pass; but, if their hopes were disappointed, the deity was assailed with childish abuse, while, if they succeeded, the vow was evaded by some less expensive sacrifice.

Yet the mere existence amongst them of Christians and of Jews caused the monotheistic idea to attract the attention of some of the more earnest and enquiring minds.

Amongst those who had endeavoured to search for the truth among the mass of conflicting dogmas and superstitions of the religions that surrounded them were Waraqah, the prophet's cousin, and Zeid ibn 'Amr, surnamed 'the Enquirer.'

These enquirers were known as 'Hanîfs, a word which originally meant 'inclining one's steps towards anything,' and therefore signified either convert or pervert.

They did not constitute a united party, but each for himself investigated the truth. There was, however, another sect who professed to have found the truth, and who preached the faith of their father Abraham, nothing more nor less, in fact, than the doctrine of the unity of God. These also called themselves 'Hanîfs, and Mohammed himself at first adopted the title as expressing the faith of Abraham[1], but subsequently changed it to Muslim.

The chief seat of the cult of the deities of Arabia was Mecca, also called Bekka, both names signifying a place of concourse; another name of the city is Umm el Qurâ, 'the mother of cities,' or metropolis. It was built about the middle of the fifth century of our era by the Qurâis on their obtaining possession of the Kaabah, the most ancient shrine in the country. It is situated in a narrow sandy valley shut in by bare mountains. The soil around the city is stony and unproductive, and the inhabitants are obliged to import their own provisions. To furnish this supply with more regularity Hâshim, Mohammed's grandfather, appointed two caravans, one in winter and the other in summer, to set out yearly; they are mentioned in the Qur'ân, Chapter CVI.

The territory of Mecca was held sacred; it was a sanctuary for man and beast, since it was unlawful to take any life there save those of the animals brought thither for sacrifice, at the time of the great gatherings of pilgrims who flocked yearly to the shrine.

The Kaabah is mentioned by Diodorus as a famous temple whose sanctity was even then revered by all the Arabians; its origin must therefore be ascribed to a very remote period.

The name, which simply means 'a cube,' was given it on account of its shape, it being built square of unhewn stones. It was supposed to have been built by Adam from a model brought from heaven, and to have been subsequently restored by Seth, and later on by Abraham and Ishmael.

The stone on which Abraham stood when rebuilding the

[1] See Qur'ân II, 129.

Kaabah is still shown there; it is called the maqâm Ibrahîm or Abraham's station, and is mentioned several times in the Qur'ân.

The well Zemzem, amongst the most venerated objects in the sacred precincts of Mecca, is believed to be the spring which Hagar discovered when she fled out into the wilderness with her son Ishmael. It was a small stream flowing from one of the surrounding hills, and this having in course of time dried up, Abd al Mu*tt*alib, Mohammed's grandfather, caused the well to be dug on the spot whence the spring originally issued.

The Kaabah, so far as the dim legends of antiquity throw any light on the subject, remained for a long period in the hands of the descendants of Ishmael, and on their migrating to other parts of the peninsula its guardianship became vested in their kinsmen, the Jorhamites. These were driven out by the Amalekites, who were in turn defeated by the combined forces of the Ishmaelites and Jorhamites, the latter of whom again became masters of the temple. The Jorhamites were defeated and deposed by a coalition of the Benu Bakr and Benu '*H*uzâ'hah, and the charge of the Kaabah remained with the last-mentioned tribe.

'Amr ibn La'hy, a chief of the Benu '*H*uzâ'hah, now assumed the political and religious chieftainship of Mecca, and it was in his reign that the idols were placed in the Kaabah. The result of this was vastly to increase the importance of the city and its temple, as the various objects to which individual tribes paid worship were then all concentrated within its precincts.

Quzâi, an ancestor of the prophet, making common cause with the Benu Kenânah, defeated the Benu Bakr and Benu '*H*uzâ'hah and restored the custody of the Kaabah to his own tribe, the Qurâi*s*.

From Quzâi it descended to his eldest son Abd ed Dar, from whom the principal offices were however transferred to his brother 'Abd Menâf. These were the privilege of supplying the pilgrims with water and food at the time of the '*Hagg*; the command of the army and civic headship of the town; and the custody of the Kaabah before alluded to.

'Abd Menâf left four sons, 'Abd Shems, Hâshim, al Mu*tt*alib, and Nâufel. To Hâshim was entrusted the guardianship of the Kaabah and the right of supplying food to the pilgrims, together with the princedom of Mecca, while to the descendants of 'Abd ed Dar was left only the office of supplying them with water.

Hâshim and his son 'Abd al Mu*tt*alib filled the office with so much liberality that the wealth of the family, though considerable, was nearly all dissipated, and the rival family of Ommaiyeh, son of 'Abd Shems, took over the more expensive offices with the prestige which they naturally carried. It was during the reign of 'Abd al Mu*tt*alib that the invasion of Mecca by the Abyssinian army under Ashram the Abraha took place; they were however repulsed with great loss. This year was afterwards known as the 'Year of the Elephant,' from the fact of these animals having been employed against the holy city. 'Abd al Mu*tt*alib's youngest son, Abd allah, married a kinswoman settled at YaTHrib (Medînah), by whom he had one posthumous child Mohammed, the future prophet.

The exact date generally given of Mohammed's birth is April 20, 571 A.D., but all that is absolutely certain is that he was born in the Year of the Elephant. All that the child inherited from his father was five camels and a slave girl.

According to the fashion of the country he was provided with a Bedawi wet nurse, one 'Halîmah, who took him with her to the tents of her people and reared him amidst the invigorating surroundings of desert life.

At the age of six Mohammed lost his mother, Amînah.

The orphan was taken care of by his grandfather 'Abd al Mu*tt*alib, who showed for him very great affection, and at his death, which happened two years later, left him to the guardianship of his son Abu Tâlib, afterwards one of the most prominent persons in Muslim history.

To support himself the young Mohammed was obliged

to tend the sheep and goats of the Meccans, an occupation which, even at the present day, is considered by the Bedawîn as derogatory to the position of a male. Of this part of his life we know but little, for although Muslim historians relate innumerable legends about him, they are for the most part obviously false, and quite unimportant to the real understanding of his life and character.

At the age of twenty-four he was employed by a rich widow, named '*H*adîgah, to drive the caravans of camels with which she carried on an extensive trade.

So well did Mohammed ingratiate himself with his employer, who was also his kinswoman, that she offered him her hand, and although she was forty years of age and he barely twenty-five, their union was eminently a happy one.

Long after her death his love for '*H*adîgah remained fresh in Mohammed's heart; he would never lose an opportunity of extolling her virtues, and would often kill a sheep and distribute its flesh to the poor in honour of her memory.

'Âyeshah, daughter of Abu Bekr, whom he married three years after '*H*adîgah's decease, was in the habit of saying that she was never jealous of any of his wives except 'the toothless old woman.'

Six children were the issue of this marriage, four girls and two boys; both of the latter died at an early age.

But of this portion of his career, too, we have no authentic information; all that is certain is that he was an honest, upright man, irreproachable in his domestic relations and universally esteemed by his fellow-citizens, who bestowed upon him the sobriquet of El Amîn, 'the trusty.'

Mohammed was a man of middle height, but of commanding presence; rather thin, but with broad shoulders and a wide chest; a massive head, a frank oval face with a clear complexion, restless black eyes, long heavy eyelashes, a prominent aquiline nose, white teeth, and a full thick beard are the principal features of the verbal portraits historians have drawn of him.

He was a man of highly nervous organization, thoughtful,

restless, inclined to melancholy, and possessing an extreme sensibility, being unable to endure the slightest unpleasant odour or the least physical pain.

Simple in his habits, kind and courteous in his demeanour, and agreeable in conversation, he gained many over to his side, as much by the charm of his manners as by the doctrine which he preached.

Mohammed had already reached his fortieth year when the first revelations came to him. They were the almost natural outcome of his mode of life and habit of thought, and especially of his physical constitution. From youth upwards he had suffered from a nervous disorder which tradition calls epilepsy, but the symptoms of which more closely resemble certain hysterical phenomena well known and diagnosed in the present time, and which are almost always accompanied with hallucinations, abnormal exercise of the mental functions, and not unfrequently with a certain amount of deception, both voluntary and otherwise.

He was also in the habit of passing long periods in solitude and deep thought; and he was profoundly impressed with the falsehood and immorality of the religion of his compatriots and with horror at their vicious and inhuman practices, and had for his best friends men, such as his cousin Waraqah and Zâid ibn Amr, who had, professedly, been long seeking after the truth and who had publicly renounced the popular religion.

At length, during one of his solitary sojournings on Mount Hirâ, a wild and lonely mountain near Mecca, an angel appeared to him and bade him 'READ[1]!' 'I am no reader!' Mohammed replied in great trepidation, whereon the angel shook him violently and again bade him read.

[1] In Arabic iqra'; a great difference of opinion exists even among Mohammedans about the exact meaning of this word. I have followed the most generally accepted tradition that it has its ordinary signification of 'reading,' and this is supported by the reference immediately afterwards to writing; others take it to mean 'recite!' Sprenger imagines it to mean 'read the Jewish and Christian scriptures,' which, however ingenious, is, as an Arab would say, bârid, singularly frigid and foreign to the spirit of the language.

This was repeated three times, when the angel uttered the five verses which commence the 96th chapter:

'READ! in the name of thy Lord, who did create—
Who did create man from congealed blood.
READ! for thy Lord is the most generous,
Who has taught the use of the pen,—
Has taught man what he did not know.'

Terribly frightened, he hastened home to his faithful wife '*H*adî*g*ah, who comforted him. The vision of the angel was not repeated, but his hallucinations and mental excitement continued to such an extent that a new fear took hold of him, and he began to wonder whether he were not, after all, possessed by a *g*inn, one of those dread supernatural beings of which I have before spoken.

Persons afflicted with epileptic or hysterical symptoms were supposed by the Arabs, as by so many other nations, to be possessed, and we find the constant complaint in the Qur'ân that he was regarded as such by his fellow-citizens. Poetic frenzy was evidently recognised by them as nearly akin to demoniacal possession, and of this charge, too, the prophet frequently endeavours to clear himself. His habit of fasting and watching throughout the night would and no doubt did increase his tendency to mental excitement and visionary hallucinations.

The celebrated 'night journey' or 'ascent into heaven,' which many of the Muslims allow to have been merely a dream, was doubtless the result of one of these fits of mental exaltation. It must be remembered, however, that to an Eastern mind the reducing it to a dream by no means detracts either from its reality or its authority, dreams being supposed to be direct revelations from God; see the Story of Joseph, Chapter XII, and the same as recorded in the Old Testament.

That he himself thoroughly believed in the reality of his revelations there can be no doubt, especially during the early part of his prophetic career. The chapters which belong to this period abound in passages which were evidently uttered in a state of complete ecstasy; but the later portions of the Qur'ân, in which more consecutive stories are told, and in which ordinances are propounded for the general guidance of the believers, or for individual cases, are of course couched in more sober language, and show traces of being composed in a calmer frame of mind.

The thought that he might be, after all, mad or possessed (ma*g*nûn) was terrible to Mohammed.

He struggled for a long time against the idea, and endeavoured to support himself by belief in the reality of the divine mission which he had received upon Mount 'Hirâ; but no more revelations came, nothing occurred to give him further confidence and hope, and Mohammed began to feel that such a life could be endured no longer. The Fatrah or 'intermission,' as this period without revelation was called, lasted for two and a half or three years.

Dark thoughts of suicide presented themselves to his mind, and on more than one occasion he climbed the steep sides of Mount 'Hirâ, or Mount Thabîr, with the desperate intention of putting an end to his unquiet life by hurling himself from one of the precipitous cliffs. But a mysterious power appeared to hold him back, and at length the long looked-for vision came, which was to confirm him in his prophetic mission.

At last the angel again appeared in all his glory, and Mohammed in terror ran to his wife '*H*adî*g*ah and cried daTHTHirûnî, 'wrap me up!' and lay down entirely enwrapped in his cloak as was his custom when attacked by the hysterical fits (which were always accompanied, as we learn from the traditions, with violent hectic fever), partly for medical reasons and partly to screen himself from the gaze of evil spirits.

As he lay there the angel again spake to him: 'O thou covered! Rise up and warn! and thy Lord magnify! and thy garments purify; and abomination shun! and grant not favours to gain increase; and for thy Lord await[1]!'

[1] Sûrah LXXIV, 1-7.

And now the revelations came in rapid succession. He no longer doubted the reality of the inspiration, and his conviction of the unity of God and of his divine commission to preach it were indelibly impressed upon his mind.

His only convert was at first his faithful wife '*H*adî*g*ah; she was always at his side to comfort him when others mocked at him, to cheer him when dispirited, and to encourage him when he wavered.

Well, indeed, did she deserve the title by which after-ages knew her of Umm el Mû'minîn, 'the mother of the believers.'

His daughters next believed; his cousin Ali, Abu Tâlib's youngest son, whom Mohammed had adopted to relieve his uncle of some portion of his family cares, soon followed; then came Zâid, his freedman, favourite companion and fellow-seeker after truth; and ere long the little band of believers was joined by Abu Bekr, a rich merchant, and man of the most upright character, who had also been his confidant during that period of doubt and mental strife. Mohammed was wont to say that, 'all the world had hesitated more or less to recognise him as the Apostle of God, except Abu Bekr alone.' Abu Bekr enjoyed immense influence with his fellow-citizens, and had by his probity earned the appellation of el Ziddîq, 'the true.'

The next converts to the new faith were two young men, Zobeir and Sa'ad ibn Waqqâz, both relations of the prophet. Abd er Rahman ibn Auf and Tal'hah, men of mark and military prowess, then joined the Muslim ranks. Othmân ibn Affân, afterwards the third Caliph, a young Arab beau, also embraced Islâm for the sake of obtaining the hand of Mohammed's daughter, Rukaiyah. The accession of these personages opened the eyes of the Qurâi*s* to the importance of the movement, but the number of the faithful was still but small.

His other converts were only women and slaves, the former being won over by the influence of '*H*adî*g*ah. Amongst the latter was an Abyssinian slave named Bilal, who subsequently underwent cruel persecutions for the faith, and on the establishment of the religion became the first mu'ezzin or 'crier,' who called to prayer in Islâm.

In the fifth year of his ministry Mohammed made another important convert, Omar ibn el '*H*a*tt*âb, a fierce soldier, who had been one of the bitterest opponents of the new religion, but who afterwards proved its chief support.

His conversion carried with it so great weight that the Mohammedan traditions relate it with miraculous attendant details. Omar and Abu Bekr supplied, the one by his vigour and promptitude in action, and the other by his persuasive eloquence and address, the want of the practical element in Mohammed's character. So thoroughly did he rely upon them and seek support from their companionship, that it was always his custom to say, 'I and Abu Bekr and Omar have been to such and such a place, or have done such and such a thing.'

To the great mass of the citizens of Mecca the new doctrine was simply the 'Hanîfism to which they had become accustomed, and they did not at first trouble themselves at all about the matter. Mohammed's claim, however, to be the Apostle of God called forth more opposition, causing some to hate him for his presumption and others to ridicule him for his pretensions; some, as we have seen above, regarded him in the light of one possessed, while another class looked upon him as a mere vulgar soothsayer.

But in preaching the unity of Allâh, Mohammed was attacking the very existence of the idols, in the guardianship of which consisted not only the supremacy of Mecca, but the welfare and importance of the state. The chiefs of the Qurâi*s* therefore began to look with no favourable eye upon the prophet, whom they regarded as a dangerous political innovator.

But Mohammed himself came of the most noble family in Mecca, and could not be attacked or suppressed without calling down upon the aggressors the certain vengeance of his protector Abu Tâlib and his clan. A deputation of the chiefs therefore waited upon Abu Tâlib and begged him to enforce silence upon his nephew, or to withdraw his protection, which latter alternative was equivalent to handing him over to the summary vengeance of his foes. This Abu Tâlib firmly but politely refused to do, and it was not until they added threats to their entreaties that he consented even to remonstrate with his nephew.

Mohammed, though deeply grieved at losing, as he feared, his uncle's protection and goodwill, exclaimed in reply, 'By Allâh! if they placed the sun on my right hand and the moon on my left, to persuade me, yet while God bids me, I will not renounce my purpose!' and bursting into tears turned to leave the place. But the kind old Abu Tâlib, moved at his nephew's tears, recalled him and assured him of his continued protection.

From his fellow-citizens Mohammed met with nothing but raillery, insults, and actual injuries, when he ventured to announce his mission in public.

In return he could only threaten them with punishment in this world and the next, setting before them the fate of those who had rejected the prophets of old, of the people of Noah and Lot, of the destruction of Pharaoh and other contumacious folk; and painting in vivid colours the dreadful torments of the future life. But the one threat seemed little likely to be realised, and in an existence after death they had no belief. So the prophet's warnings went for naught, and he himself was forced to bear with patience the contumely heaped upon him and the still deeper pain of disappointment and the sense of failure.

In proportion as the new faith incurred the open hostility of the Meccans, the position of its converts became more embarrassing. Those who had powerful protectors could still weather the storm, but the weaker ones, especially the slaves and women, had to endure the severest persecutions, and in some cases suffered martyrdom for their belief.

Some of the slaves were bought off by Abu Bekr, Mohammed's own financial position not allowing him to do this himself; others having no resource apostatized to save their lives.

Under these circumstances the prophet advised his little

band of followers to seek safety in flight, and a few of the most helpless of them accordingly emigrated to the Christian country of Abyssinia. The next year others joined them, until the little colony of Muslim emigrants numbered a hundred souls.

The Qurâi*s* were much annoyed at the escape of the Muslims, as they had hoped and determined to suppress the movement completely: they therefore sent a deputation to the Na*gg*â*s*î or king of Abyssinia, demanding the surrender of the fugitives. The Na*gg*â*s*î called his bishops around him, and summoning the refugees to the conference bade them answer for themselves. They told him how they had been plunged in idolatry and crime, and how their prophet had called them to belief in God and to the practice of a better life; then they quoted the words of the Qur'ân concerning Jesus, and finally begged the monarch not to give them up to these men, who would not only persecute them, but force them back into unbelief and sin. The Na*gg*â*s*î granted their request and sent the messengers back. The failure of this attempt increased the hostility of the Qurâi*s* towards the small remnant of the Muslims who were left in Mecca.

Almost alone, exposed to hourly danger and annoyance, it is not to be wondered at that Mohammed should for a moment have conceived the idea of a compromise.

The chiefs of Mecca cared little for their own idols, but they cared greatly for their traffic and their prestige. If the gods in the Kaabah were false and their service vain and wicked, who would visit the holy shrine? and where would then be the commercial advantages that flowed into Mecca from the pilgrims who crowded yearly to the town? Again, if they allowed the favourite deities of the neighbouring powerful tribes to be insulted or destroyed, how could they expect that these latter would accord safe conduct to their caravans or even allow them to pass through the territories unmolested?

Al 'Huzzâ, Allât, and Manât were the idols of the most important of these neighbouring tribes, and the Qurâi*s* proposed to Mohammed that he should recognise the divinity of these three deities, and promised in their turn that they would then acknowledge him to be the Apostle of Allâh.

One day, therefore, he recited before an assembly of the Qurâis the words of the Qur'ân, Chapter LIII, vers. 19, 20, and when he came to the words, 'Have ye considered Allât and Al 'Huzzâ and Manât the other third?' he added, 'They are the two high-soaring cranes, and, verily, their intercession may be hoped for!' When he came to the last words of the chapter, 'Adore God then and worship!' the Meccans prostrated themselves to the ground and worshipped as they were bidden.

A great political triumph was achieved, the proud and mocking Meccans had acknowledged the truth of the revelations, the city was converted, Mohammed's dream was realised, and he was himself the recognised Apostle of God!

But at what a sacrifice! politically he had gained the position at which he aimed, but it was at the expense of his honesty and his conviction; he had belied and stultified the very doctrine for which he and his had suffered so much. The delusion did not last long; and on the morrow he hastened to recant in the most uncompromising manner, and declared, no doubt with the fullest belief in the truth of what he was saying, that Satan had put the blasphemous words in his mouth. The passage was recited afresh, and this time it read: 'Have ye considered Allât and Al 'Huzzâ and Manât the other third? Shall there be male offspring for Him and female for you? That, then, were an unfair division! They are but names which ye have named, ye and your fathers! God has sent down no authority for them! Ye do but follow suspicion and what your souls lust after! And yet there has come to them guidance from their Lord!'

This incident is denied by many of the Muslim writers, but not only are the most trustworthy histories very explicit on the subject, but it is proved by the collateral evidence that some of the exiles returned from Abyssinia on the strength of the report that a reconciliation had been effected with the Qurâis.

His recantation brought upon Mohammed redoubled hate and opposition, but his family still stood firmly by him, and his life was therefore safe, for it was no light thing to incur the dread responsibility of the blood feud.

The Qurâis revenged themselves by placing the family under a ban, engaging themselves in writing to contract no marriage or commercial relations with any of them, to accord them no protection, and, in short, to hold no communication whatever with them. This document was solemnly suspended in the Kaabah itself.

The result of this was more than mere social disqualification, for as they could not join the Meccan caravans, and were not rich or powerful enough to equip one of their own, they lost their very means of livelihood, and were reduced to the greatest penury and distress.

Unable to contend openly with so many and such powerful foes, the whole of the Hâsimî family, pagan as well as Muslim, took refuge in the si'b or 'ravine' of Abu Tâlib, a long and narrow defile in the mountains to the east of Mecca. One man only kept aloof, and that was Abu Laheb, the uncle of the prophet, the bitterest enemy of El Islâm.

For two years the Hâsimîs lay under the ban, shut up in their ravine and only able to sally forth when the 'Hagg pilgrimage came round and the sacred months made their persons and their property for the time inviolable.

At length the Qurâis began themselves to tire of the restriction which they had imposed upon the Hâsimî clan, and were glad of an excuse for removing it. It was found that the deed on which it had been engrossed had become worm-eaten and illegible, and this being taken as an evidence of the divine disapproval of its contents, they listened to the appeal of the venerable Abu Tâlib and allowed the prisoners to come forth and mix once more freely with the rest of the world. The permission came none too soon, for their stores were gone and they were on the brink of actual starvation. During the two weary years of suffering and distress Mohammed had of course made no converts amongst the people of Mecca, and few, if any, members of his own clan had joined him during their seclusion, so that his prospects were gloomier than ever.

To add to his troubles, he lost his faithful wife '*H*adî*g*ah not long after this. Shortly afterwards he married a widow named Sâudâ; and later on he was betrothed to 'Âyeshah, daughter of Abu Bekr, then a mere child, but whom he married in three years time. This woman gained a wonderful ascendancy over the prophet, and exercised considerable influence on Islâm, both during and after his lifetime. On one occasion, when the party were on the move, 'Âyeshah was left behind with a young Arab under circumstances which gave rise to some very unpleasant rumours affecting her, and a special revelation was necessary to clear her character [1]. Two other women were presently added to his harîm, 'Hafza, daughter of 'Omar, and Zâinab, widow of a Muslim who had been slain at Bedr.

Another marriage that he contracted gave great scandal to the faithful, namely, that with the wife, also called Zâinab, of his adopted son Zâid, whom her husband divorced and offered to surrender to Mohammed on finding that the latter admired her. This also required a revelation to sanction it [2].

His uncle and protector Abu Tâlib died not long after '*H*adî*g*ah.

This last loss left him without a protector, and his life would certainly have been in imminent danger had it not been that his uncle Abu Laheb, although one of the most determined opponents of the new religion, accorded him his formal protection for the sake of the family honour. This, however, was shortly afterwards withdrawn, and Mohammed was left more alone and more exposed to danger than ever.

In the desperate hope of finding help elsewhere he set

[1] See Part I, p. 74, note 2. [2] See Chapter XXXIII, ver. 36, note.

out for *T*â'if, accompanied by his freedman and adopted son Zâid.

From *T*â'if he was driven forth by the populace, who stoned him as he fled away. Wounded and exhausted, he lay down to rest in an orchard, the proprietor of which refreshed him with some grapes, and as he retraced his steps to Mecca he had a vision by the way. It appeared to him that the hosts of the *g*inn crowded round him, adoring God, and eager to learn from him the truths of Islâm. Ten years had rolled by and the number of the believers was still very few and the prospects of Islâm darker than they were at first, when the prophet found an unexpected support in the two tribes of El 'Aus and El '*H*azra*g*, who had towards the end of the fifth century wrested the city of YaTHrib from the Jewish tribes who held it.

Some of these Arabs had embraced the Jewish religion, and many of the former masters of the city still dwelt there in the position of clients of one or other of the conquering tribes, so that it contained in Mohammed's time a considerable Jewish population.

Between the inhabitants of YaTHrib and those of Mecca there existed a strong feeling of animosity; but Mohammed, though sharing the prejudices of his compatriots, was not in a position to refuse help from whatever quarter it presented itself.

The Arab inhabitants of YaTHrib had on their part a good reason for looking with a more favourable eye upon the new prophet.

Imbued with the superstition of the Jews amongst whom they lived, they looked for the coming of a Messiah with no small apprehension of his restoring the Jewish supremacy and of their own consequent downfall.

Mohammed, after all, might be the expected Messiah; he was of their own race and it was at any rate prudent to treat with him before he should cast in his lot, as he possibly might, with their disaffected Jewish subjects.

Lastly, YaTHrib was a prey to incessant agitations and internal discords, and anything that was likely to bind the conflicting parties together by a tie of common interest could not but prove a boon to the city.

The inhabitants of YaTHrib then were, for many reasons, inclined to acknowledge the mission of Mohammed; and after sundry negotiations between the prophet and the chiefs of the city, he agreed to meet them at a part of the road between Mecca and YaTHrib, where the valley suddenly makes an abrupt descent, from which the spot was known as Akabeh.

A deputation, consisting of twelve men of the Aus and '*Hazrag* tribes, accordingly met him at the appointed spot and pledged him their word to obey his teaching.

The twelve men returned to their native city and preached the doctrine of Islâm, which was eagerly accepted by the majority of the pagan inhabitants. The Jews of YaTHrib, struck by this sudden renunciation of idolatry by their fellow-citizens, sent to beg Mohammed to send them a teacher who should instruct them in the new creed that had worked so wonderful a change.

At Mecca things were stationary, and Mohammed could do little more than wait until the time for pilgrimage should again come round and he should get fresh news from YaTHrib.

It was during this year of waiting that the celebrated night journey occurred, which has been the occasion of so much dispute to Mohammedan theologians, and has afforded such a handle to the hostile criticism of European historians. It was, as Mohammed himself persistently asserted, a vision in which he saw himself transported to heaven and brought face to face with that God who had always filled his thoughts. The story is so overlaid with spurious traditional details as to have lost, to a great extent, its real significance. It is referred to obscurely in the Qur'ân in the following passages:

'Celebrated be the praises of Him who took His servant a journey by night from the Sacred Mosque to the Remote Mosque, the precinct of which we have blessed, to show him of our signs!' (XVII, ver. 1.)

'And we made the vision which we showed thee only a cause of sedition unto men.' (XVII, ver. 62.)

'By the star when it falls, your comrade errs not, nor is he deluded! nor speaks he out of lust! It is but an inspiration inspired! One mighty in power taught him, endowed with sound understanding, and appeared, he being in the loftiest tract.

'Then drew he near and hovered o'er! until he was two bows' length off or nigher still! Then he inspired his servant what he inspired him; the heart belies not what it saw! What, will ye dispute with him on what he saw?

'And he saw him another time, by the lote tree none may pass; near which is the garden of the Abode! When there covered the lote tree what did cover it! The sight swerved not nor wandered. He saw then the greatest of the signs of his Lord.' (LIII, vers. 1-18.)

At length the wished-for time arrived, and Mohammed, who had been told by his envoy Muz'hab of the success of his mission, repaired once more to the Akabeh. Here he was met at night by seventy men from YaTHrib, who had come to the rendezvous clandestinely by twos and threes, so as not to attract attention and incur the hostility of the Qurâis.

His uncle 'Abbâs, though an unbeliever accompanied him, explained to them his nephew's position, and asked them seriously to consider the proposition which it was understood they were about to make. They declared that they were quite earnest in their desire to have Mohammed amongst them, and swore that they would defend him and his cause with their very lives. Mohammed then addressed them, recited to them some portions of the Qur'ân in which the most essential points of his doctrine were set forth, and asked them for a pledge of their good faith. This they gave in simple Bedawi fashion, one after another placing his palm in that of the prophet and taking the oath of fealty. So enthusiastic were their protestations that 'Abbâs himself was obliged to bid them be silent and urge upon them the danger and imprudence of their noisy demonstration. The treaty being thus ratified, Mohammed chose twelve naqîbs or leaders, after the number of the disciples of Jesus, and the voice of some stranger being heard close by the assembly hastily but quietly dispersed.

The Meccans, who had got a hint of the affair, taxed the YaTHrib pilgrims with having conspired with Mohammed against them, but being unable to prove the accusation, the new band of Muslims was enabled to return home in safety.

So hostile was now the attitude of the Qurâi*s* that the believers of Mecca prepared for flight, and at last there were only left in Mecca three members of the community, Mohammed himself, Abu Bekr, and Ali.

The Qurâi*s* now held a solemn council of war, at which, on the suggestion of Abu *G*ahl, it was determined that eleven men, each a prominent member of one of the noble families of the town, should simultaneously attack and murder Mohammed, and by thus dividing the responsibility should avoid the consequences of the blood feud; for, as they rightly judged, the Hâ*s*imîs, not being sufficiently powerful to take the blood revenge on so many families, would be obliged to accept the blood money instead.

Mohammed had timely warning of this design, and giving Ali his mantle bade him pretend to sleep on the couch usually occupied by himself, and so divert the attention of the would-be murderers who were watching around his house. In the meantime Mohammed and Abu Bekr escaped by a back window in the house of the latter, and the two hid themselves in a cavern on Mount THaur, an hour and a half distant from Mecca, before the Qurâi*s* had discovered the ruse and heard of their flight. A hot pursuit was immediately organized.

For three days they lay concealed, their enemies once coming so near that Abu Bekr, trembling, said, 'We are but two.' 'Nay,' said Mohammed, 'we are three; for God is with us.' The legend tells us that a spider had woven its web across the mouth of the cave, so that the Qurâi*s*, thinking that no one had entered in, passed it over in their search.

At length they ventured once more to set out, and, mounted on fleet camels, reached YaTHrib in safety. Three days after they were joined by Ali, who had been allowed to leave after a few hours' imprisonment.

This was the celebrated Hi*g*rah or 'flight,' from which the Mohammedan era dates. It took place on June 16, in the year of our Lord 622. The city of YaTHrib was henceforth known as Madînat en Nebî, 'the city of the prophet,' or simply El Medînah.

Once established at El Medînah, Mohammed proceeded to regulate the rites and ceremonies of his religion, built a mosque to serve as a place of prayer and hall of general assembly, and appointed Bilâl, the Abyssinian slave who had been so faithful throughout the former persecutions, as crier to call the believers to the five daily prayers.

His next care was to reconcile, as far as possible, the various opposing parties of the city, and this was by no means an easy task. The two tribes of El 'Aus and El '*Hazrag* could not be made entirely to lay aside their ancient rivalry, but they united so far as to make his their common cause. For this they were honoured with the title of Ansâr or 'helpers of the prophet.' The refugees from Mecca were called Muhâ*g*erûn, and to prevent any ill feeling rising up between these two classes, each of the Meccan immigrants was made to take to himself one of the Medînah Muslims, to whom he bound himself by an oath of brotherhood. This institution was, however, abolished a year and a half later, after the battle of Bedr. Of the inhabitants of Medînah, who had not joined in the invitation to Mohammed to sojourn amongst them, some left the town and went over to the Meccans; others remained behind, and though they yielded to the tide of popular opinion, and gave in their formal allegiance to the prophet, they were not completely won over to Islâm, but waited to see how matters would go, ready, as they did on several critical occasions, to desert him should his fortune show signs of a reverse. This disaffected class is spoken of in the Qur'ân by the name of Munâfiqûn or 'hypocrites,' the chief man among them being one Abdallah ibn Ubai. Although perfectly aware of their designs, Mohammed treated them with singular courtesy and forbearance, and spared no pains to win them over to his side; even when his rule was firmly established, and they were completely in his power, he made no difference in dealing with them until in the course of time they became absorbed into the general band of the faithful.

The Jews of Medînah were much harder to deal with, and although Mohammed, by adapting his religion as far as possible to their own, by appealing to their own scriptures and religious books, by according them perfect freedom of worship and political equality, endeavoured in every way to conciliate them, they treated his advances with scorn and derision. When it became obvious that Islâmism and Judaism could not amalgamate, and that the Jews would never accept him for their prophet, Mohammed withdrew his concessions one by one, changed the qiblah or point to which he turned in prayer from Jerusalem which he had at first adopted to the Kaabah at Mecca, substituted the fast of Rama*dh*ân for the Jewish fasts which he had prescribed, and, in short, regarded them as the irreconcilable enemies of his creed.

Soon afterwards he turned his attention to his native city, which had rejected him and driven him out; and feeling himself now sufficiently strong to take the offensive, he began to preach the Holy War. After some petty raids upon the enemies' caravans an event happened which brought the Muslim and the infidel armies for the first time into open collision. In January, 624 A.D., a large caravan from Mecca, which had in the autumn of the previous year escaped an attack by the Muslims, was returning from Syria laden with valuable merchandise, and Mohammed determined to capture it. His intention, however, reached the ears of Abu Sufiyân, who sent a messenger to Mecca to ask for troops for his protection, while he himself followed a different route along the coast of the Red Sea. Mohammed, without waiting for the return of his spies, marched out in the hopes of surprising Abu Sufiyân at Bedr, where the caravan usually halted, but the Meccan had been too much upon his guard, pressed on with all possible haste, and was soon out of danger. The caravan comprised most of the chief men of Mecca, besides its rich freight. Abu Sufiyân's message, therefore, asking for succour, caused a complete panic in the city. An army of nearly 1,000 men was immediately equipped and marched forth to the rescue, but on the way met a second messenger from Abu Sufiyân with the news that all danger was passed. On this 300 of them returned to Mecca, whilst others hurried to join the caravan. Mohammed was still advancing, in hopes of surprising the caravan, when he was informed of the approach of the Meccan army. After a council of war it was decided to advance and meet the enemy first, as, in the event of victory, they could afterwards pursue the caravan. Arrived at Bedr, the Muslims took up such a position that their foes could not approach the wells, and during the night the rain fell with such violence that the Meccans could scarcely march upon the sodden soil. In the morning these latter were at a great disadvantage, wearied by the state of the ground, and harassed by the blinding sun which shone straight in their faces; but Mohammed, whose numbers were far inferior, awaited the issue of the combat with no little anxiety. During the first part of the engagement the Muslims, by Mohammed's order, stood firm to their posts, whilst he encouraged them by promising the immediate reward of Paradise to those who should fall martyrs in the cause: whilst a fierce winter storm of wind which was blowing at the time, and which added to the discomfort and embarrassment of the enemy, he called the work of Gabriel with a thousand angels fighting for the faith. At length Mohammed gave the expected signal; taking up a handful he threw it towards the Meccans, and exclaimed, 'May their faces be covered with shame! Muslims to the attack!' The condition of the ground so hampered the movements of the Meccans that they were soon completely routed. Several of Mohammed's bitterest enemies were slain, and a number of prisoners and much booty taken. Of the captives, six were executed by the prophet's order, some embraced Islâm, and others were ransomed by their compatriots. This victory was so important for the cause that Mohammed himself regarded it as brought about by a special miracle, and as such it is spoken of in the Qur'ân, Chap. III, ver. 20.

Mohammed's military as well as religious supremacy was now assured in Medînah, and he lost no time in making his enemies there feel his power. The Jews first experienced the full weight of his wrath; a woman of that persuasion, who had incited her fellow-townsmen against him before the battle of Bedr, was put to death, and not long after the Benu Qâinuqâh, a Jewish tribe, who had risen against his authority, dwelling in a suburb of Medînah, were attacked, their property confiscated, and themselves sent into exile.

The war between Mecca and Medînah in the meantime continued.

Abu Sufiyân invaded the territory of Medînah, and the Muslims, on the other hand, captured a caravan belonging to the Qurâi*s*.

The Meccans, determined to revenge the defeat of Bedr, had devoted the profits of the caravan that had been the cause of the conflict to the equipment of a large army, and in January, 625 A.D., three thousand men marched on to Medînah with Abu Sufiyân at their head. The latter was accompanied by his wife Hind, who had lost her father, brother, and uncle at the battle, and longed for vengeance. They established their camp near Mount Ohod, on the road between the two cities. The Muslims were divided in opinion, whether to await the invaders in the city, or to make a sortie and attack them where they were; and at length, in spite of Mohammed's advice to the contrary, the latter plan was decided on.

They marched forth to the number of a thousand, and of these three hundred belonged to the Hypocrites, or disaffected party who deserted before the battle commenced.

Mohammed had disposed his forces so that his best trained archers covered the only vulnerable part of his army, the left flank, and these he bade keep to their posts, no matter what happened. The battle commenced with a few single combats and slight skirmishes, in which the Muslims had the advantage, and a few of the latter having reached and pillaged the enemies' camp, the archers, thinking the day already won, forgot their orders and joined in the loot. '*H*âlid, who commanded the Meccan cavalry, seized the opportunity thus afforded, and took the Muslims on the flank and completely routed them. Mohammed himself was wounded in the mouth and narrowly escaped with his life, and 'Hamzah, his uncle, surnamed the Lion of God, was slain.

The Meccans did not pursue their victory, but believing Mohammed, whom they had seen fall, to be dead, returned to their own city.

The defeat placed Mohammed in a very critical position, and he had great difficulty in restoring confidence to his followers[1].

About the beginning of the year 627 A.D. the Muslims were in great jeopardy. 4,000 Meccans and 1,000 men, gathered from the neighbouring tribes, marched upon Medînah, being instigated thereto by the Jews who had been expelled from that city.

Mohammed was only apprised of the movement at the last moment, but he at once took measures for the defence. On the advice of Salmân, a Persian captive, he caused a deep trench to be dug round the city, and earthworks to be raised in those parts where it was undefended, and behind the trench he posted his army, numbering 3,000 men.

The invading Meccans were completely checked by this mode of defence, and although the Beni Qurâidhah, a Jewish tribe, deserted to them from Mohammed's side and

[1] See Chapter III, vers. 115–168.

rendered them every assistance, their attacks were unsuccessful. At length one cold winter's night a violent storm of wind and rain arose, and a complete panic took place in the camp of the Meccans, who broke up and precipitately retired to their homes. This was the siege of the Confederates alluded to in the Qur'ân [1].

The enemy having disappeared, Mohammed at once marched against the traitorous tribe of Qurâidhah, and besieged them in their fortress, about six miles south-west of Medînah. Being quite unprepared, these were obliged to surrender after fourteen days, which they did on condition that the Benu Aus, their allies in Medînah, should decide their fate. Mohammed chose for arbitrator one of the chiefs of the Aus tribe, named Saad ibn Moâ*dh*, a fierce soldier, who was at the time dying of the wounds which he had received in the attack upon the fortress. He ordained that the men should be beheaded one and all, the women and children sold as slaves, and the property divided amongst the soldiers. This terrible sentence was promptly executed, and the men, to the number of 800, were beheaded, and the women and children bartered to the Bedawîn in exchange for arms and horses.

Mohammed's power and influence was now extending every day.

For six years neither he nor his followers had visited the Kaabah, or performed the sacred rites of the pilgrimage, and in the year 628 A.D. he resolved to attempt it. The time chosen was in the sacred month of DHu'l Qa'hdah, when the Lesser Pilgrimage was wont to be performed, rather than DHu'l 'Hi*gg*eh, that of the Greater Pilgrimage, as less likely to lead to a collision with the other tribes. Fifteen hundred men only accompanied Mohammed, bearing no other arms than those usually allowed to pilgrims, a sheathed sword for each.

The Meccans contemplated Mohammed's advance with no small apprehension, and not believing in his pacific

[1] Chapter XXXIII.

intentions, resolved to bar his progress. Mohammed, thus checked, turned aside towards 'Hudâibîyeh, on the frontier of the sacred territory.

Here, after some negotiations, a treaty was concluded in which a truce of ten years was agreed upon; any of the Meccans who pleased should be at liberty to join Mohammed, and vice versâ, any of the Muslims who chose might enter the Meccan ranks; only those who were clients of powerful chiefs were not to be allowed to become Muslims without the consent of their patrons. Mohammed and his followers were not to enter Mecca that year, but the next year they were to be permitted to do so and to remain for three days.

This was, in reality, a great triumph for Mohammed, as it recognised his position as an independent prince, while the ten years' truce not only enabled him without hindrance to propagate his doctrines at Mecca, but, by removing the constant danger in which he stood from that city, gave him the opportunity of turning his attention elsewhere.

He now not only endeavoured to reduce the Bedawîn tribes to submission, but wrote letters to the great kings and emperors of the world, to the Persian Khosrou, to the Byzantine Emperor, and to the Abyssinian Na*gg*â*s*î, peremptorily bidding them embrace the faith and submit to his rule. The replies that he received were not flattering to his pride, but he or his immediate successors were, ere long, to repeat the summons in a form that admitted neither of denial nor of delay.

One potentate only, the governor of Egypt, Maqauqas, returned a favourable answer, and he sent amongst other presents two slave girls, one of whom, a Coptic girl named Mary, Mohammed took to himself, and by so doing estranged his numerous wives, and was only reconciled by a revelation[1].

In 629 A.D., in the month of DHu'l Qa'hdah (February),

[1] See Chapter LXVI.

the long-expected pilgrimage took place. With two thousand followers the prophet entered the Holy City, and the Meccans having retired to the neighbouring hills, all passed off quietly.

In the course of the short three days' sojourn in Mecca the Muslim ranks were strengthened by the accession of two influential personages, '*H*âlid, who had conquered them at Ohod, and 'Amr, the future conqueror of Egypt.

In this year the Muslim army experienced a terrible defeat at Mûta on the Syrian frontier, in which the prophet's friend Zâid was slain. His prestige, however, was soon re-established by fresh successors and the accession of numerous border tribes.

Two years after the truce of 'Hudâibîyeh, a tribe who were under the protection of Mohammed, were attacked unawares by another tribe in alliance with the Meccans, and some Meccans in disguise were recognised amongst the assailants. This was a violation of the treaty, and Mohammed, on being appealed to by the sufferers, was nothing loth to take advantage of the opportunity afforded him for recommencing hostilities. The Meccans sent Abu Sufiyân to Medînah to offer explanations and procure a renewal of the truce, but without success. Mohammed began to make preparations for an expedition against Mecca, but concealed his plans even from his immediate followers; his Bedawîn allies were ordered either to join him at Medînah, or to meet him at certain appointed places on the route, but it was not until the last moment that his troops knew that their destination was the Holy City. While they were encamped in the immediate neighbourhood, and before the Meccans had any certain knowledge of their approach, the camp was visited at night by Abu Sufiyân, who was introduced to Mohammed by his uncle 'Abbâs, the latter having become converted to Islâm now that he saw that its cause must certainly triumph. Mohammed promised Abu Sufiyân that all those inhabitants of Mecca who should take refuge in his house or in the Kaabah or even in private houses, provided the doors were closed, should be unmolested, and dismissed him to carry this news to his fellow-citizens, not however before he and 'Abbâs had persuaded the Meccan chief to become a Muslim, which he somewhat unwillingly consented to do. There is good reason to suppose that the whole affair was arranged between Mohammed, 'Abbâs, and Abu Sufiyân, and that the meeting by night at the camp with the somewhat theatrical details with which the historians relate it, and the sudden conversion of the two hitherto irreconcilable chiefs, were part of a plan designed to save Mecca from unnecessary bloodshed now that Mohammed's increased power and the overwhelming numbers he brought with him made a capture of the city inevitable. At any rate it had this effect, the Muslim army entered Mecca almost without resistance, only a few Bedawîn under the command of '*H*âlid being assailed with arrows by some of Mohammed's bitterest opponents, whom he quickly dispersed. Mohammed, seeing him in pursuit of his assailants, was excessively angry until it was explained to him that '*H*âlid's action was unavoidable and only in self-defence.

Mohammed was at length master of the capital of Arabia; his first act was to repair to the Kaabah, and after making the circuit seven times and respectfully saluting the black stone with his staff, he entered the building and caused the idols to be destroyed. Actuated both by sound policy and by the strong feeling of attachment to his own tribe, which is inherent in every Arab's breast, he proclaimed a general amnesty, and the Meccans readily embraced Islâm and marched under its banner, hoping for the reward of Paradise, and sure of rich booty here on earth. The Bedawîn tribes in the neighbourhood gave him more trouble, but these too were brought into at least nominal subjection; the tribe of the THaqîf at *T*â'if still held out, and Mohammed attacked them in the valley of 'Honein, where they were surprised by the enemy in a narrow defile, and were in imminent danger of a defeat, had not Mohammed rallied them by appealing to them as 'Ye men of the "Sûrah of the Heifer!" Ye men of the "Tree of Fealty!"'

reminding them of the first portion of the Qur'ân revealed at Medînah, and of the oath of fealty which they had sworn as he sat beneath a tree at 'Hudâibîyeh. On this occasion he took a rich booty, and in order to conciliate the Meccan chiefs he gave them more than their fair share at the division of the spoils. This was particularly displeasing to his Medînah followers, who were only appeased by his declaring his regard for them, and promising never to desert their city or again take up his residence at Mecca. These events are alluded to in the Qur'ân, Chap. IX. After the battle of 'Honein, Mohammed laid siege to *T*â'if, and though he was unable to reduce the place, he so devastated the country around that ambassadors were sent to propose terms of capitulation; they offered to embrace Islâm, provided that their territory should be considered sacred, that they should be excused the more onerous duties of the creed, and should be allowed to retain their favourite idol Allât for at least a year. To these conditions Mohammed was at first inclined to accede, but after a night's reflection, and indignant remonstrance addressed by the fiery Omar to the THaqîfite messengers, they were definitely refused, and the tribe surrendered unconditionally.

The ninth year after the flight is known as the 'Year of Deputations,' the Bedawîn tribes one after another sending in their adhesion to his cause and acknowledging his spiritual and temporal supremacy.

In the same year Mohammed conducted the expedition against Tabûk, which was undertaken with a view to reduce the Syrian tribes to submission, they having been induced by Byzantine influence to rise in insurrection upon the frontier. Sûrah IX contains a violent denunciation of those who on various false pretences held back on the occasion. This was the last military enterprise conducted by Mohammed in person.

The Arabs, with their well-known fickleness, did not continue for long in their allegiance to Islâm and its prophet; even in Mohammed's lifetime, tribe after tribe raised the standard of revolt, and the repression of these insurrections occupied much of his time and attention during the last years of his life. With true political sagacity he saw that the only way to prevent the newly established kingdom from becoming hopelessly disintegrated was to give its members some common interest and ambition. For this reason he never relinquished his designs upon Syria, where the turbulent tribes might find scope for their warlike propensities, and where a rich booty might be gained. It was to this common bond of unity, the desire for plunder and the love of making border raids, as much as to the religious idea, that the triumph of El Islâm was due.

In March, 632 A.D., he made his last pilgrimage to Mecca, the 'Farewell Pilgrimage,' as Muslims call it, and standing upon Mount Arafât he addressed the assembled multitude, —more than forty thousand of pilgrims,—bade them stand firm by the faith that he had taught them, and called God to witness that he had delivered his message and fulfilled his mission.

In June he fell sick, and himself perceived that his end was drawing nigh.

On Monday, June 8, feeling better, he went to the Mosque of Medînah, where Abu Bekr was conducting the prayers before a crowded congregation who had flocked there to hear news of the prophet. Mohammed's entry was quite unexpected, but in spite of the weakness evident from his faltering gait, his countenance was bright, and his voice as clear and commanding as ever. Mounting the lower steps of the pulpit he said a few last words to the people, and having given some parting injunctions to Osâma, whom he had entrusted with the command of an army to Syria, Mohammed returned to his house and lay down to rest in 'Âyesha's chamber. Here, resting his head upon her bosom, the prophet of Arabia fell asleep.

The question naturally arises, how could a comparatively obscure citizen of a small Arabian town bring about results of such magnitude as Mohammed undoubtedly did?

The secret of his success was, primarily, enthusiasm combined with patriotism. Whether he believed to the full in his divine mission and revelations or not, matters but little; but it is certain that he did believe in himself as working for the good of his fellow-countrymen. He took the political and religious institutions of his country as he found them, and he strove to eradicate what was bad and to develop what was good. He knew that so long as the various tribes wasted their strength in internecine war there was no hope of their ever becoming a power; but he knew their character and temperament well enough to perceive that any scheme for bringing about national unity must fail if it involved the necessity of their submitting to any master whatever. He therefore sought to bind them together by what we may call their common religious feeling, but which really meant, as it too often does, common interests, common customs, and common superstitions. At Mecca all was ready to his hand: the Kaabah contained all the gods of the different tribes; the annual fairs and eisteddfodau (to borrow a Welsh name that exactly expresses the character of these gatherings) were held in the territory, and it was here that the historical and religious traditions of the race were circulated and kept alive. All the elements of centralisation were there, and it only wanted such a master-spirit as Mohammed's to turn their thoughts towards the common idea which should induce them to unite.

A prophet who starts in his career with no better stock-in-trade than visionary enthusiasm or deliberate imposture has but a poor chance. Musâilimah, Mohammed's rival, has left nothing behind him but his sobriquet of El KeDHDHâb, 'the liar,' and a few bitterly satirical parodies on some verses of the Qur'ân, which are still occasionally quoted by the less reverential of Muslims. El Muḳanna', the 'veiled prophet of Khorassan,' earned no more immortality than an occasional mention in Persian poetry, and the honour of being the hero of an English popular poem. Mutanebbî, 'the would-be prophet,' as his name signifies, who flourished in the tenth century of our era, was an Arab of the Arabs, and one of the greatest poets of his age. He, too, set up as a prophet, but with so little success that he had to retire from the business at an early period of his career. It was probably his wonderful facility in language that induced him to imitate Mohammed's example, and rely upon the 'miraculous' eloquence of his language in support of his pretensions to inspiration. He, however, missed the opportunities which Mohammed had ; he was no great reformer himself, and there was no urgent need of a reform at the time. Moreover, he was entirely destitute of religious feeling, and, even in his earliest poems, so blasphemes and sneers at holy names that his most devoted commentators are frequently at a loss to find excuses for him.

In forming our estimate of Mohammed's character, therefore, and of the religion which we are accustomed to call by his name, we must put aside the theories of imposture and enthusiasm, as well as that of divine inspiration. Even the theory of his being a great political reformer does not contain the whole truth; and although it is certain that his personal character exercised a most important influence on his doctrine, yet it is not by any means evident that it even moulded it into its present shape.

The enthusiasm which he himself inspired, and the readiness with which such men as Abu Bekr and Omar, Arabs of the noblest birth, ranged themselves amongst his followers, who consisted for the most part of men of the lowest rank, slaves, freedmen, and the like, prove that he could have been no mere impostor.

The early portions of the Qur'ân are the genuine rhapsodies of an enthusiast who believed himself inspired, and Mohammed himself points to them in the later Sûrahs as irrefragable proofs of the divine origin of his mission. In his later history, however, there are evidences of that tendency to pious fraud which the profession of a prophet necessarily involves. Although commenced in perfect good faith, such a profession must place the enthusiast at last in an embarrassing position, and the very desire to prove the truth of what he himself believes may reduce him to the alternative of resorting to a pious fraud or of relinquishing all the results which he has previously attained.

At the outset of his career he turned to the Jews, imagining that, as he claimed to restore the original religion of Abraham, and appealed to the Jewish scriptures for confirmation of his teaching, they would support him. Disappointed in this quarter, he treated them with more bitter hostility than any other of his opponents.

In the latter part of his career he took but little notice either of the Jews or Christians, and when he does mention the latter it is without any of the conciliatory spirit which he at first displayed to them, and they are not only sharply reproved for their errors, but are included in the general mass of infidels against whom the true believers are to fight.

Mohammed styles himself in the Qur'ân En Nebîy el'ummîy (Chap. VII, vers. 156 and 158), which may be interpreted either 'the illiterate prophet' or 'the prophet of the Gentiles,' as the word 'Ummîyûn in Chap. II, ver. 73 means rather 'those who have no scriptures.'

Mohammedans themselves differ very much as to whether the prophet could read or write, the Sunnîs denying it and the Shî'ahs declaring that he was able to do both. The evidence of the fact, though, is very untrustworthy, and in the traditional accounts of the occasions on which he is said to have written, the words may mean nothing more than that he dictated the documents in question. In the Qur'ân, XXIX, 47, it is merely said that he never 'recited a book before this,' and the passages in Chap. XCVI, vers. 1–6, which begin 'Read,' and in which the angel Gabriel is supposed to exhibit the Umm al Kitâb (see p. 2, note 2), and to command him to read it, the act implied may be nothing more than an intuitive perception of the contents of the book thus mysteriously shown to him.

It is probable that he could neither read nor write, and it is almost certain that he could not have done so sufficiently to have made use of any of the Jewish or Christian scriptures.

The oral Jewish and Christian traditions incorporated in the Qur'ân were, no doubt, current among the Jewish and

Christian tribes; there is not the least evidence in support of the accusation made against Mohammed by Christian writers, that the greater part of his revelations were due to the suggestions of a Christian monk. The person referred to in the Qur'ân, Chapter XVI, ver. 105, is probably Salmân the Persian; the Persian legends being in the Arab mind the very archetype of those 'old folks' tales' to which his revelations were so often compared by his contemporaries.

Other stories, such as those of 'Âd and Thamûd; the legends of their great forefather Abraham; of the Seil al 'Arim, or the bursting of the dyke at Marab, were all commonplaces of the folk lore of the country.

He, however, told them over again with the additional particulars which he had derived from Jewish and Christian sources, and appealed to this additional information in proof of the divine origin of his version.

The city of YaTHrib, better known afterwards as El Medînah, 'the city,' contained many Jewish inhabitants, and Mecca itself was no doubt also frequented by Jewish Arabs, and the influence of their beliefs and superstitions is apparent throughout the Qur'ân.

Christianity too, as we have seen, contributed considerably to the new religion, though not to so great an extent as Judaism.

It is clear, however, that Mohammed was not acquainted with the originals themselves, either of the Jewish or Christian scriptures. The only passage of the Old Testament quoted in the Qur'ân is in Chapter XXI, vers. 104, 105, 'And already have we written in the Psalms after the reminder that "the earth my righteous servants shall inherit,"' which is an Arabic paraphrase of Psalm xxxvii, ver. 29, 'The righteous shall inherit the land.' The well-known exclusiveness of the Jews and their unwillingness that any Gentile hand should touch their holy Book, renders it extremely improbable that even this sentence was borrowed direct from the scriptures themselves, even if Mohammed could have understood the language in which they are written.

The Qur'ân appeals several times to the prophecies concerning Mohammed which are alleged to exist in the New and Old Testaments: thus in Chap. II, 141, 'Those to whom we have given the Book know him as they know their own sons, although a sect of them do surely hide the truth, the while they know;' and again, VI, 20, 'Those to whom we have brought the Book know him as they know their sons,—those who lose their souls do not believe.'

The allusion is said to be to the promise of the Paraclete in John xvi. 7, the suggestion being that the word *παράκλητος* in the Greek has been substituted for *περικλυτός*, which would be exactly translated by the name A'hmed, or Mohammed. Mohammed, however, certainly had not access to the Greek Testament, and it is doubtful whether an Arabic version even existed at the time, Syriac only being the ecclesiastical language of the Christians of the day: it is more probable that Mohammed may have received the suggestion from some of his Christian friends.

The monotheistic idea, which is the key-word to El Islâm, was not new to the Arabs, but it was distasteful, and particularly so to the Qurâi*s*, whose supremacy over the other tribes, and whose worldly prosperity arose from the fact that they were the hereditary guardians of the national collection of idols kept in the sanctuary at Mecca. Mohammed's message, therefore, sounded like a revolutionary watchword, a radical party-cry, which the conservative Meccans could not afford to despise, and which they combated very energetically. The prophet, therefore, in the first place, met with but little success. '*H*adî*g*ah accepted her husband's mission without hesitation, so did her cousin Waraqah; and Zâid, 'the enquirer,' a man who had spent his life in seeking for the truth, and in fighting against this same idolatry that was so repugnant to Mohammed's ideas, at once gave in his adherence to the new doctrine. For three years, however, only fourteen converts were added to the Muslim church.

The mission of Mohammed, then, appealed forcibly to the Arabs on many grounds. Compared with the prevalent idolatry of the time, the idea as presented was so grand, so simple, and so true, that reason could scarcely hesitate between the two systems, unless, as in the case of the Qurâis, self-interest were thrown into the scale. Side by side with the religion of the Jews and Christians, as practised in Arabia at least, it appeared more spiritual and more divine, and presented the truths of both religions without the blemishes. It harmonized with the traditional Semitic belief, Arab as well as Jewish, of the coming of a Messiah, or at least of a prophet, who should reveal the truth at last, and set right the order of things which had spiritually and temporally gone so wrong. And lastly, it made no call on their credulity; it only asked them to believe what they might well accept as self-evident, and it only laid claim to one miracle, that of the marvellous eloquence of its delivery, and this neither friends nor foes could deny. It must not be forgotten that this claim of the Qur'ân to miraculous eloquence, however absurd it may sound to Western ears, was and is to the Arab incontrovertible.

In order to understand the immense influence which the Qur'ân has always exercised upon the Arab mind, it is necessary to remember that it consists not merely of the enthusiastic utterances of an individual, but of the popular sayings, choice pieces of eloquence, and favourite legends current among the desert tribes for ages before his time. Arabic authors speak frequently of the celebrity attained by the ancient Arabic orators, such as Shâibân Wâil, but unfortunately no specimen of their works have come down to us. The Qur'ân, however, enables us to judge of the nature of the speeches which took so strong a hold upon their countrymen.

The essence of Mohammedanism is its assertion of the unity of God, as opposed to polytheism and even to trinitarianism. And this central truth was, we repeat, nothing new; it was, as Mohammed said of it, the ancient faith of Abraham, and it was upon that faith that the greatness of the Jewish nation was founded; nay, it was the truth which Christ himself made more fully known and understood.

One great difference between Judaism and Islâm is that the former is not a proselytising religion, while the latter emphatically is so. All the laws and ordinances of the Pentateuch, all the revelations of the Old Testament, are for the Jew alone, and the Gentile was excluded with jealous care from the enjoyment of any of the divine privileges until Christianity proclaimed that revelation was for the world at large. The Arab, on the contrary, was enjoined to propagate his religion. 'There is no god but God,' and man must be 'resigned to His will,' and if he will not, he must be made to; this is what Islâm or 'resignation' really means.

But, it may be asked, why, if Mohammed preached nothing more than the central truth of Judaism and Christianity, did he not rather accept one or other of these creeds, than found a new one? To answer this question, we must regard Judaism and Christianity not as they are understood now, but as they existed in Arabia in Mohammed's time. Judaism was effete, Christianity corrupt. The Hebrew nation had fallen, and Magian superstitions and Rabbinic inventions had obscured the primeval simplicity of the Hebrew faith and marred the grandeur of its law. The Christians were forgetful alike of the old revelation and of the new, and neglecting the teachings of their Master, were split up into numerous sects—'Homoousians and Homoiousians, Monothelites and Monophysites, Jacobites and Eutychians,' and the like—who had little in common but the name of Christians, and the cordial hatred with which they regarded each other.

Mohammed certainly wished his religion to be looked upon as a further fulfilment of Christianity, just as Christianity is the fulfilment of Judaism. He regards our Lord with particular veneration, and even goes so far as to call Him the 'Spirit' and 'Word' of God; 'the Messiah, Jesus the son of Mary, is but the apostle of God and His Word, which He cast into Mary and a spirit from Him' (Sûrah IV, 169). The reservation, 'is but the apostle,' &c., is directed against the misconception of the Christian doctrine which was then prevalent in Arabia, and which was the only one with which Mohammed was acquainted. With the Arab Christian, the Trinity meant nothing more nor less than tritheism, and these three the Father, Virgin-Mother, and Son.

The doctrine of the unity of God, as preached by Mohammed, was a protest against the dualism of Persia as well as the degenerate Christianity of the time and the polytheism of the Arabs who were his contemporaries. Thus the Chapter of Cattle (VI) commences with the words, 'Praise belongs to God who created the heavens and the earth, and brought into being the darkness and the light,' which negatives the Manichæan theory that the two principles of light and darkness were uncreate and eternal, and by their admixture or antagonism gave birth to the material universe.

As for the angelism and demonology of the Qur'ân, they are a mixture of local superstitions, Persian and Jewish tradition. The system was certainly not due to Mohammed's invention, but was evolved out of what he had heard from Jewish, Christian, and other sources, and regarded as revelation, and coloured by his individual local beliefs.

It is a curious thing that the rite of circumcision is not mentioned in the Qur'ân; but there is no doubt that Mohammed insisted upon it as a compromise for more cruel and dangerous practices [1].

The Qur'ân itself is not a formal and consistent code either of morals, laws, or ceremonies.

Revealed 'piecemeal,' particular passages being often promulgated to decide particular cases, it cannot fail to contain many things that are at variance with, or flatly contradict others.

It has, however, a certain unity notwithstanding; for Mohammed had his doctrine of the unity of God, according to the 'Hanîfite conception, always before his mind: he had the immemorial customs of his country and their tribal

[1] See note to vol. ii, p. 110, of Burton's 'Pilgrimage to El Medina and Mecca.'

usages to guide him in his decisions, only instead of being bound by these usages he was able, by virtue of his office of prophet, to alter or abrogate such as appeared to him not to conduce to the welfare of society. The religious observances and ceremonies he retained were also to a great extent forced upon him; the injunctions to prayer and fasting were necessary to keep alive the religious fervour of the converts, and, indeed, to give the character of a religion to the movement and distinguish it from a mere political reform. The ceremonies of the pilgrimage could not be entirely done away with. The universal reverence of the Arab for the Kaabah was too favourable and obvious a means for uniting all the tribes into one confederation with one common purpose in view. The traditions of Abraham, the father of their race and the founder of Mohammed's own religion, as he always declared him to be, no doubt gave the ancient temple a peculiar sanctity in the prophet's eyes, and although he had at first settled upon Jerusalem as his Qiblah, he afterwards reverted to the Kaabah itself. Here, then, Mohammed found a shrine to which, as well as at which, devotion had been paid from time immemorial: it was the one thing which the scattered Arabian nation had in common—the one thing which gave them even the shadow of a national feeling; and to have dreamed of abolishing it, or even of diminishing the honours paid to it, would have been madness and ruin to his enterprise. He therefore did the next best thing, he cleared it of idols and dedicated it to the service of God. Again, the 'Ha*gg* was the occasion on which the tribes assembled at Mecca and, therefore, not only the cause of trading and mutual profit amongst themselves, but upon it depended entirely the commercial prosperity of the Qurâi*s*.

It has been objected to Islâm that neither its doctrines nor its rites are original. No religion, certainly no sacred books of a religion, ever possessed entire originality. The great principles of morality, and the noble thoughts which are common to humanity, must find their way into the Scriptures, if these are to have any hold upon men; and it would, indeed, be strange if the writers, however inspired, left no trace in their writings of what they had seen, heard, or read. The New Testament, it is well known, contains much that is not original. Many of the parables &c., as a late eminent Orientalist once pointed out, are to be found in the Talmud. We know that St. Paul drew upon classic Greek sources for many of his most striking utterances, not even disdaining to quote the worldly wisdom of the comedian Menander; and there is at least a curious coincidence between the words used in describing the blindness that fell on the apostle just before his conversion, and its subsequent cure, with the description given by Stesichorus in his 'Palinodia' of a similar incident connected with his own conversion to the worship of the Dioscuri. Even the most divine sentiment in the Lord's Prayer, 'Forgive us our trespasses as we forgive those who trespass against us,' is expressed almost in so many words in the advice given by Nestor to the angered Achilles in the first book of Homer's Iliad.

Judged then by the standard which we apply to other creeds, Mohammed's religion stands forth as something strikingly new and original, since it sets before his countrymen, for the first time, the grand conception of one God, which was, as he asserted, the faith of their father Abraham, but which their fetishism had so long obscured.

The Arabs made use of a rhymed and rhythmical prose, the origin of which it is not difficult to imagine. The Arabic language consists for the most part of triliteral roots, i.e. the single words expressing individual ideas consist generally of three consonants each, and the derivative forms expressing modifications of the original idea are not made by affixes and terminations alone, but also by the insertion of letters in the root. Thus **ẓaraba** means 'he struck,' and **qatala**, 'he killed,' while ma**ẓrûb** and ma**qtûl** signify 'one struck' and 'one killed.' A sentence, therefore, consists of a series of words which would each require to be expressed in clauses of several words in other languages, and it is easy to see how a next following sentence, explanatory of or completing the first, would be much more clear and forcible if it consisted of words of a similar shape and implying similar modifications of other ideas. It follows then that the two sentences would be necessarily symmetrical, and the presence of rhythm would not only please the ear but contribute to the better understanding of the sense, while the rhyme would mark the pause in the sense and emphasize the proposition.

The Qur'ân is written in this rhetorical style, in which the clauses are rhythmical though not symmetrically so, and for the most part end in the same rhyme throughout the chapter.

The Arabic language lends itself very readily to this species of composition, and the Arabs of the desert in the present day employ it to a great extent in their more formal orations, while the literary men of the towns adopt it as the recognised correct style, deliberately imitating the Qur'ân.

That the best of Arab writers has never succeeded in producing anything equal in merit to the Qur'ân itself is not surprising. In the first place, they have agreed beforehand that it is unapproachable, and they have adopted its style as the perfect standard; any deviation from it therefore must of necessity be a defect. Again, with them this style is not spontaneous as with Mohammed and his contemporaries, but is as artificial as though Englishmen should still continue to follow Chaucer as their model, in spite of the changes which their language has undergone. With the prophet the style was natural, and the words were those used in every-day ordinary life, while with the later Arabic authors the style is imitative and the ancient words are introduced as a literary embellishment. The natural consequence is that their attempts look laboured and unreal by the side of his impromptu and forcible eloquence.

That Mohammed, though, should have been able to challenge even his contemporaries to produce anything like the Qur'ân, 'And if ye are in doubt of what we have revealed unto our servant, then bring a chapter like it . . . But if ye do it not, and ye surely shall do it not, &c.,' is at first sight surprising, but, as Nöldeke[1] has pointed out, this challenge really refers much more to the subject than to the mere style,—to the originality of the conception of the unity of God and of a revelation supposed to be couched in God's own words. Any attempt at such a work must of necessity have had all the weakness and want of prestige which attaches to an imitation. This idea is by no means foreign to the genius of the old Arabs; thus the learned grammarian and rhetorician 'Harîrî excuses himself in the preface to his celebrated 'Assemblies' for any shortcomings, which might possibly be detected in a composition professedly modelled on that of another, by quoting an ancient poem:

> ''Twas this affected me, that while I lay
> Snatching a breath of sleep for drowsiness,
> There wept a dove upon the Aikah bough
> Trilling her weeping forth with sweetest notes:
> Ah, had I wept—ere she began to weep—
> For Sâudâ's love, my soul had found relief!
> But 'twas her weeping that excited mine,
> And he who comes first must be always best!'

Amongst a people who believed firmly in witchcraft and soothsaying and who though passionately fond of poetry, believed that every poet had his familiar spirit who inspired his utterances, it was no wonder that the prophet should be taken for 'a soothsayer,' for 'one possessed with an evil spirit,' or for 'an infatuated poet[2].'

Each chapter of the Qur'ân is called in Arabic a sûrah, a word which signifies a course of bricks in a wall, and is generally used in the body of the work for any connected or continuous portion complete in itself.

[1] Geschichte des Qorâns, p. 43.

[2] Mohammed may well have repudiated the charge of being a poet, for he is only credited with one verse, and that an involuntary one:

> Ana 'nnabîyu lâ Kadhib;
> Ana 'bnu 'Abd el Muttalib.
> 'I am the prophet who lies not;
> I am the son of bd el Muttalib.'

The word Qur'ân, 'a reading,' comes from the verb qara'a, 'to read,' though some lexicographers derive it from qarana, 'to join,' and interpret it as meaning the 'collected whole.' It is also called El Forqân, 'the discrimination,' a word borrowed from the Hebrew and also applied in the Qur'ân to divine inspiration generally.

The individual portions of the Qur'ân were not always written down immediately after their revelation, as we find that Mohammed often repeated them several times until he had learnt them by heart, and the book itself shows that he occasionally forgot them and even altered and supplemented them: 'Whatever verse we may annul or cause thee to forget, we will bring a better one than it, or one like it' (Chapter II, ver. 100). On other occasions he employed an amanuensis, as, for instance, Abdallah ibn Sa'hd ibn Abî Sar'h (see Part I, p. 126, note 2) and Zâid ibn THâbit; and tradition relates that he would frequently direct in which Sûrah the passage dictated was to be placed. That the Qur'ân was, or that even the individual Sûrahs were, however, arranged in the present order by the prophet himself is impossible, both from internal evidence and that of tradition.

At the prophet's death no collected edition of the Qur'ân existed. Scattered fragments were in the possession of certain of his followers, written down at different times and on the most heterogeneous materials, but by far the greater portion was preserved only in the memories of men whom death might at any moment carry off. The death of many Muslim warriors at the battle of Yemâmah opened the eyes of the early Caliphs to the danger that the 'Book of God' might be, ere long, irrevocably lost: they accordingly provided, to the best of their power, against such a contingency. Abu Bekr,—or rather Omar, during his reign,—was the first to take the matter in hand, and employed Zâid ibn THâbit the Ansârî, a native of Medînah, who had acted as amanuensis to Mohammed, to collect and arrange the text. This he did from 'palm-leaves, skins, blade-bones, and the hearts of men,' and presented to the Caliph a copy of the Qur'ân, which did not probably differ greatly from that which we now possess. As we have already seen, the whole was strung together without any reference to the chronological order, and with very little regard to the logical connection of various passages. The longer Sûrahs were placed at the beginning and the short ones at the end, although the order of their revelation was for the most part just the reverse. And, lastly, many odd verses appear to have been inserted into various Sûrahs for no other reason than that they suit the rhyme.

The text was so far fixed by Zâid, but not the reading of it. In the first place, the vowel points, which make often a very great difference in the meaning of a word, were probably hardly ever, if at all, used; again, many persons were still alive who themselves remembered portions of the Qur'ân by heart, but who did not agree as to individual words, or who remembering the sense only substituted some of the locutions of their own tribe for the actual words of Mohammed.

These tribal dialects often differed diametrically in the use of particular words; thus i'*h*fa'un means 'to conceal' in the dialect of one tribe and 'to display' in that of another; when such words occurred, as they often do, in the Qur'ân, they could not fail to give rise to disputes as to their interpretation.

In the present recension of the Qur'ân there are comparatively few various readings recognised, but it is clear that great variations existed from the very first. On more than one occasion Mohammed himself dictated the same passage to different persons with different readings; and the 'traditional saying' ascribed to him, that 'the Qur'ân was revealed according to seven modes of reading,' shows what latitude he himself allowed. The other interpretation of this tradition, namely, that 'the Qur'ân may be read according to the seven Arabic dialects,' was obviously invented to check the tendency to perversion of the text according to individual fancy, and is plainly refuted by the fact that the persons to whom the saying was uttered, and who had appealed to the prophet to decide upon the reading of a certain text, were both of the tribe of Qurâis.

At length, some twenty years afterwards, the Caliph Othmân, alarmed at the bitter feelings and open quarrels which these differences of reading and interpretation had already engendered, determined to prevent the Muslims from differing amongst themselves in their way of reading the word of God as the Jews and Christians did. He accordingly appointed a commission, consisting of Zâid, the original editor, with three men of the Qurâis (Mohammed's own tribe), to decide, once for all. upon the text and to fix the reading definitely according to the pure Qurâis idiom.

When this edition was completed, Othmân sent copies to all the principal cities in the empire, and caused all the previous copies to be burned. These copies were perhaps not themselves free from small discrepances; the few slight various readings which have, as I have shown, crept in, are most of them mere matters of orthography, and the rest are unimportant to the general sense. The last named will be found mentioned in the notes to the passages in which they occur in the course of the following translation.

Othmân's recension has remained the authorised text, and has been adopted by all schools of Mohammedan theologians from the time it was made (A.D. 660) until the present day.

In this no further attempt was made at chronological arrangement than in the preceding one. The individual Sûrahs have prefixed to them the name of the place, Mecca or Medînah, at which they were revealed; but this indication, though derived from authentic tradition, is not a sufficient guide, since in many places verses have been inserted in a Meccan Sûrah which were evidently revealed at Medînah, and vice versâ. To clear away this difficulty, and to propose an intelligible chronological arrangement of the Sûrahs, has been the aim of scholars, both Arabic and European; but no one has treated the subject in so critical or masterly a manner as Nöldeke, and his arrangement may be taken as the best which Arabic tradition, combined with European criticism, can furnish.

To arrive at a decision on this point we must consider first the historical event, if any, to which each text refers; next, the style generally; and lastly, the individual expressions used. Thus, in addressing the Meccans the words yâ aiyuha 'nnâs, 'O ye folk!' occur, while the expression yâ aiyuha 'llaDHîn âmanû is used in speaking to the people of Medînah; though sometimes the former phrase occurs in a verse of a Medînah Sûrah.

The Sûrahs resolve themselves into two great classes, those revealed at Mecca and those revealed at Medînah after the flight; and these are easily distinguished both by their style and subject-matter. The earlier ones especially are grander in style, and testify in every verse to the mental exaltation of the prophet and the earnest belief which he certainly had at this time in the reality and truth of his divine mission.

The Qur'ân falls naturally into these two classes, which represent, in fact, the first development of Mohammed's prophetic office at Mecca. and the later career as a leader and lawgiver after the flight at Medînah.

Sûrahs belonging to the first period of his career are therefore ascribed to Mecca, and those of the latter period to Medînah, although the actual place at which they were delivered may be in certain cases doubtful.

One of the next earliest Sûrahs is that entitled Abu Laheb. Mohammed had at length called together his clansmen, the Banû Hâshim, and bade them accept the new doctrine of Allah's unity. Hereupon 'Abd el 'Huzzah, surnamed Abu Laheb, 'he of the flame,' indignantly exclaimed, 'Perdition to you! is that what thou hast called us for?' Mohammed then proclaimed the Sûrah bearing Abu Laheb's name, in which he enunciates a terrible curse against him and his wife Umm *G*emîl, and made of him an irreconcilable foe.

The CVIth Sûrah also belongs undoubtedly to an early

period. In it Mohammed bids the Qurâis 'serve the Lord of this House,' for the two trading caravans they yearly sent out in winter and summer respectively.

In the Meccan Sûrahs Mohammed's one and steady purpose is to bring his hearers to a belief in the one only God; this he does by powerful rhetorical displays rather than logical arguments, by appealing to their feelings rather than their reason; by setting forth the manifestations of God in his works; by calling nature to witness to His presence; and by proclaiming His vengeance against those who associate other gods with Him, or attribute offspring to Him. The appeal was strengthened by glowing pictures of the happiness in store for those who should believe, and by frightful descriptions of the everlasting torments prepared for the unbelievers.

The short Sûrah entitled 'Unity' is said, on the traditional authority of Mohammed himself, to be equivalent in value to two-thirds of the Qur'ân.

'Say, "He is God, one God the eternal. He begets not, and is not begotten; nor is there like unto Him, one."'

This protest is not aimed at the Christian doctrines alone, for the Arab, as we have seen, asserted that their angels and deities were daughters of Allâh, the supreme God.

In the earlier chapters, too, the prophetic inspiration, the earnest conviction of the truth of his mission, and the violent emotion which his sense of responsibility caused him are plainly shown.

The style is curt, grand, and often almost sublime; the expressions are full of poetical feeling, and the thoughts are earnest and passionate, though sometimes dim and confused, indicating the mental excitement and doubt through which they struggled to light.

In the second period of the Meccan Sûrahs, Mohammed appears to have conceived the idea of still further severing himself from the idolatry of his compatriots, and of giving to the supreme deity Allâh another title, Ar-Ra'hmân, 'the merciful one.'

The Meccans, however, seem to have taken these for

the names of separate deities[1], and the name is abandoned in the later chapters.

In the Sûrahs of the second Meccan period we first find the long stories of the prophets of olden time, especial stress being laid upon the punishment which fell upon their contemporaries for disbelief; the moral is always the same, namely, that Mohammed came under precisely similar circumstances, and that a denial of the truth of his mission would bring on his fellow-citizens the self-same retribution.

They also show the transition stage between the intense and poetical enthusiasm of the early Meccan chapters and the calm teaching of the later Medînah ones. This change is gradual, and even in the later and most prosaic we find occasionally passages in which the old prophetic fire flashes out once more.

The three periods again are marked by the oaths which occur throughout the Qur'ân. In the first period they are very frequent and often long, the whole powers of nature being invoked to bear witness to the unity of God and the mission of His Apostle; in the second period they are shorter and of rarer occurrence; in the last period they are absent altogether.

To understand the Medînah Sûrahs we must bear in mind Mohammed's position with respect to the various parties in that city.

In Mecca he had been a prophet with little honour in his own country, looked on by some as a madman, and by others as an impostor, both equally grievous to him, while his following consisted only of the poorest and meanest of his fellow-townsmen.

His own clansmen, for the reason that they were his clansmen and for no other, resented the affronts against him.

In Medînah he appears as a military leader and a prince, though as yet possessing far from absolute authority. Around him in the city were, first, the true believers who had fled with him, El Muhâgerîn; next, the in-

[1] See Part II, p. 13, note 1.

habitants of YaTHrib, who had joined him and who were called El Ansâr, 'the helpers;' and lastly, a large class who are spoken of by the uncomplimentary name of Munâfiqûn or 'hypocrites,' consisting of those who went over to his side from fear or compulsion, and lastly those 'in whose heart is sickness,' who, though believing on him, were prevented by tribal or family ties from going over to him openly.

Abdallâh ibn Ubai was a chief whose influence operated strongly against Mohammed, and the latter was obliged to treat him for a long time almost as an equal, even after he had lost his political power.

The other party at Medînah was composed of the Jewish tribes settled in and around the city of YaTHrib. The Jews were at first looked to as the most natural and likely supporters of the new religion, which was to confirm their own.

These various parties together with the pagan Arabs of Mecca and the Christians are the persons with whom the Medînah Sûrahs chiefly deal.

The style of the Medînah Sûrahs resembles that of the third period of the Meccan revelations, the more matter-of-fact nature of the incidents related or the precepts given accounting in a great measure for the more prosaic language in which they are expressed.

As in the Meccan Sûrahs it is possible to arrive at a tolerably accurate notion of their chronological order by noting the events to which they refer, and comparing them with the history itself; although the doubtful authority of many of the traditions and the frequent vagueness of the allusions in the Qur'ân itself leave much uncertain.

In the Medînah Sûrahs the prophet is no longer merely trying to convert his hearers by examples, promises, and warnings; he addresses them as their prince and general, praising or blaming them for their conduct, and giving them laws and precepts as occasion required.

Nöldeke has given a masterly analysis of the various historical and other allusions, and has reduced as far as possible the heterogeneous mass of materials to such order that we may accept his arrangement as at least the most accurate hitherto proposed.

Since, however, many passages are no doubt misplaced and inserted in Sûrahs to which they did not originally belong, nothing but a comprehensive view of the contents of the whole Qur'ân, studied side by side with the history of Mohammed and his contemporaries, will enable us to arrive at an actual decision on the exact chronological sequence of the revelation.

To assist in the investigation of this most important subject I have subjoined a précis of the contents of each chapter.

The following is Nöldeke's chronological order of the Sûrahs:—

Meccan Sûrahs.

First Period (from the first to the fifth year of Mohammed's mission): XCVI, LXXIV, CXI, CVI, CVIII, CIV, CVII, CII, CV, XCII, XC, XCIV, XCIII, XCVII, LXXXVI, XCI, LXXX, LXVIII, LXXXVII, XCV, CIII, LXXXV, LXXIII, CI, XCIX, LXXXII, LXXXI, LIII, LXXXIV, C, LXXIX, LXXVII, LXXVIII, LXXXVIII, LXXXIX, LXXV, LXXXIII, LXIX, LI, LII, LVI, LXX, LV, CXII, CIX, CXIII, CXIV, I.

Second Period (the fifth and sixth year of his mission): LIV, XXXVII, LXXI, LXXVI, XLIV, L, XX, XXVI, XV, XIX, XXXVIII, XXXVI, XLIII, LXXII, LXVII, XXIII, XXI, XXV, XVII, XXVII, XVIII.

Third Period (from the seventh year to the flight): XXXII, XLI, XLV, XVI, XXX, XI, XIV, XII, XL, XXVIII, XXXIX, XXIX, XXXI, XLII, X, XXXIV, XXXV, VII, XLVI, VI, XIII.

Medînah Sûrahs.

II, XCVIII, LXIV, LXII, VIII, XLVII, III, LXI, LVII, IV, LXV, LIX, XXXIII, LXIII, XXIV, LVIII, XXII, XLVIII, LXVI, LX, CX, XLIX, IX, V.

The mysterious letters which are placed at the beginning of certain chapters of the Qur'ân are explained in various ways by the Muslim commentators. Some suppose them to be part of the revelation itself, and to conceal sublime and inscrutable mysteries; others think that they stand for the names of Allâh, Gabriel, Mohammed, and so on.

Nöldeke has the ingenious theory that they were monograms of the names of the persons from whom Zâid and his companions obtained the portions to which they are prefixed; thus, A L R would stand for Ez-zubâir, A L M R for Al-Mu*gh*âirah, *T* H for Tal'Hah, and so on. A comparison of the Arabic letters themselves with the names suggested makes the hypothesis a very probable one. They may have been mere numerical or alphabetical labels for the boxes of scraps on which the original was written; the authors of the Commentary known as El Jelâlâin, however, give the prevailing opinion amongst Muslim scholars when they say, 'God alone knows what He means by these letters.'

The Sûrahs are subdivided into 'âyât, 'verses' (literally 'signs'), which, although they for the most part mark a distinct pause either in the rhyme or sense, are sometimes mere arbitrary divisions irrespective of either.

Besides these, the Qur'ân is divided into sixty equal portions, called a'hzâb (sing. 'hizb), each subdivided into four equal parts; another division is that into thirty 'a*g*zâ' (sing. *g*uz') or 'sections,' so that the whole may be read through during the month of Rama*dh*ân: these are again subdivided into rukû'h (sing. rak'hah), 'acts of bowing.' By these, rather than by chapter and verse (Sûrah and 'Âyah), the Muslims themselves quote the Book.

Besides the name Qur'ân it is known as El Furqân, 'the Discrimination,' El Mus'haf, 'the Volume,' El Kitâb, 'the Book,' and EDH-DHikr, 'the Reminder.' The title attached to each Sûrah is taken from some striking word which occurs in it.

The creed of Mohammed and the Qur'ân is termed Islâm, 'Resignation,' scil. to the will of God. The religion, as understood and practised, is based upon four rules or fundamental principles:

1. The Qur'ân itself.

2. 'HadîTH (pl. 'a'hâdîTH), the 'traditional' sayings of the prophet which supplement the Qur'ân, and provide for cases of law or ceremonial observance on which it is silent. They also deal with the life of Mohammed and the circumstances attending the revelations, and are therefore of great use in the exegesis of the Book itself. Although the Muslim authorities have been very strict in the canons laid down for the reception or rejection of these traditions, tracing them from hand to hand up to their original sources, a great deal of uncertainty exists as to the authenticity of many of them. The laws embodied in the traditions are called the Sunnah.

3. Igmâ'h or the 'consensus' of opinion of the highest authorities in the Muslim church upon points concerning which neither the Qur'ân nor the 'HadîTH are explicit.

4. Qiyâs or 'Analogy,' that is, the reasoning of the theological authorities by analogy from the Qur'ân, 'HadîTH, and Igmâ'h, where anything in any one or more is still left undecided.

The first principle of the Muslim faith is a belief in Allâh, who, as we have seen, was known to the Arabs before Mohammed's time, and under the title Allâh ta'hâlâ, 'Allâh the most high,' was regarded as the chief god of their pantheon. The epithet ta'hâlâ is, properly speaking, a verb meaning 'be He exalted,' but is used, as verbs sometimes are in Arabic[1], as an epithet. The name Allâh, 'God,' is composed of the article al, 'the,' and ilâh, 'a god,' and is a very old Semitic word, being connected with the el and elohîm of the Hebrew, and entering into the composition of a large proportion of proper names in Hebrew, Nabathean, and Arabic.

According to Muslim theology, Allâh is eternal and everlasting, one and indivisible, not endued with form, nor circumscribed by limit or measure; comprehending all things, but comprehended of nothing.

[1] See my Arabic Grammar, p. 256.

His attributes are expressed by ninety-nine epithets used in the Qur'ân, which in the Arabic are single words, generally participial forms, but in the translation are sometimes rendered by verbs, as, 'He hears' for 'He is the hearer.'

These attributes constitute the Asmâ' el 'Husnâ, 'the good names[1],' under which God is invoked by the Muslims; they are ninety-nine in number, and are as follows:—

1. ar-Ra'hmân, the Merciful.
2. ar-Ra'hîm, the Compassionate.
3. al-Mâlik, the Ruler.
4. al-Qaddûs, the Holy.
5. as-Salâm, Peace.
6. al-Mû'min, the Faithful.
7. al-Muhâimun, the Protector.
8. al-'Hazîz, the Mighty.
9. al-*G*abbâr, the Repairer.
10. al-Mutakabbir, the Great.
11. al-Khâliq, the Creator.
12. al-Bâri', the Creator.
13. al-Muzawwir, the Fashioner.
14. al-*Gh*affâr, the Forgiver.
15. al-Qahhâr, the Dominant.
16. al-Wahhâb, the Bestower.
17. ar-Razzâq, the Provider.
18. al-Fattâ'h, the Opener.
19. al-'Âlim, the Knowing.
20. al-Qâbiz, the Restrainer.
21. al-Bâsi*t*, the Spreader.
22. al-'Hâfiz, the Guardian.
23. ar-Râfi', the Exalter.
24. al-Mu'hizz, the Honourer.
25. al-Muzîl, the Destroyer.
26. as-Samî'h, the Hearer.
27. al-Bazîr, the Seer.
28. al-'Hâkim, the Judge.
29. al-'Hadl, Justice.
30. al-La*t*îf, the Subtle.
31. al-'*H*abîr, the Aware.
32. al-'Halîm, the Clement.
33. al-'Ha*th*îm, the Grand.
34. al-*Gh*afûr, the Forgiving.
35. a*s*-*S*akûr, the Grateful.
36. al-'Halî, the Exalted.
37. al-Kabîr, the Great.
38. al-'Hâfiz, the Guardian.
39. al-Muqît, the Strengthener.
40. al-Hasîb, the Reckoner.
41. al-*G*alîl, the Majestic.
42. al-Karîm, the Generous.
43. ar-Raqîb, the Watcher.
44. al-Mu*g*îb, the Answerer of Prayer.
45. al-Wasî'h, the Comprehensive.
46. al-'Hakîm, the Wise.
47. al-Wadûd, the Loving.
48. al-Ma*g*îd, the Glorious.
49. al-Bâ'hiTH, the Raiser.
50. a*s*-*S*ahîd, the Witness.
51. al-Haqq, Truth.
52. al-Wakîl, the Guardian.
53. al-Qawwî, the Strong.
54. al-Matîn, the Firm.
55. al-Walî, the Patron.
56. al-Hamîd, the Laudable.
57. al-Mu'hsî, the Counter.

[1] See Chapter VII, ver. 179.

58. al-Mubdî, the Beginner.
59. al-Mu'hîd, the Restorer.
60. al-Mo'hyî, the Quickener.
61. al-Mumît, the Killer.
62. al-'Hâiy, the Living.
63. al-Qâiyûm, the Subsisting.
64. al-Wâgid, the Existing.
65. al-Magîd, the Glorious.
66. al-Wâhid, the One.
67. az-Zamad, the Eternal.
68. al-Qâdir, the Powerful.
69. al-Muqtadir, the Prevailing.
70. al-Muwa'h'hir, the Deferrer.
71. al-Muqaddim, the Bringer-forward.
72. al-Awwal, the First.
73. al-Â'hir, the Last.
74. ath-Thâhir, the Apparent.
75. al-Bâtin, the Innermost.
76. al-Wâlî, the Governor.
77. al-Muta'hâl, the Exalted.
78. al-Barr, Righteousness.
79. at-Tawwâb, the Relenting.
80. al-Muntaqim, the Avenger.
81. al-'Hafû, the Pardoner.
82. ar-Ra'ûf, the Kind.
83. Mâlik al Mulk, the Ruler of the Kingdom.
84. Dhu'lgalâl wa'l ikrâm, Lord of Majesty and Liberality.
85. al-Muqsit, the Equitable.
86. al-Gâmi'h, the Collector.
87. al-Ghanî, the Independent.
88. al-Mughnî, the Enricher.
89. al-Mu'htî, the Giver.
90. al-Mâni'h, the Withholder.
91. az-Zârr, the Distresser.
92. an-Nâfi'h, the Profiter.
93. an-Nûr, Light.
94. al-Hâdî, the Guide.
95. al-Badî'h, the Incomparable.
96. al-Bâqî, the Enduring.
97. al-Wârith, the Inheritor.
98. ar-Rasîd, the Rightly-directing.
99. az-Zabûr, the Patient.

These names are used by Muslims in their devotions, the rosary (masba'hah) being employed to check their repetition. Such an exercise is called a DHikr or 'remembrance,' a word that is also applied to a recitation of the whole or portions of the Qur'ân and to the devotional exercises of the dervishes.

The formula 'In the name of the merciful and compassionate God,' with which every chapter but one of the Qur'ân begins, appears to have been adopted from the Persian Zoroastrian phrase, Benâm i Yezdân i ba'hsâyisgar dâdâr, 'In the name of God the merciful, the just;' the later Parsee form Benâm i 'hudawandi ba'hsâyenda ba'hsâyisgar is the exact equivalent of the Mohammedan phrase.

Besides a belief in God, the Qur'ân requires belief in the existence of angels; they are pure, without distinction of sex, created of fire, and neither eat nor drink nor propagate their species.

The archangels are, Gibra'îl, 'Gabriel' (also called er Rû'h el Amîn, 'the faithful spirit,' or er Rû'h el Qudus, 'the holy spirit'), God's messenger by whom the Qur'ân was revealed to Mohammed ; Mikâ'îl, the guardian angel of the Jews[1]; Isrâfîl, the archangel who will sound the last trumpet at the resurrection ; Azrâ'îl, the angel of death.

Two angels are appointed to each human being, who stand one on his right and one on his left hand, to record his every action.

One angel, called Ra*z*wân, 'goodwill,' presides over heaven ; and one, named Mâlik, 'the ruler,' over hell[2].

Munkir and Nakîr are the two angels who preside at 'the examination of the tomb.' They visit a man in his grave directly after he has been buried, and examine him concerning his faith. If he acknowledge that there is but one God and that Mohammed is his prophet, they suffer him to rest in peace, otherwise they beat him with iron maces till he roars so loud that he is heard by all from east to west except by men and *g*inns. They then press the earth down on the corpse, and leave it to be torn by dragons and serpents till the day of resurrection.

The angelology of Islâm is apparently traceable to Jewish sources, though the ancient Arab cult had no doubt borrowed some portion of it from the Persians, whence too it was introduced into Judaism.

The notions of the bridge over hell, Es Sirâ*t*, and of the partition wall, El Aarâf, between paradise and hell[3], are also common to the Jewish and Magian traditions.

Iblîs or *S*aitân, 'the devil' or 'Satan,' was originally an angel who fell from paradise on account of his proudly refusing to adore Adam[4].

Besides the angels there are the *g*inn (collectively *g*ânn), of whom I have before spoken. They are created out of

---

[1] See Part I, p. 13, note 2.

[2] Mâlik is evidently identical with Moloch, as *G*ehennum, hell, is the same as the Gehenna of the Bible.

[3] See Part I, p. 138, note 1.

[4] See Chapter II, ver. 32.

fire and are both good and evil, the latter being generally called 'Ifrît.' Their abode is Mount Qâf, the mountain chain which encircles the world. These are the creatures over whom Solomon held control, and a tribe of whom were converted to Islâm by Mohammed's preaching on his return from *T*â'if[1].

The two classes of beings, human and superhuman, by which the world is inhabited are called ETH-THaqalân, 'the two weighty matters,' or el 'Hâlamûn, 'the worlds,' as in the expression in the Opening Chapter, 'Lord of the worlds.'

Heaven, according to the Qur'ân and the traditions, consists of seven divisions:

*G*annat al '*H*uld (Chapter XXV, 16), the Garden of Eternity.
Dâr as Salâm (Chapter VI, 127), the Abode of Peace.
Dâr al Qarâr (Chapter XL, 42), the Abode of Rest.
*G*annat 'Hadn (Chapter IX, 72), the Garden of Eden.
*G*annat al Mâ'wâ (Chapter XXXII, 19), the Garden of Resort.
*G*annat an Na'hîm (Chapter VI, 70), the Garden of Pleasure.
*G*annat al 'Hilliyûn (Chapter LXXXIII, 18), the Garden of the Most High.
*G*annat al Firdaus (Chapter XVIII, 107), the Garden of Paradise.

Of the presumed sensual character of the Muslim paradise much has been written. It appears, however, from the Qur'ân, to be little more than an intense realisation of all that a dweller in a hot, parched, and barren land could desire, namely, shade, water, fruit, rest, and pleasant companionship and service.

Hell contains also seven divisions[2]:

*G*ehennum (Chapter XIX, 44), Gehenna.
La*th*â (Chapter LXX, 15), the Flaming Fire.
Hu*t*amah (Chapter CIV, 4), the Raging Fire that splits everything to pieces.
Sa'hîr (Chapter IV, 11), the Blaze.
Saqar (Chapter LIV, 58), the Scorching Fire.
*G*ahîm (Chapter II, 113), the Fierce Fire.
Hâwiyeh (Chapter CL, 8), the Abyss.

[1] See above, p. xxx.

[2] Cf. Chapter XV, ver. 44.

As to the condition of the soul between death and the resurrection, Islâm has no authoritative teaching; the general opinion is that there is a limbo somewhere or other in which the spirits of the good repose, while those of the wicked are imprisoned elsewhere in a foul dungeon to await their doom.

A great many wonderful signs are to precede the judgment day, of which we need only notice the coming of Mehdi or 'guide,' who shall have the same name as Mohammed himself, and whose father's name shall be the same as his father's name, and who shall govern the Arabians, and fill the earth with righteousness; the appearance of Ed-da*gg*âl, 'the antichrist;' the release of Gog and Magog[1]; and the convulsions in heaven and earth described in the Qur'ân itself.

The chief prophets recognised by the Qur'ân are the following: each of whom is said to have had a special revelation, and to possess an appropriate title:

Adam, *Z*afîy allâh, the Chosen of God.
Noah, Nabîy allâh, the Prophet of God.
Abraham, '*H*alîla 'llâh, the Friend of God.
Jesus, Rû'ha 'llâh, the Spirit of God.
Mohammed, Rusûl allâh, the Apostle of God.

Mohammed is also called 'the seal of the prophets,' and the saying traditionally attributed to him, 'There is no prophet after me,' makes it unlawful to expect the advent of another.

Besides these, there are the minor apostles sent to particular tribes, the stories of some of whom are related in the Qur'ân.

The practical duties of Islâm are, 1. The profession of faith in the unity of God, and the mission of Mohammed. 2. Prayer. 3. Fasting. 4. Almsgiving. 5. Pilgrimage.

The first consists in the repetition of the Kelimah or creed, 'There is no god but God, and Mohammed is the Apostle of God.'

[1] See Part II, p. 25.

Prayer consists of the recital of a certain prescribed and invariable formula at five stated times of the day, namely: 1. Between dawn and sunrise. 2. After the sun has begun to decline. 3. Midway between this. 4. Which is said shortly after sunset. 5. At nightfall. These are farẓ or 'incumbent;' all others are nafl, 'supererogatory,' or sunnah, 'in accordance with the practices of the prophet.' The prayers are preceded by wuẓû'h, 'ablution;' they are commenced in a standing position, qiyâm, the hands being so held that the thumbs touch the lobes of the ears, and the face being turned towards the qiblah, that is, in the direction of Mecca. During the prayers inclinations of the body, rukû'h [1], are made, of which a certain number only are incumbent.

The time for prayer is called from the minarets of the mosques by Mu'eDHDHins or 'criers,' in the following words:

'God is great!' (four times). 'I bear witness that there is no god but God' (twice). 'I bear witness that Mohammed is the Apostle of God' (twice). 'Come hither to prayers!' (twice). 'Come hither to salvation!' (twice). 'God is great! There is no other god but God!' and in the early morning the crier adds, 'Prayer is better than sleep!'

This formula appears to have been used by Bilâl, Mohammed's own crier, on the establishment of the first mosque in Medînah. It is called the aDHân or 'call.'

The word 'mosque' is a corruption of masgid, 'a place of adoration' (sigdah), and is applied to the whole precincts of a Muslim place of worship. Another name is *g*âmi'h, 'the assembling,' especially applied to a cathedral mosque.

The mosques are always open for public prayers, but on Fridays a special service is held, followed by a '*H*u*t*bah or 'homily.'

Another of the duties incumbent on every believer

[1] 'The lowering of the head, by a person praying [or in prayer], after the act of standing, in which the recitation [of portions of the Ḳur-án] is performed, so that the palms of the hand reach the knees, or so that the back becomes depressed,' Lane's Arabic-English Lexicon.

is that of fasting between dawn and sunset throughout Rama*dh*ân, the ninth month of the Muslim year. The fast is a most rigorous one, not even a drop of water being allowed to pass the lips even when Rama*dh*ân occurs in the hot season. Only the sick and infirm are allowed exemption.

One night between the twenty-first and twenty-ninth of Rama*dh*ân, the exact date being uncertain, is called the Lailat el Qadr or 'night of power;' in it the Qur'ân was said to have been revealed [1].

Zakât, 'almsgiving [2]' or 'poor rate,' must be given either in money, stock, or goods, and consists of the bestowal in charity of about one-fortieth of all such property as shall have been a year in the owner's possession. In Mohammed's time the zakât was a contribution by his followers to the expenses of the war against the infidels.

Sadaqah is the name applied to any charitable gifts beyond that prescribed by law, especially to the offerings on the 'hîd al fi*t*r, or 'feast of breaking fast,' at the expiration of Rama*dh*ân.

Waqf is a religious bequest or endowment.

The 'Ha*gg* or 'pilgrimage,' the last of the five incumbent practices of the religion, is a very ancient institution, and one which, as we have seen, Mohammed could not, if he would, have abolished.

The ceremonies observed during the season of the pilgrimage are as follows:—

Arrived at the last of the mîqât, or six stages in the immediate vicinity of Mecca, the pilgrim divests himself of his ordinary clothes and assumes the i'hrâm or 'garb of sanctity.' This consists of two wrappers without seams, one of which is bound round the waist, and the other thrown loosely over the shoulders, the head being left uncovered. After putting on this it is unlawful to anoint the head, shave this or any other part of the body, pare the nails, or wear any other garment than the i'hrâm.

[1] Cf. Chapter XCVII, ver. 1.

[2] The word originally meant 'purity.'

On reaching Mecca he performs the legal ablutions, proceeds to the Sacred Mosque, and having saluted the 'black stone,' makes the tawâf or circuit of the Kaabah seven times, three times quickly and four times at a slow walk.

He then visits the Maqâm Ibrâhîm or Abraham's station, and afterwards returns and kisses the black stone.

Passing through the gate of the haram leading to Mount Zafâ, he runs seven times between the summit of that hill and that of Merwah[1].

On the eighth day, called tarwî'h, the pilgrims assemble in the valley of Minâ, where they pass the night.

As soon as morning prayers are over they 'rush tumultuously' to Mount Arafât, stay there until sunset, and then proceed to a place called Muzdalifeh, where they again pass the night.

The next day is the 'Hîd al Az'hâ, when the pilgrims again repair to the valley of Minâ, and go through the ceremony of throwing stones at three pillars, called *G*amrah. This is in commemoration of Abraham, or, as some say, of Adam, who, meeting the devil at the same spot, drove him away with stones.

The next ceremony is the sacrifice of some animal, a camel, sheep, or goat, in Minâ; after which they divest themselves of the pilgrim garb and get themselves shaved, their nails pared, &c.

The pilgrim should then rest at Mecca for the three following days, the âiyâm et ta*s*rîq or 'days of drying up,' scil. the blood of the sacrifices.

The sacrifice is said to have been instituted in commemoration of Abraham's proposed sacrifice of his son Ishmael (not Isaac as in the Bible) in accordance with the divine command.

The pilgrimage must be performed from the seventh to the tenth of the month Dhu'l 'Hi*gg*eh. A visit at any other time of the year is termed 'Homrah, 'visitation,' and though meritorious, has not the same weight as the 'Ha*gg* itself.

[1] See p. xiii and Chapter II, ver. 153.

The Kaabah is revisited before the pilgrim leaves Mecca, and the ceremony of the Tawâf again performed. From Mecca the pilgrim proceeds to Medînah to visit the tomb of the prophet. He is then entitled to assume the title of El 'Hâ*gg* (in Persian and Hindustânî corrupted into 'Hâ*g*î).

It is worth remarking that the word 'Ha*gg* is identical with the Hebrew word used in Exodus x. 9, where the reason assigned for the departure of the Israelites is that they may 'hold a feast ('hagg) unto the Lord' in the wilderness.

Islâm inculcates the doctrine of predestination, every act of every living being having been written down from all eternity in the Lau'h el Ma hfû*th*, 'the preserved tablet.' This predestination is called taqdîr, 'meting out,' or qismeh, 'apportioning.' The reconciliation of such a doctrine with the exercise of free-will, and the difficulty, if it be accepted, of avoiding the ascription of evil as well as good to God, have furnished materials for never-ending disputes amongst Muslim theologians, and have given rise to innumerable heresies. As the present introduction is only intended to furnish the reader with the necessary information to enable him to understand the Qur'ân and its system, I will not dwell upon these and kindred matters which belong to the later history of the creed.

One of the greatest blots on El Islâm is that it keeps the women in a state of degradation, and therefore effectually prevents the progress of any race professing the religion. For this Mohammed is only so far responsible that he accepted without question the prevalent opinion of his time, which was not in favour of allowing too great freedom to women, so that when he had ameliorated their condition by modifying the unjust laws of divorce, by enjoining kindness and equity upon his followers in the treatment of their wives, and by sternly repressing the barbarous custom of female infanticide, he thought, no doubt, that he had done enough for them. Similarly he provided for the better and kinder treatment of slaves, but it could never enter his mind that slavery was in itself a wrong or impolitic institution. The real fault lies in the unelastic nature of the religion: in his desire to shield it from change and to prevent his followers from 'dividing into sects,' the founder has made it impossible for Islâm to throw off certain customs and restrictions which, however convenient and even necessary to the Arabs at the time, became grievous and unsuitable for other nations at distant periods and in distant lands. The institution of the 'Ha*gg* pilgrimage, for example, was an admirable one for consolidating the Arab tribes, but it is burdensome and useless to the Muslim communities now that they extend over nearly half the civilized world.

That Mohammed had a due respect for the female sex, as far as was consistent with the prevailing state of education and opinion, is evident both from his own faithful affection to his first wife '*H*adîgah, and from the fact that 'believing women' are expressly included in the promises of a reward in the future life which the Qur'ân makes to all who acknowledge one God and do good works.

The language of the Qur'ân is universally acknowledged to be the most perfect form of Arab speech. The Qurâi*s*, as the guardians of the national temple and the owners of the territory in which the great fairs and literary festivals of all Arabia were held, would naturally absorb into their own dialect many of the words and locutions of other tribes, and we should consequently expect their language to be more copious and elegant than that of their neighbours. At the same time we must not forget that the acknowledged claims of the Qur'ân to be the direct utterance of the divinity have made it impossible for any Muslim to criticise the work, and it became, on the contrary, the standard by which other literary compositions had to be judged. Grammarians, lexicographers, and rhetoricians started with the presumption that the Qur'ân could not be wrong, and other works therefore only approached excellence in proportion as they, more or less, successfully imitated its style. Regarding it, however, from a perfectly impartial and unbiassed standpoint, we find that it expresses the thoughts and ideas of a Bedawî Arab in Bedawî language and metaphor. The language is noble and forcible, but it is not elegant in the sense of literary refinement. To Mohammed's hearers it must have been startling, from the manner in which it brought great truths home to them in the language of their every-day life.

There was nothing antiquated in the style or the words, no tricks of speech, pretty conceits, or mere poetical embellishments; the prophet spoke with rude, fierce eloquence in ordinary language. The only rhetorical ornament he allowed himself was that of making his periods more or less rhythmical, and most of his clauses rhyme,—a thing that was and still is natural to an Arab orator, and the necessary outcome of the structure of the Arabic tongue [1].

It is often difficult to enter thoroughly into the spirit of the old Arab poets, Mohammed's contemporaries or immediate predecessors, because we cannot completely realise the feelings that actuated them or identify ourselves with the society in which they moved. For this reason they have always something remote and obsolete about them, however clear their language and meaning may be. With the Qur'ân it is not so. Mohammed speaks with a living voice, his vivid word-painting brings at once before the mind the scene he describes or conjures up, we can picture his very attitude when, having finished some marvellously told story of the days of yore, uttered some awful denunciation, or given some glorious promise, he pauses suddenly and says, with bitter disappointment, 'These are the true stories, and there is no god but God; and yet ye turn aside!'

To translate this worthily is a most difficult task. To imitate the rhyme and rhythm would be to give the English an artificial ring from which the Arabic is quite free; and the same objection lies against using the phraseology of our authorised version of the Bible: to render it by fine or stilted language would be quite as foreign to the spirit of

[1] How natural this was to an Arab may be inferred from the anecdote related in Part I, note 2, p. 126; see also p. lv.

the original: while to make it too rude or familiar would be to err equally on the other side. I have, therefore, endeavoured to take a middle course; I have translated each sentence as literally as the difference in structure between the two languages would allow, and when possible I have rendered it word for word. Where a rugged or commonplace expression occurs in the Arabic I have not hesitated to render it by a similar English one, even where a literal rendering may perhaps shock the reader.

To preserve this closeness of rendering, I have had in several instances to make use of English constructions which, if not incorrect from a strictly grammatical point of view, are, I am aware often inelegant. Thus a peculiarity of the Arabic is to use the same preposition with a passive verb as the active and transitive verb required; for instance, *gh*aẓaba 'halâihi, 'he was angered against him,' in the passive, *gh*uẓiba 'halâihi, 'he was angered-against,' and the preservation of this construction is often absolutely necessary to retain the force of the original.

An instance of this occurs in the Opening Chapter, where the words ellaDHîna an'hamta 'halâihim, *gh*âiral ma*gh*ẓûbi 'halâihim are rendered, 'of those thou art gracious to, not of those thou art wroth with;' in Sale's translation, 'of those to whom thou hast been gracious, not of those against whom thou art incensed;' the placing the preposition before the verb gives a completely different ring to the English to that of the Arabic, to say nothing of the absence of that colloquial freedom which distinguishes the original.

I have, as far as possible, rendered an Arabic word by the same English word wherever it occurs; in some cases, however, where the Arabic word has more than one signification, or where it would distort the sense to retain the same expression, I have not scrupled to alter it.

Some of the Arabic words that occur in the Qur'ân are ambiguous, and have given rise to numerous differences of opinion among commentators. Thus the word istawâ is applied to God, and is interpreted in some passages to mean 'he directed himself by his will to the heaven' (Lane), and in others to mean 'he stood straight or erect' (Lane). The expression occurs often in the Qur'ân as descriptive of God's taking up a certain position with regard to the throne or highest heaven, and Muslim theologians have never ceased to debate concerning the exact nature of this position. El *Gh*azzâlî says that He 'istawâ' upon the throne in the manner he has himself described, and in the sense He himself means, but not by actual contact or local situation, while the throne itself is sustained by Him. To render it then by 'sitting' or 'ascending' would be to adopt a particular view of a very debatable question, and to give to the Arabic word a precision of meaning which it does not possess. The root of the word contains the notions of 'equality of surface' or 'uniformity,' of 'making' or 'fashioning,' and of 'being or going straight.' I have, therefore, adopted a rendering which has a similar confusion of significations, and translated it 'made for,' as in Chapter II, ver. 27, 'He made for the heavens.' Where no question can arise concerning its interpretation, as, for instance, when it is used of a rider balancing himself on the back of his camel, I have rendered it simply 'settled [1].'

The notes that I have appended are only such as are absolutely necessary for understanding the text; for a full account of all the historical allusions, Arabic, Jewish, and Magian legends, with which the native commentators illustrate the Qur'ân, the reader is referred to the notes in Sale's translation. The version of that eminent scholar fully deserves the consideration it has so long enjoyed, but from the large amount of exegetical matter which he has incorporated in his text, and from the style of language employed, which differs widely from the nervous energy and rugged simplicity of the original, his work can scarcely be regarded as a fair representation of the Qur'ân.

Rodwell's version approaches nearer to the Arabic, but even in that there is too much assumption of the literary

[1] See Chapter XLIII, ver. 12.

style. The arrangement of the Sûrahs in chronological order, too, though a help to the student, destroys the miscellaneous character of the book, as used by the Muslims, and as Mohammed's successors left it.

In my rendering I have, for the most part, kept to the interpretation of the Arabic commentator Bâi*dh*âvî, and have only followed my own opinion in certain cases where a word or expression, quite familiar to me from my experience of every-day desert life, appeared to be somewhat strained by these learned schoolmen. Chapter XXII, ver. 64, is an instance in which a more simple rendering would be preferable, though I have only ventured to suggest it in a note [1].

I am fully sensible of the shortcomings of my own version, but if I have succeeded in my endeavour to set before the reader plainly what the Qur'ân is, and what it contains, my aim will have been accomplished.

E. H. PALMER.

St. John's College, Cambridge,
March, 1880.

[1] See Part II, p. 63, note.

ABSTRACT

OF THE

CONTENTS OF THE QUR'ÂN.

I. The Opening Chapter. (Mecca.)

Prayer for guidance.

II. The Chapter of the Heifer. (Medînah.)

The Qur'ân a guidance. Rebuke to misbelievers: parable of one who kindles a fire. God is not ashamed of trifling similitudes. The creation of man: Adam taught 'the names:' Iblîs refuses to adore him: the temptation and fall. The children of Israel: their trials in Egypt: the golden calf: the manna and quails: bidden to enter the city and say 'hi*tt*atun. Moses strikes the rock: he bids the people slaughter a dun cow to discover a murder. Charge against the Jews of corrupting the Scriptures. The golden calf: the mountain held over them. Gabriel reveals the Qur'ân: Hârût and Mârût. Believers are not to say râ'hinâ, but un*th*urnâ. Verses which are annulled will be replaced by better ones. Paradise not exclusively for Jews and Christians. Mosques to be free. Story of Abraham: he rebuilds the Kaabah: was a 'Hanîf. The qiblah fixed. Zafâ and Merwah may be compassed. Proofs of God's unity. Lawful and unlawful food. The law of retaliation for homicide. Testators. The fast of Rama*dh*ân. Rites of the pilgrimage: its duration. Fighting for religion lawful during the sacred months. Wine and gaming forbidden. Marriage with idolaters unlawful. The law of divorce. Of suckling children. The Muhâ*g*erîn to be rewarded. The children of Israel demand a king. Saul (*T*âlût): the shechina: the ark. Saul and Gideon confounded. Goliath. Jesus. The âyat el kursîy ('verse of the throne') asserting the self-subsistence and omnipresence of God. Nimrod and Abraham. Almsgiving. No compulsion in religion. Proofs of the resurrection: Ezekiel's vision of the dry bones referred to: Abraham and the birds. Almsgiving recommended. Usurers denounced. Laws relating to debt and trading. Persons mentally incapable are to act by agents. The believers' prayer.

III. The Chapter of Imrân's Family. (Medînah.)

God's unity and self-subsistence. The Qur'ân confirmatory of previous Scriptures. The verses are either decisive or ambiguous. Example of Pharaoh's punishment. The battle of Bedr. Islâm the true religion. Future torment eternal. Obedience to God and the Apostle enjoined. Conception of the Virgin Mary; she is brought up by Zachariah. Birth of John: the annunciation of the Virgin. Birth and infancy of Jesus: the miracle of the birds of clay: the disciples: allusion to Mohammed's dispute with a Christian deputation from Nagran. Abraham a 'Hanîf. Reproof to Jews who pretend to believe and then recant; and who pervert the Scriptures. No distinction to be made between the prophets. The Jews rebuked for prohibiting certain kinds of food. The foundation of the Kaabah. Abraham's station. Pilgrimage enjoined. Schism and misbelief reproved. Battle of Ohod referred to. The victory at Bedr due to angelic aid. Usury denounced. Fate of those who rejected the prophets of old. Mohammed's death must not divert the believers from their faith. Promise of God's help. Further account of the battle of Bedr. The Muslim martyrs to enter Paradise. The victory of Bedr more than counterbalanced the defeat at Ohod. The hypocrites detected and reproved. Death the common lot even of apostles. Prayer for the believers. Exhortation to vie in good works and be patient.

IV. The Chapter of Women. (Medînah.)

God creates and watches over man. Women's dowries. Administration of the property of orphans and idiots. Distribution of property among the heirs. Witnesses required to prove adultery. Believers are not to inherit women's estates against their will: no false charge of adultery to be made with a view of keeping a woman's dowry. Women whom it is unlawful to marry. Men are superior to women: punishment of refractory wives. Arbitration between man and wife. Duty towards parents, kinsmen, orphans, the poor, neighbours, &c. Almsgiving for appearance sake a crime. Believers must not pray when drunk or polluted. Sand may be used for purification when water is not to be had. Charge against

Jews of perverting the Scriptures and saying râ'hinâ: they are threatened with transformation, like those who broke the Sabbath, for their unbelief. Idolatry the unpardonable sin. Some who have the Scriptures believe. Trusts to be paid back. Quarrels to be referred to God and the Apostle only. The Apostle will intercede for the believers. Mohammed commanded to settle their differences. Believers to take precautions in sallying forth to battle. They are exhorted to fight, and promised Paradise if they fall. Obedience to the prophet is obedience to God. Salutation to be returned. The hypocrites. Deserters are to be slain, unless they have taken refuge with a tribe in league with the Muslims. Penalty for killing a believer by mistake. Believers are not to plunder others on the mere pretence that they are infidels. Fate of the half-hearted Muslims who fell at Bedr. Precautions to be taken against an attack during prayers. Exhortation to sincerity in supporting the faith. Rebuke to the pagan Arabs for their idolatry and superstitious practices. Islâm the best religion, being that of Abraham the 'Hanîf. Laws respecting women and orphans: equity and kindness recommended. Partiality to one wife rather than another reproved. Fear of God inculcated. God does not pardon the unstable in faith or the hypocrites. No middle course is allowed. The Jews were punished for demanding a book from heaven. Of old they asked Moses to show them God openly and were punished. They are reproached for breaking their covenant with God, for calumniating Mary, and for pretending that they killed Jesus, whereas they only killed his similitude, for God took him to Himself. Certain lawful foods forbidden the Jews for their injustice and usury. Mohammed is inspired in the same manner as the other apostles and prophets. Jesus is only an Apostle of God and His Word and a spirit from Him. Doctrine of the Trinity denounced. God has not begotten a son. The law of inheritance in the case of remote kinship.

V. The Chapter of the Table. (Mẹdînah.)

Believers are to fulfil their compacts. Brute beasts, except those hereafter mentioned, are lawful; but chase during the pilgrimage is unlawful. The rites and sacrifices of the pilgrimage are lawful. The Muslims are not to bear ill-will against the Qurâis who prevented them at 'Hudâibîyeh from making the pilgrimage. Forbidden meats. The food of Jews and Christians is lawful to Muslims: so too their women. Ablutions before prayers. Rules for purification in cases of pollution. The Muslims are bidden to remember the oath of fealty (at 'Akabah), and how God made a similar covenant with the children of Israel, and chose twelve wardens. Mohammed is warned against their treachery as well as against the Christians. Refutation of the doctrine that Christ is God; and of the idea that the Jews and Christians are 'sons of God' and His beloved. Mohammed sent as a warner and herald of glad tidings. Moses bade the children of Israel invade the Holy Land and they were punished for hesitating. Story of the two sons of Adam: the crow shows Cain how to bury the body of Abel. Gravity of homicide. Those who make war against God and His Apostle are not to receive quarter. Punishment for theft. Mohammed is to judge both Jews and Christians by the Qur'ân, in accordance with their own Scriptures, but not according to 'their lusts.' Or would they prefer to be judged according to the unjust laws of the time of the pagan Arabs? The Muslims are not to take Jews and Christians for patrons. The hypocrites hesitate to join the believers: they are threatened. Further appeal to the Jews and Christians: fate of those before them who were transformed for their sins. The Jews reproved for saying that 'God's hand is fettered.' Some of them are moderate, but the greater part are misbelievers. The prophet is bound to preach his message. Sabæans, Jews, and Christians appealed to as believers. Prophets of old were rejected. Against the worship of the Messiah and the doctrine of the Trinity. Jews and idolaters are the most hostile to the Muslims; and the Christians are nearest in love to them. Expiation for an inconsiderate oath. Wine and gambling forbidden. Game not to be hunted or eaten during pilgrimage. Expiation for violating this precept: fish is lawful at this time. Rites of the 'Ha*gg* to be observed. Believers must not ask about painful things till the whole Qur'ân is revealed. Denunciation of the superstitious practices of the pagan Arabs with respect to certain cattle. Witnesses required when a dying man makes his testament. The mission of Jesus: the miracles of the infancy: the apostles ask for a table from heaven as a sign: Jesus denies commanding men to worship him and his mother as gods.

VI. The Chapter of Cattle. (Mecca.)

Light and darkness are both created by God. Rebuke to idolaters. They are exhorted to take warning by the fate of those of old, who rejected the prophets. Had the revelation been a material book they would have disbelieved it: if the prophet had been an angel he would have come in the guise of a man. Attributes of God. Mohammed bidden to become a Muslim. Those who have the Scriptures ought to recognise Mohammed as the one foretold in them. The idolaters will be disappointed of the intercession of their gods on the judgment day. They deny the resurrection day now, but hereafter they will have awful proof of its truth. The next world is preferable to this. Prophets aforetime were also mocked at and they were patient. God could send them a sign if He pleased. Beasts, birds, and the like are communities like men: their fate is all written in the Book: they too shall be gathered on the judgment day. Arguments in proof of the supreme power of God. Mohammed is only a messenger: he is to disclaim miraculous power: is not to repulse believers: he is bidden to abjure idolatry and not follow the lusts of the Meccans. God's omniscience. He takes men's souls to Himself during sleep: sends guardian angels to watch over them: preserves men in danger by land and sea. Mohammed is not to join in discussions on religion with idolaters, nor to associate with those who make a sport of it. Folly of idolatry set forth: God the creator: Abraham's perplexity in seeking after the true God: worships successively the stars, the moon, and the sun, but is convinced that they are not gods by seeing them set. Turns to God and becomes a 'Hanîf. Other prophets of old were inspired: the Qur'ân is also a special revelation from God to the Meccans, fulfilling their Scriptures; but the Jews have perverted or suppressed parts of them. Denunciation of one who falsely pretended to be inspired. The creation a proof of God's unity. Rebuke to those who call the *g*inn His partners, or attribute offspring to Him. Idolaters are not to be abused lest they too speak ill of God. The Meccans would not have believed even if a sign had been given them. Mohammed is to trust to God alone. Men are not to abstain from food over which God's name has been pronounced. God will vindicate His messenger. Belief or the reverse depends on God's grace. The *g*inns and false gods, together with their worshippers, will be condemned to everlasting torment. God never punishes without first sending an apostle with warning. The threatened doom cannot be averted. Denunciation of the idolatrous practices of the Arabs: setting apart portions of the produce of the land for God and for the idols, and defrauding God of His portion: infanticide: declaring cattle and tilth inviolable. God created all fruits and all cattle; both are therefore lawful. Argument proving the absurdity of some of these customs. Enumeration of the only kinds of food that are unlawful. The prohibition to the Jews of certain food was only on account of their sins. God's revealed word is the only certain argument. Declaration of things really forbidden, namely, harshness to parents, infanticide, abominable sins, and murder. The property of orphans is to be respected, and fair dealing to be practised. No soul compelled beyond its capacity. The Qur'ân to be accepted on the same authority as the book of Moses was. Faith required now without signs: no later profession on the judgment day shall profit them. Good works to be rewarded tenfold, but evil works only by the same amount. Islâm is the religion of Abraham the 'Hanîf: a belief in one God, to whom all prayer and devotion is due. Each soul shall bear its own burden. The high rank of some of the Meccans is only a trial from the Lord whereby to prove them.

VII. The Chapter of Al Aarâf. (Mecca.)

Mohammed is bidden to accept the Qur'ân fearlessly. The Meccans must take warning by the fate of those who rejected the prophets of old. The creation and fall of Adam. Iblîs allowed to tempt mankind. Men are to go to Mosque decently clad. God has only prohibited sinful actions. Men are warned not to reject the mission of the apostles: their punishment at and after death if they do so. The happiness of believers in Paradise. Description of Al Aarâf, the partition between heaven and hell. Immediate belief in the Qur'ân required. God the Creator. Humble and secret prayer enjoined. Proofs of God's goodness. Noah sent to warn his people: he is saved in the ark while they are drowned. Hûd sent to 'Âd: they reject his preaching and are punished. Zâli'h sent to Thamûd: produces the she-camel as a sign: the people hamstring her and are punished. Lot sent to the people of Sodom: their punishment. Sho'hâib sent to Midian: his people reject him and are destroyed. Thus city after city was destroyed for rejecting the apostles. Moses sent to Pharaoh: the miracles of the snake and the white hand. The magicians contend with Moses, are overcome, and believe. Pharaoh punishes them. The slaughter of the firstborn: the plagues of Egypt. The Israelites are delivered. Moses communes with God, who appears to him on the Mount. The giving of the Law. The golden calf. Moses' wrath against Aaron. The seventy elders. The coming of Mohammed 'the illiterate prophet' foretold. Some Jews are just and rightly guided. The division into twelve tribes. The miracle of smiting the rock: the manna and quails: the command to enter the city, saying 'hi*tt*atun, and punishment for disobedience. The Sabbath-breaking city: the transformation of the wicked inhabitants into apes. The dispersion of the Jews. The mountain held over the Jews. The covenant of God with the posterity of Adam: 'Am I not your Lord[1]?' Humiliation of one who having foretold the coming of a prophet in the time of Mohammed would not acknowledge the latter as such. Many both of the *g*inn and of mankind predestined for hell. The names of God are not to be perverted[2]. Mohammed is not 'possessed.' The coming of 'the Hour.' Creation of Adam and Eve: conception and birth of their first child, ''Abd el 'Hareth:' their idolatry. Idols are themselves servants of God: they have neither life nor senses. Mohammed is bidden to treat his opponents with mildness. The mention of God's name repels devilish influences. Men are recommended to listen to the Qur'ân and to humble themselves before God, whom the angels adore.

VIII. The Chapter of the Spoils. (Medînah.)

Spoils belong to God and the Apostle. Who are the true believers. The expedition of Mohammed against the caravan from Syria under Abu Sufiân. The miraculous victory at Bedr. Address to the Meccans who, fearing an attack from Mohammed, took sanctuary in the Kaabah, and prayed to God to decide between themselves and him. Exhortation to believe and avoid treachery. Plots against Mohammed frustrated by divine interference. The revelation treated as old folks' tales. Rebuke of the idolaters for mocking the Muslims at prayer. Offer of an amnesty to those

[1] This is constantly alluded to in Persian mystical poetry as Rozialast, 'the day of "Am I not?"'

[2] As Allâh, not Allât, the name of a goddess. See p. 160, note 1.

who will believe. Exhortation to fight the infidels: division of the spoils: description of the battle. The enemy made to seem few in the Muslims' eyes, while they seemed more numerous than they really were. The infidels forsaken by Satan, their leader, on the day of battle. Fate of the hypocrites. Warning from Pharaoh's fate. The infidels who break their treaty. Treachery to be met with the like. God will help the prophet against the traitors. A few enduring believers shall conquer a multitude of infidels. The Muslims are reproved for accepting ransom for the captives taken at Bedr. The spoils are lawful. The Muhâ*g*erîn who fled with Mohammed, and the inhabitants of Medînah who gave him refuge, are to form ties of brotherhood[1].

IX. The Chapter of Repentance or Immunity. (Medînah.)

(This chapter is without the initial formula 'In the name of the merciful,' &c.)

An immunity for four months proclaimed to such of the idolaters as have made a league with the prophet; but they are to be killed wherever found when the sacred months have expired. An idolater seeking refuge is to be helped in order that he may hear the word of God. None are to be included in the immunity but those with whom the league was made at the Sacred Mosque. They are not to be trusted. Exhortation to fight against the Meccans. Idolaters may not repair to the mosques of God. Reproof to Abu 'l 'Abbâs, the prophet's uncle, who, while refusing to believe, claimed to have done enough in supplying water to the pilgrims and in making the pilgrimage himself. The Muhâ*g*erîn are to hold the first rank. Infidels are not to be taken for patrons even when they are fathers or brothers. Religion is to be preferred to ties of kinship. The victory of 'Honein. The idolaters are not to be allowed to enter the Sacred Mosque at Mecca another year. The infidels are to be attacked. The Jews denounced for saying that Ezra is the son of God: the assumption of the title 'Rabbi' reproved. Diatribe against Jewish doctors and Christian monks. Of the sacred months and the sin of deferring them. Exhortation to the Muslims to march forth to battle. Allusions to the escape of Mohammed and Abu Bekr from Mecca and their concealment in a cave. Rebuke to those who seek to be excused from fighting,

[1] See Introduction, p. xxxiv.

and to those who sought to excite sedition in the Muslim ranks. Reproof to the hypocrites and half-hearted and to those who found fault with the prophet for his use of the alms (zakât). Proper destination of the alms. Hypocrites and renegades denounced: they are warned by the example of the people of old, who rejected the prophets. Rewards promised to the true believers. Continued denunciation of the hypocrites and of those who held back from the fight. Mohammed is not to pray at the grave of any one of them who dies: their seeming prosperity is not to deceive him. Happiness in store for the Apostle, the believers, and the Muhâgerîn. Those who may lawfully be excused military service. The desert Arabs are among the worst of the 'hypocrites;' though some believe. Some people of Medînah also denounced as hypocrites: others have sinned, but confessed: others wait for God's pleasure. Denunciation of some who had set up a mosque from motives of political opposition. Mohammed is not to sanction this mosque, but rather to use that of Qubâ', founded by him while on his way from Mecca to Medînah during the Flight. God has bought the persons and wealth of the believers at the price of Paradise. The prophet and the believers must not ask forgiveness for the idolaters however near of kin. Abraham only asked pardon for his idolatrous father in fulfilment of a promise. The three Ansârs who refused to accompany Mohammed to Tabûk are forgiven. The people of Medînah and the neighbouring Arabs blamed for holding back on the occasion. All sacrifices for the sake of the religion are counted to them. Exhortation to fight rigorously against the infidels. Reproof to those who receive the revelation suspiciously. God will stand by His Apostle.

X. The Chapter of Jonah. (Mecca.)

No wonder that the Qur'ân was revealed to a mere man. Misbelievers deem him a sorcerer. God the creator and ruler: no one can intercede with Him except by His permission. Creation is a sign of His power. Reward hereafter for the believers. Man calls on God in distress, but forgets Him when deliverance comes. Warning from the fall of former generations. The infidels are not satisfied with the Qur'ân: Mohammed dare not invent a false revelation. False gods can neither harm nor profit them. People require a sign. God saves people in dangers by land and sea. This life is like grass. Promise of Paradise and threat of Hell.

Fate of the idolaters and false gods at the last day. God the Lord of all. Other religions are mere conjecture. The Qur'ân could only have been devised by God. The Meccans are challenged to produce a single sûrah like it. Unbelievers warned of the last day by the fate of previous nations. Reproval of those who prohibit lawful things. God is ever watchful over the prophet's actions. Happiness of the believers: the infidels cannot harm the prophet. Refutation of those who ascribe offspring to God. Mohammed encouraged by the story of Noah and the other prophets of old. Fate of Pharaoh and vindication of Moses and Aaron. The People of the Book (Jews and Christians) appealed to in confirmation of the truth of the Qur'ân. The story of Jonas. The people of Nineveh saved by repenting and believing in time. The people are exhorted to embrace Islâm, the faith of the 'Hanîf. God alone is powerful. Belief or unbelief affect only the individual himself. Resignation and patience inculcated.

XI. The Chapter of Hûd. (Mecca.)

The Qur'ân a book calling men to believe in the unity of God: nothing is hidden from Him: He is the creator of all. Men will not believe, and deem themselves secure because their punishment is deferred. They demand a sign, or say the Qur'ân is invented by the prophet; but they and their false gods together cannot bring ten such sûrahs. Misbelievers threatened with future punishment, while believers are promised Paradise. Noah was likewise sent, but his people objected that he was a mere mortal like themselves and only followed by the meaner sort of men. He also is accused of having invented his revelation: he is saved in the ark and the unbelievers drowned: he endeavours to save his son. The ark settles on Mount *G*ûdî. Hûd was sent to 'Âd: his people plotted against him and were destroyed, while he was saved. Zâli'h was sent to Thamûd: the she-camel given for a sign. The people hamstring her and perish. Abraham entertains the angels who are sent to the people of Lot: he pleads for them. Lot offers his daughters to the people of Sodom, to spare the angels: he escapes by night, and Sodom is destroyed. Sho'hâib is sent to Midian; and his people, rejecting his mission, perish too. Moses sent to Pharaoh, who shall be punished at the resurrection. The Meccans too shall be punished: they are threatened with the judgment day, when they shall be sent to hell, while the believers are in Paradise. The Meccans are bidden to take warning by the fate of the cities whose stories are related above. These stories are intended to strengthen the prophet's heart: he is bidden to wait and leave the issue to God.

XII. The Chapter of Joseph. (Mecca.)

The Qur'ân revealed in Arabic that the Meccans may understand: it contains the best of stories. Story of Joseph: he tells his father his dream: Jacob advises him to keep it to himself. Jealousy of Joseph's brethren: they conspire to throw him in a pit: induce his father to let him go with them: they cast him in the pit, and bring home his shirt covered with 'lying blood.' Travellers discover him and sell him into Egypt: he is adopted by his master: his mistress endeavours to seduce him: his innocence proved. His mistress shows him to the women of the city to excuse her conduct: their amazement at his beauty. He is imprisoned: interprets the dreams of the baker and the cupbearer. Pharaoh's dream: Joseph is sent for to expound it. He is appointed to a situation of trust in the land. His brethren arrive and do not recognise him: they ask for corn and he requires them to bring their youngest brother as the condition of his giving it to them. The goods they had brought to barter are returned to their sacks. Benjamin is sent back. Joseph discovers himself to him. Joseph places the king's drinking cup in his brother's pack: accuses them all of the theft: takes Benjamin as a bondsman for the theft. They return to Jacob, who in great grief sends them back again to bring him news. Joseph discovers himself to them, and sends back his shirt: Jacob recognises it by the smell. Jacob goes back with them to Egypt. This story appealed to as a proof of the truth of the revelation.

XIII. The Chapter of Thunder. (Mecca.)

The Qur'ân a revelation from the Lord, the creator and governor of all. Misbelievers are threatened: God knows all, and the recording angels are ever present. Lightning and thunder celebrate God's praises. All in heaven and earth acknowledge Him. God sends rain and causes the torrents to flow: the scum thereof is like the dross on smelted ore. The righteous and the believers are promised Paradise; and the misbelievers are threatened with hell-fire. Exhortation to believe in the Merciful. Were the

Qur'ân to convulse nature they would not believe. Further threats against misbelievers. God notes the deeds of every soul. Stratagem unavailing against Him. Paradise and Hell. Mohammed bidden to persevere in asserting the unity of God. Had he not followed the Qur'ân God would have forsaken him. Other apostles have had wives and children: none could bring a sign without God's permission: for every period there is a revelation. God can annul or confirm any part of His revelation which He pleases: he has the 'Mother of the Book' (i. e. the Eternal Original). Whether Mohammed live to see his predictions fulfilled or not, God only knows: his duty is only to preach the message. The conquests of Islâm pointed to. God will support the prophet against misbelievers.

XIV. The Chapter of Abraham. (Mecca.)

The Qur'ân revealed to bring men from darkness into light. God is Lord of all. No apostle sent except with the language of his own people. Moses sent to Pharaoh. The people of Noah, 'Âd, and Thamûd objected that their prophets were mortals like themselves. The prophets relied on God who vindicated them. Frightful description of hell. Misbelievers are like ashes blown away by a stormy wind. Helplessness of the damned: Satan will desert them. But believers are in Paradise. A good word is like a good tree whose root is in the earth and whose branches are in the sky, and which gives fruit in all seasons. A bad word is as a tree that is felled. God's word is sure. Idolaters are threatened with hell-fire. God is the creator of all: He subjects all things to man's use. Abraham prayed that the territory of Mecca might be a sanctuary. The unjust are only respited till the judgment day. The ruins of the dwellings of those who have perished for denying the mission of their apostles are a proof of the truth of Mohammed's mission. The Lord will take vengeance at the last day, when sinners shall burn in hell with shirts of pitch to cover them. The Qur'ân is a warning and an admonition.

XV. The Chapter of El '*H*agr. (Mecca.)

Misbelievers will one day regret their misbelief. No city was ever destroyed without warning. The infidels mockingly ask Mohammed to bring down angels to punish them. So did the sinners of old act towards their apostles. There are signs enough in the zodiac, guarded as they are from the devils who are pelted with shooting-stars if they attempt to listen. All nature is under God's control. Man created from clay, and the *g*inn from smokeless fire. The angels bidden to adore Adam. Iblîs refuses; is cursed and expelled; but respited until the day of judgment. Is allowed to seduce mankind. Hell, with its seven doors, promised to misbelievers, and Paradise to believers. Story of Abraham's angelic guests: they announce to him the birth of a son: they proceed to Lot's family. The crime and punishment of the people of Sodom. The ruined cities still remain to tell the tale. Similar fate of the people of the Grove and of El '*H*a*g*r. The Hour draws nigh. The Lord the Omniscient Creator has sent the Qur'ân and the 'seven verses of repetition' (the Opening Chapter). Mohammed is not to grieve at the worldly success of unbelievers. Those who 'dismember the Qur'ân[1]' are threatened with punishment. Mohammed is encouraged against the misbelievers.

XVI. THE CHAPTER OF THE BEE. (Mecca.)

God's decree will come to pass. He sends the angels to instruct His servants to give warning that there is no other God. The creation and ordering of all natural objects are signs of His power. The false gods are inanimate and powerless. God is but one. The unbelievers who call the revelation old folks' tales must bear the burden of their own sins. On the resurrection day their 'associates' will disown them. Reception by the angels of the wicked and the good in Hell and in Paradise. The infidels strenuously deny the resurrection. The Muhâ*g*erîn are promised a good reward. The Jews and Christians to be asked to confirm the Qur'ân. All nature adores God. Unity of God affirmed. When in distress men turn to God, but forget Him and become idolaters when deliverance comes. The practice of setting aside part of their produce for the idols reproved. The practice of female infanticide, while they ascribe daughters to God, is reproved, and disbelief in the future life also rebuked. Satan is the patron of the infidels. The Qur'ân sent down as a guidance and mercy. The rain which quickens the dead earth, and the cattle which give milk, and the vines which give fruit and wine are signs. The bee is inspired from the Lord to build hives and to use those made first by men. Its honey is lawful. The rich Arabs are reproved for

[1] Here used for the Scriptures generally.

their treatment of their slaves. Helplessness of the false gods illustrated by the parable of the slave and of the dumb man. Goodness of God in providing food and shelter for men. Idolaters shall be disowned by the false gods at the resurrection. Every nation shall have a witness against it on that day. Justice and good faith inculcated, especially the duty of keeping to a treaty once made. Satan has no power over believers. Verses of the Qur'ân abrogated: the Holy Spirit (Gabriel) is the instrument of the revelation. Suggestion that Mohammed is helped by some mortal to compose the Qur'ân: this cannot be, as the person hinted at speaks a foreign language and the Qur'ân is in Arabic. Denunciation of misbelievers. Warning of the fate Mecca is to expect if its inhabitants continue to disbelieve. Unlawful foods. God will forgive wrong done through ignorance. Abraham was a 'Hanîf. The ordinance of the Sabbath. Mohammed is to dispute with his opponents kindly. The believers are not to take too savage revenge. They are exhorted to patience and trust in God.

XVII. The Chapter of the Night Journey. (Mecca.)

Allusion to the 'Night Journey' from the Sacred Mosque (at Mecca) to the Remote Mosque (at Jerusalem). Moses received the Book. Noah was a faithful servant. Israel's two sins and their punishment. The Qur'ân a guide and glad tidings. Man prays for evil and is hasty. Night and day are two signs. Every man's augury is round his neck. Each one shall have a book on the resurrection day with an account of his deeds. Each is to bear the burden of his own sins. No city is destroyed till warned by an apostle. Choice of good in this world or the next. Mohammed is not to associate others with God. Kindness to parents enjoined. Moderation to be practised. Infanticide and fornication are sins. Homicide is to be avenged except for just cause. Honesty and humility inculcated. The angels are not the daughters of God. If there were other gods they would rebel against God: all in the heavens praise Him. Unbelievers cannot understand the Qur'ân. The unity of God unacceptable to the Meccans. The resurrection. Idolaters not to be provoked. Some prophets preferred over others. False gods themselves have recourse to God. All cities to be destroyed before the judgment day. Had Mohammed been sent with signs, the Meccans would have disbelieved them like Thamûd. The Vision (of the Night Journey) and the

Zaqqûm Tree of Hell are causes of contention. Iblîs' disobedience and fall: he is given permission to delude men. Safety by land and sea a special mercy from God. All shall have justice at the last day. The Thaqîf tribe at *T*â'if nearly seduced Mohammed into promulgating an unauthorised sentence. Injunction to pray. Man is ungrateful. Departure of the Spirit. Mankind and *g*inns together could not produce the like of the Qur'ân. Signs demanded of Mohammed: he is only a mortal. Fate of those who disbelieve in the resurrection. Moses brought nine signs, but Pharaoh disbelieved in them: his fate: the children of Israel succeeded him in his possessions. The Qur'ân was revealed as occasion required: those who believe the Scriptures recognise it. God and the Merciful One are not two gods, for God has no partner.

XVIII. The Chapter of the Cave. (Mecca.)

The Qur'ân is a warning especially to those who say God has begotten a son. Mohammed is not to grieve if they refuse to believe. Story of the Fellows of the Cave. Their number known only to God. Mohammed rebuked for promising a revelation on the subject. He is enjoined to obey God in all things, and not to be induced to give up his poorer followers. Hell-fire threatened for the unbeliever and Paradise promised to the good. Parable of the proud man's garden which was destroyed while that of the humble man flourished. This life is like the herb that springs up and perishes. Good works are more lasting than wealth and children. The last day. Iblîs refuses to adore Adam: the men are not to take him for a patron. They shall be forsaken by their patrons at the last day. Men would believe but that the example of those of yore must be repeated. Misbelievers are unjust and shall not be allowed to understand, or be guided. But God is merciful. Story of Moses and his servant in search of El '*H*id*h*r: they lose their fish at the confluence of the two seas: they meet a strange prophet, who bids Moses not question anything he may do: he scuttles a ship, kills a boy, and builds up a tottering wall: Moses desires an explanation, which the stranger gives and leaves him. Story of Dhu 'l Qarnâin: he travels to the ocean of the setting sun: builds a rampart to keep in Gog and Magog: these are to be let loose again before the judgment day: reward and punishment on that day. Were the sea ink it would not suffice for the words of the Lord. The prophet is only a mortal.

XIX. The Chapter of Mary. (Mecca.)

Zachariah prays for an heir: he is promised a son, who is to be called John: is struck dumb for three days as a sign. John is born and given the Book, judgment, grace, and purity. Story of Mary: the annunciation: her delivery beneath a palm tree: the infant Jesus in the cradle testifies to her innocence and to his own mission. Warning of the day of judgment. Story of Abraham: he reproves his father, who threatens to stone him: Abraham prays for him: Isaac and Jacob are born to him. Moses communes with God and has Aaron for a help. Ishmael and Idrîs mentioned as prophets. Their seed when the signs of the merciful are read fall down adoring. The Meccans, their successors, are promised reward in Paradise if they repent and believe. The angels only descend at the bidding of the Lord. Certainty of the resurrection: punishment of those who have rebelled against the Merciful. Reproof to one who said he should have wealth and children on the judgment day. The false gods shall deny their worshippers then. The devils sent to tempt unbelievers. The gathering of the judgment day. All nature is convulsed at the imputation that the Merciful has begotten a son. This revelation is only to warn mankind by the example of the generations who have passed away.

XX. The Chapter of *T.* H. (Mecca.)

The Qur'ân a reminder from the Merciful, who owns all things and knows all things. There is no god but He. His are the excellent names. Story of Moses: he perceives the fire and is addressed from it by God in the holy valley *T*uvâ: God shows him the miracle of the staff turned to a snake and of the white hand: sends him to Pharaoh: Moses excuses himself because of the impediment in his speech. Aaron is given him as a minister. Moses' mother throws him in the sea: his sister watches him: he is restored to his mother. Slays an Egyptian and flees to Midian. Moses and Aaron go to Pharaoh and call on him to believe: Pharaoh charges them with being magicians: their contest with the Egyptian magicians, who believe and are threatened with punishment by Pharaoh. Moses leads the children of Israel across the sea by a dry road: Pharaoh and his people are overwhelmed: the covenant on Mount Sinai: the miracle of the manna and quails. Es Sâmarîy makes the calf in Moses' absence. Moses seizes his brother angrily by the beard and destroys the calf. Misbelievers threatened with the terrors of the resurrection day: fate of the mountains on that day: all men shall be summoned to judgment: no intercession shall avail except from such as the Merciful permits. The Qur'ân is in Arabic that people may fear and remember. Mohammed is not to hasten on its revelation. Adam broke his covenant with God. Angels bidden to adore Adam: Iblîs refuses: tempts Adam: Adam, Eve, and Iblîs expelled from Paradise. Misbelievers shall be gathered together blind on the resurrection day. The Meccans pass by the ruined dwellings of the generations who have been aforetime destroyed for unbelief: but for the Lord's word being passed they would have perished too. Mohammed is exhorted to bear their insults patiently and to praise God throughout the day. Prayer enjoined. The fate of those of yore a sufficient sign. Let them wait and see the issue.

XXI. The Chapter of the Prophets. (Mecca.)

Men mock at the revelation: they say it is a 'jumble of dreams,' and that Mohammed is a poet, and they ask for a sign. The prophets of old were but mortal: the people who rejected them perished. Heaven and earth were not created in sport. Truth shall crush falsehood. All things praise God. If there were other gods than He heaven and earth would be corrupted. All former prophets were taught that there is no god but God. The Merciful has not begotten children: the angels are only his servants. The separation of earth from heaven, the creation of living things from water, the steadying of the earth by mountains and placing the sky as a roof over it, and the creation of the night and day and of the sun and moon are signs. No one was ever granted immortality: every soul must taste of death. The unbelievers mock at Mohammed and disbelieve in the Merciful. Man is hasty. The infidels are threatened with punishment in the next world. Those who mocked at the prophets of old perished. No one shall be wronged at the last day. Moses and Aaron received a scripture. Abraham destroys the images which his people worshipped: he tells them that it was the largest idol which did it: he is condemned to be burnt alive; but the fire is miraculously made cool and safe. Abraham, Lot, Isaac, and Jacob all inspired. Lot was brought safely out of a city of wrong-doers. Noah also was saved. David and Solomon give judgment about a field. The mountains and birds are made subject to David: he is taught the art of making coats of mail. The wind and the demons are subjected to Solomon. Job was saved. Ishmael, Idrîs, and Dhu 'l Kifl were patient and entered into the mercy of the Lord. Dhu 'nnûn (Jonah) was saved in the fish's belly. Zachariah had his prayer granted and a son (John) given him. The Spirit was breathed into the Virgin Mary. But their followers have divided into sects. A city once destroyed for unbelief shall not be restored till Gog and Magog are let loose. The promise draws nigh. Idolaters shall be the pebbles of hell. But the elect shall be spared the terror of that day; when the heavens shall be rolled up as Es-Sigill rolls up books. As is written in the Psalms, 'The righteous shall inherit the earth.' Mohammed sent as a mercy to the worlds. God is one God: He knows all: He is the Merciful.

XXII. The Chapter of the Pilgrimage. (Mecca.)

Terrors of the last day; yet men dispute about God and follow devils. The conception, birth, growth, and death of men, and the growth of herbs in the ground are proofs of the resurrection. But some dispute, others waver between two opinions. The most desperate means cannot thwart the divine decrees. God will decide between the Jews, Christians, Sabæans, Magians, and Idolaters on the judgment day. All nature adores God. The misbelievers are threatened with hell-fire, and the believers promised Paradise. Punishment threatened to those who prohibit men from visiting the Sacred Mosque. Abraham when bidden to cleanse the Kaabah was told to proclaim the pilgrimage. The rules of the 'Ha*gg* enjoined. Cattle are lawful food. Warning against idolatry and exhortation to become 'Hanîfs. Sacrifices at the Kaabah are enjoined. All men have their appointed rite. The name of God is to be mentioned over cattle when slaughtered. Camels may be sacrificed and eaten. God will defend believers, but loves not misbelieving traitors. Those who have been driven from their homes for acknowledging God's unity are allowed to fight. If men did not fight for such a cause, all places of worship would be destroyed. The people of Noah, 'Âd, Thamûd, Abraham, and Lot called their prophets liars and were allowed to range at large, but at last they were punished. Their cities were destroyed and the ruins are visible to travellers still. Mohammed is only sent to warn the Meccans of a like fate. Satan contrives to suggest a wrong reading to the prophet while reading the Qur'ân [1]. The kingdom shall be God's upon the judgment day. Those who flee or are slain in the cause shall be provided for and rewarded. Believers who take revenge and are again attacked will be helped. All nature is subject to God. Every nation has its rites to observe. The idolaters treat the revelation with scorn. The false gods could not even create a fly. Exhortation to worship God and fight for the faith of Abraham, whose religion the Muslims profess. God is the sovereign and helper.

XXIII. The Chapter of Believers. (Mecca.)

The humble, chaste, and honest shall prosper. The creation, birth, death, and resurrection of man: God's goodness in providing for men's sustenance. Noah sent to his people, who reject him because he is a mere mortal: they are drowned, and he is saved in the ark. Moses and Aaron were also called liars. Mary and her son the cause of their followers' division into sects. The God-fearing encouraged. The Qurâis rebuked for their pride, and for denying Mohammed, and calling him possessed. They are reminded of the famine and defeat they have already experienced. Doctrine of the resurrection. The unity of God: He has no offspring: is omniscient. Mohammed is encouraged not to care for the false accusations of the Meccans, but to seek refuge in God. Punishment, on the day of resurrection, of those who mocked at the little party of believers.

XXIV. The Chapter of Light. (Medînah.)

(This chapter deals with the accusation of unchastity against Ayesha.)

Punishment of the whore and the whoremonger. Witnesses required in the case of an imputation of unchastity to a wife. Vindication of Ayesha's character and denunciation of the accusers. Scandalmongers rebuked and threatened with punishment at the last day. Believers are not to enter other persons' houses without permission or in the absence of the owners. Chastity and modest deportment enjoined particularly upon women. Those by whom women may

[1] An allusion to the tradition of Mohammed's acknowledgment of the goddesses Allât, Al 'Huzzâ, and Manât. See Introduction, pp. xxvi and xxvii.

be seen unveiled. Slaves to be allowed to purchase their freedom. Slave girls not to be compelled to prostitute themselves. God the Light of the Heavens. Nothing keeps the believer from the service of God; but the unbeliever's works are like the mirage on a plain or like darkness on a deep sea. All nature is subject to God's control. Reproof to a sect who would not accept the prophet's arbitration. Actual obedience required rather than an oath that they will be obedient. Belief in the unity of God, steadfastness in prayer, and the giving of alms enjoined. Slaves and children not to be admitted into an apartment without asking permission, when the occupant is likely to be undressed. Rules for the social intercourse of women past child-bearing, and of the blind, lame, or sick. Persons in whose houses it is lawful to eat food. Salutations to be exchanged on entering houses. Behaviour of the Muslims towards the Apostle. He is to be more respectfully addressed than other people.

XXV. The Chapter of the Discrimination. (Mecca.)

The 'Discrimination' sent down as a warning that God is one, the creator and governor of all; yet the Meccans call it 'old folks' tales:' they object that the prophet acts and lives as a mere mortal, or is crazy. Hell-fire shall be the punishment of those who disbelieve in the resurrection. Description of the judgment day. The Qurâis object that the Qur'ân was revealed piecemeal. Moses and Aaron and Noah were treated like Mohammed, but those who called them liars were punished: 'Âd and Thamûd perished for the same sin: the ruins of the cities of the plain are existing examples: yet they will not accept the prophet. God controls the shadow; gives night for a repose; quickens the dead earth with rain. He lets loose the two seas, but places a barrier between them. He has created man. He is the loving and merciful God. The Qurâis object to the 'Merciful' as a new God. The lowly and moderate are His servants: they abstain from idolatry, murder, false witness, and frivolous discourse. These shall be rewarded. God cares nothing for the rejection of his message by the infidels: their punishment shall be lasting.

XXVI. The Chapter of the Poets. (Mecca.)

Mohammed is not to be vexed by the people's unbelief. Though called a liar now, his cause shall triumph in the end. Moses sent to Pharaoh: he fears lest he may be killed for slaying the Egyptian. Pharaoh charges him with ingratitude. Their dispute about God. Pharaoh claims godhead himself. The miracles of the rod and the 'white hand.' Moses' contest with the magicians: the magicians are conquered and believe: Pharaoh threatens them with condign punishment. The Israelites leave Egypt and are pursued. The passing of the Red Sea and destruction of Pharaoh and his hosts. The story of Abraham: he preaches against idolatry. Noah is called a liar and vindicated. Hûd preaches to the people of 'Âd, and Zâli'h to Thamûd: the latter hamstring the she-camel and perish. The crime and punishment of the people of Sodom. The people of the Grove and the prophet Sho'hâib. The Qur'ân revealed through the instrumentality of the Faithful Spirit (Gabriel), in plain Arabic. The learned Jews recognise its truth from the prophecies in their own Scriptures. The devils could not have brought it. Mohammed is to be meek towards believers and to warn his clansmen. Those upon whom the devils do descend, namely, the poets who 'wander distraught in every vale.'

XXVII. The Chapter of the Ant. (Mecca.)

The Qur'ân a guidance to believers. God appears to Moses in the fire: Moses is sent to Pharaoh with signs, but is called a 'sorcerer.' David and Solomon endowed with knowledge. Solomon taught the speech of birds. His army of men, *g*inns, and birds marches through the valley of the ant. One ant bids the rest retire to their holes lest Solomon and his hosts crush them. Solomon smiles and answers her. He reviews the birds and misses the hoopoe, who, returning, brings news of the magnificence of the queen of Sheba. Solomon sends him back with a letter to the queen. A demon brings him her throne. She comes to Solomon; recognises her throne; marvels at the palace with a glass floor, which she mistakes for water: becomes a Muslim. Thamûd reject Zâli'h and perish. Lot is saved, while the people of Sodom are destroyed. The Lord the God of nature; the only God and creator. Certainty of the resurrection. The ruins of ancient cities an example. The Qur'ân decides disputed points for the Jews. Mohammed bidden to trust in God, for he cannot make the deaf to hear his message. The beast that shall appear at the resurrection. Terrors of the last day. The prophet bidden to worship 'the Lord of this land,' to recite the Qur'ân, and to become a Muslim.

XXVIII. The Chapter of the Story. (Mecca.)

The history of Moses and Pharaoh: the latter and his vizier Hâmân oppress the children of Israel. Moses is exposed on the river by his mother: he is adopted by Pharaoh: his sister watches him, and his mother is engaged to nurse him. He grows up and slays the Egyptian: flees to Midian: helps the two maidens to draw water: serves their father Sho'hâib for ten years and then marries his daughter. God appears to him in the fire in the holy valley of *T*uvâ, in Sinai. Is sent with his brother Aaron to Pharaoh. Hâmân builds Pharaoh a high tower to ascend to the God of Moses. His punishment. Moses gives the law. These stories are proofs of Mohammed's mission. The Arabs reject the book of Moses and the Qur'ân as two impostures. Those who have the Scriptures recognise the truth of the Qur'ân. The Meccans warned by the example of the cities of old that have perished. Disappointment of the idolaters at the day of judgment. Helplessness of the idols before God. Qarûn's great wealth: the earth opens and swallows him up for his pride and his insolence to Moses. Mohammed encouraged in his faith and purpose.

XXIX. The Chapter of the Spider. (Mecca.)

Believers must be proved. Kindness to be shown to parents; but they are not to be obeyed if they endeavour to lead their children to idolatry. The hypocrites stand by the Muslims only in success. The unbelievers try to seduce the believers by offering to bear their sins. Noah delivered from the deluge. Abraham preaches against idolatry. Is cast into the fire, but saved: flees from his native land: Isaac and Jacob born to him. Lot and the fate of the inhabitants of Sodom. Midian and their prophet Sho'hâib. 'Âd and Thamûd. Fate of Qarûn, Pharaoh, and Hâmân. Similitude of the spider. Mohammed bidden to rehearse the Qur'ân. Prayer enjoined. Those who have the Scriptures are to be mildly dealt with in disputation. They believe in the Qur'ân. Mohammed unable to read. Signs are only in the power of God. The idolaters reproved, and threatened with punishment. The believers promised reward. God provides for all. This world is but a sport. God saves men in dangers by sea, yet they are ungrateful. The territory of Mecca inviolable. Exhortation to strive for the faith.

XXX. The Chapter of the Greeks. (Mecca.)

Victory of the Persians over the Greeks: prophecy of the coming triumph of the latter. The Meccans warned by the fate of former cities. The idols shall forsake them at the resurrection: the believers shall enter Paradise. God is to be praised in the morning and evening and at noon and sunset. His creation of man and of the universe and His providence are signs. He is the incomparable Lord of all. Warning against idolatry and schism. Honesty inculcated and usury reproved. God only creates and kills. Corruption in the earth through sin. The fate of former idolaters. Exhortation to believe before the sudden coming of the judgment day. God's sending rain to quicken the earth is a sign of His power. Mohammed cannot make the deaf hear his message. Warning of the last day.

XXXI. The Chapter of Loqmân. (Mecca.)

The Qur'ân a guidance to believers. Denunciation of one who purchased Persian legends and preferred them to the Qur'ân. God in nature. Other gods can create nothing. Wisdom granted to Loqmân: his advice to his son. The obstinacy of the infidels rebuked. If the sea were ink and the trees pens they would not suffice to write the words of the Lord. God manifest in the night and day, in the sun and moon, and in rescuing men from dangers by sea. God only knows the future.

XXXII. The Chapter of Adoration. (Mecca.)

The Qur'ân is truth from the Lord. God the creator and governor. The resurrection. Conduct of true believers when they hear the word: their reward: the punishment of misbelievers: description of hell. The people are exhorted to believe and are admonished by the fate of the ruined cities they see around them: they are warned of the judgment day.

XXXIII. The Chapter of the Confederates. (Medînah.)

Mohammed is warned against the hypocrites. Wives divorced by the formula 'thou art henceforth to me like my mother's back' are not to be considered as real mothers and as such regarded as unlawful. Neither are adopted sons to be looked upon as real sons. The real ties of kinship and consanguinity are to supersede the tie of sworn brotherhood[1]. God's covenant with the prophets. Miraculous interference in favour of the Muslims when besieged by the confederate army at Medînah. Conduct of the 'hypocrites' on the occasion. Departure of the invaders. Siege and defeat of the Benu Qurâi*th*ah Jews: the men are executed: their women and children are sold into slavery and their property confiscated. Laws for the prophet's wives: they are to be discreet and avoid ostentation. Encouragement to the good and true believers of either sex. Vindication of Mohammed's conduct in marrying Zâinab the divorced wife of his freedman and adopted son Zâid (who is mentioned by name). No term need be observed in the case of women divorced before cohabitation. Peculiar privileges granted to Mohammed in the matter of women. Limitation of his license to take wives. Muslims are not to enter the prophet's house without permission: after eating they are to retire without inconveniencing him by familiar discourse: are to be very modest in their demeanour to his wives: are not to marry any of his wives after him. Those relations who are permitted to see them unveiled. God and His angels bless the prophet. Slander of misbelievers will be punished. The women are to dress modestly. Warning to the hypocrites and disaffected at Medînah. The fate of the infidels at the last judgment. Man alone of all creation undertook the responsibility of faith.

XXXIV. The Chapter of Sebâ. (Mecca.)

The omniscience of God. Those who have received knowledge recognise the revelation. The unbelievers mock at Mohammed for preaching the resurrection. The birds and mountains sing praises with David: iron softened for him: he makes coats of mail. The wind subjected to Solomon: a fountain of brass made to flow for him: the *g*inns compelled to work for him: his death only discovered by means of the worm that gnawed the staff that supported his corpse. The prosperity of Sebâ: bursting of the dyke (el 'Arim) and ruin of the town. Helplessness of the false gods: they cannot intercede for their worshippers when assembled at the last day. Fate of the misbelievers on that day: the proud and the weak shall dispute as to which misled the others. The affluence of the Meccans will only increase their ruin. The angels shall disown the worshippers of false gods. The Meccans accuse

[1] See Introduction, p. xxxiv.

Mohammed of imposture; so did other nations deal with their prophets and were punished for it. Mohammed is cleared of the suspicion of insanity. The wretched plight of the misbelievers on the last day.

XXXV. The Chapter of the Angels, or, the Creator. (Mecca.)

Praise of God, who makes the angels his messengers. God's unity: apostles before Mohammed were accused of imposture. Punishment in store for the unbelievers. Mohammed is not to be vexed on their account. God sends rain to quicken the dead earth: this is a sign of the resurrection. The power of God shown in all nature: the helplessness of the idols. They will disclaim their worshippers at the resurrection. No soul shall bear the burden of another. Mohammed cannot compel people to believe: he is only a warner. Other nations have accused their prophets of imposture, and perished. Reward of the God-fearing, of believers, and of those who read and follow the Qur'ân: punishment of hell for the infidels. The idolaters shall be confounded on the judgment day. The Qurâis in spite of their promises and of the examples around them are more arrogant and unbelieving than other people. If God were to punish men as they deserve he would not leave so much as a beast on the earth; but He respites them for a time.

XXXVI. The Chapter of Y. S. (Mecca.)

Mohammed is God's messenger, and the Qur'ân is a revelation from God to warn a heedless people. The infidels are predestined not to believe. All men's works shall be recorded. The apostles of Jesus rejected at Antioch: 'Habîb en Na*gg*âr exhorts the people to follow their advice: he is stoned to death by the populace: Gabriel cries out and the sinful people are destroyed. Men will laugh at the apostles who come to them; but they have an example in the nations who have perished before them. The quickening of the dead earth is a sign of the resurrection. God's power shown in the procreation of species. The alternation of night and day, the phases of the moon, the sun and moon in their orbits, are signs of God's power. So too the preservation of men in ships at sea. Almsgiving enjoined: the unbelievers jeer at the command. The sudden coming of the judgment day. Blessed state of the believers in Paradise, and misery of the unbelievers in hell. Mohammed is no mere poet. The Qur'ân an admonition. God's providence. The false gods will not be able to help their worshippers. Proofs of the resurrection.

XXXVII. The Chapter of the Ranged. (Mecca.)

Oath by the angels ranged in rank, by those who drive the clouds, and by those who rehearse the Qur'ân that God is one alone! They guard the gates of heaven, and pelt the devils who would listen there with shooting-stars. Do the Meccans imagine themselves stronger than the angels that they mock at God's signs and deny the resurrection? The false gods and the Meccans shall recriminate each other at the judgment day. They say now, 'Shall we leave our gods for a mad poet?' They shall taste hell-fire for their unbelief, while the believers are in Paradise. Description of the delights thereof: the maidens there: the blessed shall see their unbelieving former comrades in hell. Immortality of the blessed. Ez Zaqqûm the accursed tree in hell: horrors of that place. The posterity of Noah were blessed. Abraham mocks at and breaks the idols. He is condemned to be burnt alive, but is delivered: is commanded to offer up his son Ishmael as a sacrifice; obeys, but his son is spared. His posterity is blessed. Moses and Aaron too left a good report behind them; so too did Elias, who protested against the worship of Baal. Lot was saved. Jonas was delivered after having been thrown overboard and swallowed by a fish. The gourd. Jonas is sent to preach to the people of the city (of Nineveh). The Meccans rebuked for saying that God has daughters, and for saying that He is akin to the *g*inns. The angels declare that they are but the humble servants of God. The success of the prophet and the confusion of the infidels foretold.

XXXVIII. The Chapter of S. (Mecca.)

Oath by the Qur'ân. Example of former generations who perished for unbelief and for saying that their prophets were sorcerers and the Scriptures forgeries: the Meccans are warned thereby. Any hosts of the confederates shall be routed. Fate of the people of Noah, 'Âd, Pharaoh, Thamûd, and Lot: the Meccans must expect the same. Mohammed exhorted to be patient of what they say: he is reminded of the powers bestowed on David. The parable of the ewe lambs proposed to David by the two antagonists. David exhorted not to follow lust. The heaven and earth were not created in vain as the misbelievers think: the Qur'ân a reminder. Solomon lost in admiration of his horses neglects his devotions, but repenting slays them. A *g*inn in Solomon's likeness is set on his throne to punish him: he repents, and prays God for a kingdom such as no one should ever possess again. The wind and the devils made subject to him. The patience of Job. Abraham, Isaac, and Jacob: Elisha and Dhu 'l Kifl. Happiness of the righteous in Paradise. Misery and mutual recrimination of the wicked in hell. Mohammed only sent to warn people and proclaim God's unity. The creation of man and disobedience of Iblîs, who is expelled: he is respited till the judgment day that he may seduce people to misbelief. But he and those who follow him shall fill hell.

XXXIX. The Chapter of the Troops. (Mecca.)

Rebuke to the idolaters who say they serve false gods as a means of access to God himself. The unity of God, the creator and controller of the universe. His independence and omnipotence. Ingratitude of man for God's help. Difference between the believers and unbelievers. Mohammed is called to sincerity of religion and to Islâm: he is to fear the torment at the judgment day if he disobeys the call. Hell-fire is prepared for the infidels. Paradise promised to those who avoid idolatry. The irrigation of the soil and the growth of corn are signs. The Qur'ân makes the skins of those who fear God creep. Threat of the judgment day. The Meccans are warned by the fate of their predecessors not to reject the Qur'ân. Parable showing the uncertain position of the idolaters. Mohammed not immortal. Warning to those who lie against God, and promise of reward to those who assert the truth. Mohammed is not to be frightened with the idols of the Meccans. Their helplessness demonstrated. The Qur'ân is a guide, but the prophet cannot compel men to follow it. Human souls are taken to God during sleep, and those who are destined to live on are sent back. No intercession allowed with God. The doctrine of the unity of God terrifies the idolaters. Prayer to God to decide between them. The infidels will regret on the resurrection day. Ingratitude of man for God's help in trouble. The Meccans are warned by the fate of their predecessors. Exhortation to repentance before it is too late. Salvation of the God-fearing. God the creator and controller of everything. Description of the last judgment. All souls driven in troops to heaven or to hell.

XL. The Chapter of the Believer. (Mecca.)

Attributes of God. Mohammed encouraged by the fate of other nations who rejected their apostles. The angels' prayer for the believers. Despair in hell of the idolaters. The terrors of the judgment day. God alone the omniscient judge. The vestiges of former nations are still visible in the land to warn the people. The story of Moses and Pharaoh: the latter wishes to kill Moses; but a secret believer makes a long appeal: Pharaoh bids Hâmân construct a tower to mount up to the God of Moses. God saves the believer, and Pharaoh is ruined by his own devices. Mutual recrimination of the damned. Exhortation to patience and praise. Those who wrangle about God rebuked. The certain coming of the Hour. The unity of God asserted and His attributes enumerated. Idolatry forbidden. The conception, birth, life, and death of man. Idolaters shall find out their error in hell. Mohammed encouraged to wait for the issue. Cattle to ride on and to eat are signs of God's providence. The example of the nations who perished of old for rejecting the Apostle.

XLI. The Chapter 'Detailed.' (Mecca.)

The Meccans are called on to believe the Qur'ân. The creation of the heavens and the earth. Warning from the fate of 'Âd and Thamûd. The very skins of the unbelievers shall bear witness against them on the day of judgment. Punishment of those who reject the Qur'ân. The angels descend and encourage those who believe. Precept to return good for evil. Refuge to be sought with God against temptation from the devil. Against sun and moon worship. The angels praise God, though the idolaters are too proud to do so. The quickening of the earth with rain is a sign. The Qur'ân a confirmation of previous scriptures. If it had been revealed in a foreign tongue the people would have objected that they could not understand it, and that the prophet being an Arab should have had a revelation in his own language. Moses' scripture was also the subject of dispute. God is omniscient. The false gods will desert their worshippers at the resurrection. Man's ingratitude for God's help in trouble. God is sufficient witness of the truth.

XLII. THE CHAPTER OF COUNSEL. (Mecca.)

The Qur'ân inspired by God to warn 'the Mother of cities' of the judgment to come. God is one, the creator of all things, who provides for all. He calls men to the same religion as that of the prophets of old, which men have broken up into sects. Mohammed has only to proclaim his message. Those who argue about God shall be confuted. None knows when the Hour shall come but God. The idolaters shall only have their portion in this life. God will vindicate the truth of His revelation. His creation and providence signs of His power. Men's misfortunes by land and sea are due to their own sins. The provision of the next world is best for the righteous. It is not sinful to retaliate if wronged, though forgiveness is a duty. The sinners shall have none to help them on the day of judgment: they are exhorted to repent before it comes. Ingratitude of man. God controls all. No mortal has ever seen God face to face: He speaks to men only through inspiration or His apostles. This Qur'ân was revealed by a spirit to guide into the right way.

XLIII. THE CHAPTER OF GILDING. (Mecca.)

The original of the Qur'ân is with God. The example of the nations of old who mocked at the prophets. God the creator. Men are bidden to praise Him who provides man with ships and cattle whereon to ride. The Arabs are rebuked for attributing female offspring to God, when they themselves repine when a female child is born to any one of them. They are also blamed for asserting that the angels are females. The excuse that this was the religion of their fathers will not avail: it is the same as older nations made: their fate. Abraham disclaimed idolatry. The Meccans were permitted to enjoy prosperity only until the Apostle came; and now that he has come they reject him. They are reproved for saying that had the prophet been a man of consideration at Mecca and *T*â'if they would have owned him. Misbelievers would have had still more wealth and enjoyment, but that men would have then all become infidels. Those who turn from the admonition shall be chained to devils, who shall mislead them. God will take vengeance on them whether Mohammed live to see it or not: he is encouraged to persevere. Moses was mocked by Pharaoh, whom he was sent to warn. But Pharaoh and his people were drowned. Answer to the Arabs who objected that Jesus too must come under the ban against false gods. But Jesus did not assume to be a god. Threat of the coming of the Hour. The joys of Paradise and the terrors of Hell. The damned shall beg Mâlik to make an end of them. The recording angels note down the secret plots of the infidels. God has no son: He is the Lord of all.

XLIV. The Chapter of Smoke. (Mecca.)

Night of the revelation of the Qur'ân. Unity of God. Threat of the last day, when a smoke shall cover the heavens, and the unbelievers shall be punished for rejecting the prophet and saying he is taught by others or distracted. Fate of Pharaoh for rejecting Moses: fate of the people of Tubbâ'h. The judgment day: the tree Zaqqûm and the punishment of hell. Paradise and the virgins thereof. The Qur'ân revealed in Arabic for an admonition.

XLV. The Chapter of the Kneeling. (Mecca.)

God revealed in nature: denunciation of the infidels: trading by sea a sign of God's providence. The law first given to Israel, then to Mohammed in the Qur'ân. Answer to the infidels who deny the resurrection, and warning of their fate on that day.

XLVI. The Chapter of El A'hqâf. (Mecca.)

God the only God and creator. The unbelievers call Mohammed a sorcerer or a forger. The book of Moses was revealed before, and the Qur'ân is a confirmation of it in Arabic. Conception, birth, and life of man. Kindness to parents and acceptance of Islâm enjoined. The misbelievers are warned by the example of 'Âd, who dwelt in A'hqâf; and by that of the cities whose ruins lie around Mecca. Allusion to the *g*inns who listened to Mohammed's preaching at Na'*h*leh on his return from *T*â'if. Warning to unbelievers of the punishment of the last day.

XLVII. The Chapter of Mohammed, also called Fight. (Medînah.)

Promise of reward to believers. Exhortation to deal severely with the enemy. Description of Paradise and of Hell. Reproof to some pretended believers and hypocrites who hesitate to obey the command to make war against the unbeliever. Their secret malice shall be revealed. Exhortation to believe, and to obey God and the Apostle, and sacrifice all for the faith.

XLVIII. The Chapter of Victory. (Medînah.)

Announcement of a victory[1]. God comforts the believers and punishes the hypocrites and idolaters. The oath of fealty: the cowardice and excuses of the desert Arabs with regard to the expedition of El 'Hudâibîyeh. Those left behind wish to share the spoils gained at Khâibar. The incapacitated alone are to be excused. The oath of fealty at the Tree[2]. God prevented a collision between the Meccans and the Muslims when the latter were prohibited from making the pilgrimage. Prophecy of the pilgrimage to be completed the next year.

XLIX. The Chapter of the Inner Chambers. (Medînah.)

Rebuke to some of the Muslims who had presumed too much in the presence of the Apostle, and of others who had called out rudely to him: also of a man who had nearly induced Mohammed to attack a tribe who were still obedient; of certain Muslims who contended together; of others who use epithets of abuse against each other; who entertain unfounded suspicions. Exhortation to obedience and reproof of the hypocrites.

L. The Chapter of Q. (Mecca.)

Proofs in nature of a future life. Example of the fate of the nations of old who rejected the apostles. Creation of man: God's proximity to him: the two recording angels: death and resurrection. The last judgment and exhortation to believe.

LI. The Chapter of the Scatterers. (Mecca.)

Oaths by different natural phenomenon that the judgment day will come. Story of Abraham's entertaining the angels: the destruction of Sodom. Fate of Pharaoh, of 'Âd, of Thamûd, and of the people of Noah. Vindication of Mohammed against the charges of imposture or madness.

LII. The Chapter of the Mount. (Mecca.)

Oath by Mount Sinai and other things. Terrors of the last day. Bliss of Paradise. Mohammed is neither a madman, soothsayer, poet, nor imposter. Reproof of the Meccans for their superstitions, and for proudly rejecting the prophet.

---

[1] See note to the passage in the translation.

[2] See Introduction, p. xl.

LIII. The Chapter of the Star. (Mecca.)

Oath by 'the star' that Mohammed's vision of his ascent to heaven was not a delusion. Description of the same. The amended passage relating to Allât, El 'Huzzah, and Manât[1]. Wickedness of asserting the angels to be females. God's omniscience. Rebuke of an apostate who paid another to take upon him his burden at the judgment day. Definition of the true religion, and enumeration of God's attributes.

LIV. The Chapter of the Moon. (Mecca.)

'The splitting asunder of the moon.' Mohammed accused of imposture. The Meccans warned by the stories of Noah and the deluge, of Thamûd, the people of Sodom, and Pharaoh. The sure coming of the judgment.

LV. The Chapter of the Merciful. (Mecca.)

An enumeration of the works of the Lord, ending with a description of heaven and hell. A refrain runs throughout this chapter, 'Which then of your Lord's bounties do ye twain deny?'

LVI. The Chapter of the Inevitable. (Mecca.)

Terrors of the inevitable day of judgment: description of heaven and hell. Proofs in nature. None but the clean may touch the Qur'ân. The condition of a dying man.

LVII. The Chapter of Iron. (Medînah.)

God the controller of all nature. Exhortation to embrace Islâm. Those who do so before the taking of Mecca are to have the precedence. Discomfiture of the hypocrites and unbelievers at the last day. The powers vouchsafed to former apostles.

LVIII. The Chapter of the Wrangler. (Medînah.)

Abolition of the idolatrous custom of divorcing women with the formula 'thou art to me as my mother's back.' God's omniscience and omnipresence: He knows the secret plottings of the disaffected. Discourse on the duties of true believers. Denunciation of those who oppose the Apostle.

LIX. The Chapter of the Emigration. (Medînah.)

The chastisements of the Jews who would not believe in the

[1] See Introduction, pp. xxvi, xxvii.

Qur'ân. The division of the spoils. The treacherous conduct of the hypocrites. The power of the Qur'ân. God's mighty attributes.

LX. The Chapter of the Tried. (Medînah.)

Exhortations to the Muslims not to treat secretly with the Qurâis. Abraham's example. Other idolaters who have not borne arms against them may be made friends of. Women who desert from the infidels are to be tried before being received into Islâm; if they are really believers they are ipso facto divorced. The husbands are to be recompensed to the amount of the women's dowries.

LXI. The Chapter of the Ranks. (Mecca.)

Believers are bidden to keep their word and to fight for the faith. Moses was disobeyed by his people. Jesus prophesies the coming of A'hmed: the Christians rebuked.

LXII. The Chapter of the Congregation. (Medînah.)

God has sent the 'illiterate prophet.' The Jews rebuked for unbelief. Muslims are not to leave the congregation during divine service for the sake of merchandise.

LXIII. The Chapter of the Hypocrites. (Medînah.)

The treacherous designs of the hypocrites revealed.

LXIV. The Chapter of Cheating. (Place of origin doubtful.)

God the creator: the resurrection: the unity of God. Wealth and children must not distract men from the service of God.

LXV. The Chapter of Divorce. (Medînah.)

The laws of divorce. The Arabs are admonished, by the fate of former nations, to believe in God. The seven stories of heaven and earth.

LXVI. The Chapter of Prohibition. (Medînah.)

The prophet is relieved from a vow he had made to please his wives. The jealousies in his harem occasioned by his intrigue with the Coptic slave-girl Mary. Exhortation to hostilities against the infidels. The example of the disobedient wives of Noah and Lot: and of the good wife of Pharaoh: and of the Virgin Mary.

LXVII. THE CHAPTER OF THE KINGDOM. (Mecca.)

God the lord of the heavens; the marvels thereof. The discomfiture of the misbelievers in Hell. The power of God exhibited in nature. Warnings and threats of punishment.

LXVIII. THE CHAPTER OF THE PEN (also called NÛN). (Mecca.)

Mohammed is neither mad nor an impostor. Denounced by an insolent opponent. Example from the fate of the owner of the 'gardens.' Unbelievers threatened. Mohammed exhorted to be patient and not to follow the example of Jonah.

LXIX. THE CHAPTER OF THE INFALLIBLE. (Mecca.)

The infallible judgment. Fate of those who denied it, of 'Âd, Thamûd, and Pharaoh. The deluge and the last judgment. Vindication of Mohammed from the charge of having forged the Qur'ân.

LXX. THE CHAPTER OF THE ASCENTS. (Mecca.)

An unbeliever mockingly calls for a judgment on himself and his companions. The terrors of the judgment day. Man's ingratitude. Adultery denounced. Certainty of the judgment day.

LXXI. THE CHAPTER OF NOAH. (Mecca.)

Noah's preaching to the antediluvians: their five idols also worshipped by the Arabs: their fate.

LXXII. THE CHAPTER OF THE *G*INN. (Mecca.)

A crowd of *g*inns listen to Mohammed's teaching at Na'*h*leh: their account of themselves. Mohammed exhorted to persevere in preaching.

LXXIII. THE CHAPTER OF THE ENWRAPPED. (Mecca.)

Mohammed when wrapped up in his mantle is bidden to arise and pray: is bidden to repeat the Qur'ân and to practise devotion by night: he is to bear with the unbelievers for a while. Pharaoh rejected the Apostle sent to him. Stated times for prayer prescribed. Almsgiving prescribed.

LXXIV. THE CHAPTER OF THE COVERED. (Mecca.)

Mohammed while covered up is bidden to arise and preach[1].

[1] This part of the sûrah is the second revelation after the appearance of the archangel Gabriel on Mount Hirâ; see Introduction, p. xx.

Denunciation of a rich infidel who mocks at the revelation. Hell and its nineteen angels. The infidels rebuked for demanding material scriptures as a proof of Mohammed's mission.

LXXV. THE CHAPTER OF THE RESURRECTION. (Mecca.)

The resurrection. Mohammed is bidden not to be hurried in repeating the Qur'ân so as to commit it to memory. Dying agony of an infidel.

LXXVI. THE CHAPTER OF MAN. (Mecca.)

Man's conception and birth. Unbelievers warned and believers promised a reward. Exhortation to charity. Bliss of the charitable in Paradise. The Qur'ân revealed by degrees. Only those believe whom God wills.

LXXVII. THE CHAPTER OF THOSE SENT. (Mecca.)

Oath by the angels who execute God's behests. Terrors of the last day. Hell and heaven.

LXXVIII. THE CHAPTER OF THE INFORMATION. (Mecca.)

Another description of the day of judgment, hell, and heaven.

LXXIX. THE CHAPTER OF THOSE WHO TEAR OUT. (Mecca.)

The coming of the day of judgment. The call of Moses. His interview with Pharaoh: chastisement of the latter. The creation and resurrection.

LXXX. THE CHAPTER 'HE FROWNED.' (Mecca.)

The prophet rebuked for frowning on a poor blind believer. The creation and resurrection.

LXXXI. THE CHAPTER OF THE FOLDING UP. (Mecca.)

Terrors of the judgment day. The female child who has been burned alive will demand vengeance. Allusion to the prophet's vision of Gabriel on Mount Hirâ. He is vindicated from the charge of madness.

LXXXII. THE CHAPTER OF THE CLEAVING ASUNDER. (Mecca.)

Signs of the judgment day. Guardian angels.

LXXXIII. THE CHAPTER OF THOSE WHO GIVE SHORT WEIGHT. (Mecca.)

Fraudulent traders are warned. Si*gg*în, the register of the acts of the wicked. Hell and heaven.

LXXXIV. THE CHAPTER OF THE RENDING ASUNDER. (Mecca.)

Signs of the judgment day. The books of men's actions. The resurrection. Denunciation of misbelievers.

LXXXV. THE CHAPTER OF THE ZODIACAL SIGNS. (Mecca.)

Denunciation of those who persecuted believers. Example of the fate of Pharaoh and Thamûd.

LXXXVI. THE CHAPTER OF THE NIGHT STAR. (Mecca.)

By the night star! every soul has a guardian angel. Creation and resurrection of man. The plot of the infidels shall be frustrated.

LXXXVII. THE CHAPTER OF THE MOST HIGH. (Mecca.)

Mohammed shall not forget any of the revelation save what God pleases. The revelation is the same as that given to Abraham and Moses.

LXXXVIII. THE CHAPTER OF THE OVERWHELMING. (Mecca.)

Description of the last day, heaven, and hell.

LXXXIX. THE CHAPTER OF THE DAWN. (Mecca.)

Fate of previous nations who rejected the apostles. Admonition to those who rely too much on their prosperity.

XC. THE CHAPTER OF THE LAND. (Mecca.)

Exhortation to practise charity.

XCI. THE CHAPTER OF THE SUN. (Mecca.)

Purity of the soul brings happiness. Example of Thamûd.

XCII. THE CHAPTER OF THE NIGHT. (Mecca.)

Promise of reward to believers and of punishment to idolaters.

XCIII. THE CHAPTER OF THE FORENOON. (Mecca.)

Mohammed encouraged and bidden to remember how God has

cared for him hitherto; he is to be charitable in return, and to publish God's goodness.

XCIV. THE CHAPTER OF 'HAVE WE NOT EXPANDED?' (Mecca.)

God has made Mohammed's mission easier to him.

XCV. THE CHAPTER OF THE FIG. (Place of origin doubtful.)

The degradation of man: future reward and punishment.

XCVI. THE CHAPTER OF CONGEALED BLOOD. (Mecca.)

Mohammed's first call to 'Read' the Qur'ân. Denunciation of Abu Laheb for his opposition.

XCVII. THE CHAPTER OF 'POWER.' (Place of origin doubtful.)

The Qur'ân revealed on 'the night of power.' Its excellence: angels descend thereon.

XCVIII. THE CHAPTER OF THE MANIFEST SIGN. (Place of origin doubtful.)

Rebuke to Jews and Christians for doubting the manifest sign of Mohammed's mission.

XCIX. THE CHAPTER OF THE EARTHQUAKE. (Place of origin doubtful.)

The earthquake preceding the judgment day.

C. THE CHAPTER OF THE CHARGERS. (Mecca.)

Oath by the charging of war horses. Man is ungrateful: certainty of the judgment.

CI. THE CHAPTER OF THE SMITING. (Mecca.)

The terrors of the last day and of hell-fire.

CII. THE CHAPTER OF THE CONTENTION ABOUT NUMBERS. (Place of origin doubtful.)

Two families of the Arabs rebuked for contending which was the more numerous. Warning of the punishment of hell.

CIII. THE CHAPTER OF THE AFTERNOON. (Mecca.)

Believers only shall prosper.

CIV. THE CHAPTER OF THE BACKBITER. (Mecca.)

Backbiters shall be cast into hell.

CV. The Chapter of the Elephant. (Mecca.)

The miraculous destruction of the Abyssinian army under Abraha al Asram by birds when invading Mecca with elephants.

CVI. The Chapter of the Qurâis. (Mecca.)

The Qurâis are bidden to give thanks to God for the trade of their two yearly caravans.

CVII. The Chapter of 'Necessaries.' (Place of origin doubtful.)

Denunciation of the unbelieving and uncharitable.

CVIII. The Chapter of El Kâuthar. (Mecca.)

Mohammed is commanded to offer the sacrifices out of his abundance. Threat that his enemies shall be childless.

CIX. The Chapter of the Misbelievers. (Mecca.)

The prophet will not follow the religion of the misbelievers.

CX. The Chapter of Help. (Mecca.)

Prophecy that men shall join Islâm by troops.

CXI. The Chapter of Abu Laheb. (Mecca.)

Denunciation of Abu Laheb and his wife, who are threatened with hell-fire.

CXII. The Chapter of Unity. (Place of origin doubtful.)

Declaration of God's unity.

CXIII. The Chapter of the Daybreak. (Place of origin doubtful.)

The prophet seeks refuge in God from evil influences.

CXIV. The Chapter of Men. (Place of origin doubtful.)

The prophet seeks refuge in God from the devil and his evil suggestions.

THE QUR'ÂN.

THE QUR'ÂN.

The Opening Chapter.

(I. Mecca.)

In the name of the merciful and compassionate God.

Praise belongs to God, the Lord of the worlds,
the merciful, the compassionate, the ruler of the
day of judgment! Thee we serve and Thee we ask
for aid. [5] Guide us in the right path, the path of
those Thou art gracious to [1]; not of those Thou art
wroth with; nor of those who err.

[1] See Preface.

The Chapter of the Heifer.

(II. Medina.)

In the name of the merciful and compassionate God.

A. L. M.[1] That[2] is the book! there is no doubt therein; a guide to the pious, who believe in the unseen, and are steadfast in prayer, and of what we have given them expend in alms; who believe in what is revealed to thee, and what was revealed before thee, and of the hereafter they are sure. These are in guidance from their Lord, and these are the prosperous. [5] Verily, those who misbelieve, it is the same to them if ye warn them or if ye warn them not, they will not believe. God has set a seal upon their hearts and on their hearing; and on their eyes is dimness, and for them is grievous woe. And there are those among men who say, 'We believe in God and in the last day;' but they do not believe. They would deceive God and those who do believe; but they deceive only themselves and they do not perceive. In their hearts is a sickness, and God has made them still more sick, and for them is grievous woe because they lied. [10] And when it is said to them, 'Do not evil in the earth,' they say, 'We do but what is right.' Are not they the evildoers? and yet they do not perceive. And when it is said to them, 'Believe as other men believe,' they say, 'Shall we

[1] For an explanation of these and similar letters see Introduction.

[2] Although the Arabic demonstrative pronoun means 'that,' the translators have hitherto always rendered it 'this,' forgetting that it is not an address to the reader, but supposed to be Gabriel's words of inspiration to Mohammed while showing him the Umm al Kitâb —the 'Eternal original of the Qur'ân;' cf. Chapter X, which begins 'Read,' and others.

believe as fools believe?' Are not they themselves the fools? and yet they do not know. And when they meet those who believe, they say, 'We do believe;' but when they go aside with their devils, they say, 'We are with you; we were but mocking!' God shall mock at them and let them go on in their rebellion, blindly wandering on.

[15] Those who buy error for guidance, their traffic profits not, and they are not guided. Their likeness is as the likeness of one[1] who kindles a fire; and when it lights up all around, God goes off with their light, and leaves them in darkness that they cannot see. Deafness, dumbness, blindness, and they shall not return! Or like a storm-cloud from the sky, wherein is darkness and thunder and lightning; they put their fingers in their ears at the thunder-clap, for fear of death, for God encompasses the misbelievers. The lightning well-nigh snatches off their sight, whenever it shines for them they walk therein; but when it is dark for them they halt; and if God willed He would go off with their hearing and their sight; verily, God is mighty over all.

O ye folk! serve your Lord who created you and those before you; haply ye may fear! [20] who made the earth for you a bed and the heaven a dome; and sent down from heaven water, and brought forth therewith fruits as a sustenance for you; so make no peers for God, the while ye know!

And if ye are in doubt of what we have revealed unto our servant, then bring a chapter like it, and call your witnesses other than God if ye tell truth. But if ye do it not, and ye shall surely do it not, then

[1] This change of number is of frequent occurrence in the Qur'ân, and is not incompatible with the genius of the Arabic language.

fear the fire whose fuel is men and stones[1], prepared for misbelievers. But bear the glad tidings to those who believe and work righteousness, that for them are gardens beneath which rivers flow; whenever they are provided with fruit therefrom they say, 'This is what we were provided with before,' and they shall be provided with the like[2]; and there are pure wives for them therein, and they shall dwell therein for aye.

Why, God is not ashamed to set forth a parable of a gnat[3], or anything beyond; and as for those who believe, they know that it is truth from the Lord; but as for those who disbelieve, they say, 'What is it that God means by this as a parable? He leads astray many and He guides many;'—but He leads astray only the evildoers; [25] who break God's covenant after the fixing thereof, and cut asunder what God has ordered to be joined, and do evil in the earth;—these it is who lose.

How can ye disbelieve in God, when ye were dead and He made you alive, and then He will kill you and then make you alive again, and then to Him will ye return? It is He who created for you all that is in the earth, then he made for the heavens and fashioned them seven heavens; and He knows all things.

And when thy Lord said unto the angels, 'I am about to place a vicegerent in the earth,' they said,

---

[1] That is, the idols.

[2] The vagueness is in the original; it is variously interpreted 'fruits like each other,' or 'like the fruits of earth.'

[3] This is in answer to the objections that had been taken against the mention of su.h small things as the 'spider' and the 'bee,' which give their names to two of the chapters of the Qur'ân.

'Wilt Thou place therein one who will do evil therein and shed blood? [30] we celebrate Thy praise and hallow Thee.' Said (the Lord), 'I know what ye know not.' And He taught Adam the names, all of them; then He propounded them to the angels and said, 'Declare to me the names of these, if ye are truthful[1].' They said, 'Glory be to Thee! no knowledge is ours but what Thou thyself hast taught us, verily, Thou art the knowing, the wise.' Said the Lord, 'O Adam declare to them their names;' and when he had declared to them their names He said, 'Did I not say to you, I know the secrets of the heavens and of the earth, and I know what ye show and what ye were hiding?' And when we said to the angels, 'Adore Adam,' they adored him save only Iblîs, who refused and was too proud and became one of the misbelievers. And we said, 'O Adam dwell, thou and thy wife, in Paradise, and eat therefrom amply as you wish; but do not draw near this tree or ye will be of the transgressors. And Satan made them backslide therefrom and drove them out from what they were in, and we said, 'Go down, one of you the enemy of the other, and in the earth there is an abode and a provision for a time.' [35] And Adam caught certain words from his Lord, and He turned towards him, for He is the compassionate one easily turned. We said, 'Go down therefrom altogether and haply there may come from me a guidance, and whoso follows my guidance, no fear is theirs, nor shall they grieve.

[1] That is, truthful in their implied suggestion that man would be inferior to themselves in wisdom and obedience. The whole tradition here alluded to of the creation accords with the Talmudic legends, and was probably current among the Jewish Arab tribes.

But those who misbelieve, and call our signs lies, they are the fellows of the Fire, they shall dwell therein for aye.'

O ye children of Israel! remember my favours which I have favoured you with; fulfil my covenant and I will fulfil your covenant; me therefore dread. Believe in what I have revealed, verifying what ye have got, and be not the first to disbelieve in it, and do not barter my signs for a little price, and me do ye fear. Clothe not truth with vanity, nor hide the truth the while ye know. [40] Be steadfast in prayer, give the alms, and bow down with those who bow. Will ye order men to do piety and forget yourselves? ye read the Book, do ye not then understand? Seek aid with patience and prayer, though it is a hard thing save for the humble, who think that they will meet their Lord, and that to Him will they return.

O ye children of Israel! remember my favours which I have favoured you with, and that I have preferred you above the worlds. Fear the day wherein no soul shall pay any recompense for another soul, [45] nor shall intercession be accepted for it, nor shall compensation be taken from it, nor shall they be helped.

When we saved you from Pharaoh's people who sought to wreak you evil and woe, slaughtering your sons and letting your women live; in that was a great trial for you from your Lord. When we divided for you the sea and saved you and drowned Pharaoh's people while ye looked on. When we treated with Moses forty nights, then ye took the calf after he had gone and ye did wrong. Yet then we forgave you after that; perhaps ye may be grateful. [50] And when we gave Moses the Scriptures and the Discrimination; perhaps ye will be guided. When Moses said to his people, 'O my people! Ye have wronged yourselves in taking this calf; repent unto your Creator and kill each other[1]; that will be better for you in your Creator's eyes; and He turned unto you, for He is the compassionate one easily turned.' And when ye said to Moses, 'O Moses! we will not believe in thee until we see God manifestly,' and the thunderbolt caught you while ye yet looked on. Then we raised you up after your death; perhaps ye may be grateful. And we overshadowed you with the cloud, and sent down the manna and the quails; 'Eat of the good things we have given you.' They did not wrong us, but it was themselves they were wronging. [55] And when we said, 'Enter this city[2] and eat therefrom as plentifully as ye wish; and enter the gate worshipping and say 'hi*tt*atun[3]. So will we pardon you your sins and give increase unto those who do well.'

But those who did wrong changed it for another[4] word than that which was said to them: and we sent down upon those who did wrong, wrath from heaven for that they had so sinned.

---

[1] Cf. Exodus xxxii. 24, 26, 27.

[2] According to some commentators, Jerusalem; and according to others, Jericho.

[3] The word means Remission, or laying down the burden (of sins).

[4] Some say the expression they used was habbah fi sha'hîrah, 'a grain in an ear of barley,' the idea being apparently suggested by the similarity between the words 'hi*tt*ah, as given above, and 'hin*t*ah, 'a grain of wheat.' The commentators add that they crept in in an indecent posture instead of entering reverently as they were bidden.

When Moses, too, asked drink for his people and we said, 'Strike with thy staff the rock,' and from it burst forth twelve springs; each man among them knew his drinking place. 'Eat and drink of what God has provided, and transgress not on the earth as evildoers.'

And when they said, 'O Moses, we cannot always bear one kind of food; pray then thy Lord to bring forth for us of what the earth grows, its green herbs, its cucumbers, its garlic, its lentils, and its onions.' Said he, 'Do ye ask what is meaner instead of what is best? Go down to Egypt,--there is what ye ask.' Then were they smitten with abasement and poverty, and met with wrath from God. That was because they had misbelieved in God's signs and killed the prophets undeservedly; that was for that they were rebellious and had transgressed.

Verily, whether it be of those who believe, or those who are Jews or Christians or Sabæans, whosoever believe in God and the last day and act aright, they have their reward at their Lord's hand, and there is no fear for them, nor shall they grieve.

[60] And when we took a covenant with you and held the mountain over you[1]; 'Accept what we have brought you with strong will, and bear in mind what is therein, haply ye yet may fear.'

Then did ye turn aside after this, and were it not for God's grace towards you and His mercy, ye would have been of those who lose. Ye know too of those among you who transgressed upon the

[1] The Mohammedan legend is that this was done by the angel Gabriel to terrify the people into obedience.

Sabbath, and we said, 'Become ye apes, despised and spurned [1].'

Thus we made them an example unto those who stood before them, and those who should come after them, and a warning unto those who fear.

And when Moses said to his people, 'God bids you slaughter a cow [2],' they said, 'Art thou making a jest of us?' Said he, 'I seek refuge with God from being one of the unwise.' They said, 'Then pray thy Lord for us to show us what she is to be.' He answered, 'He saith it is a cow, nor old, nor young, of middle age between the two; so do as ye are bid.' [65] They said, 'Pray now thy Lord to show us what her colour is to be.' He answered, 'He saith it is a dun cow, intensely dun, her colour delighting those who look upon her.'

Again they said, 'Pray thy Lord to show us what she is to be; for cows appear the same to us; then we, if God will, shall be guided.' He answered, 'He saith, it is a cow, not broken in to plough the earth or irrigate the tilth, a sound one with no blemish on her.' They said, 'Now hast thou brought the truth.' And they slaughtered her, though they came near leaving it undone.

When too ye slew a soul and disputed thereupon, and God brought forth that which ye had hidden, then we said, 'Strike him with part of her.' Thus

---

[1] The tradition is that some inhabitants of Elath (Akabah) were transformed into apes for catching fish on the Sabbath in David's time. Other commentators say that the expression is only figurative.

[2] The legend embodied in this passage and what follows appears to be a distorted account of the heifer ordered by the Mosaic law to be slain in expiation of a murder, the perpetrator of which had not been discovered. Deut. xxi. 1-9.

God brings the dead to life and shows you His signs, that haply ye may understand.

Yet were your hearts hardened even after that, till they were as stones or harder still, for verily of stones are some from which streams burst forth, and of them there are some that burst asunder and the water issues out, and of them there are some that fall down for fear of God; but God is never careless of what ye do.

[70] Do ye crave that they should believe you when already a sect of them have heard the word of God and then perverted it[1] after they had understood it, though they knew?

And when they meet those who believe they say, 'We believe,' but when one goes aside with another they say, 'Will ye talk to them of what God has opened up to you, that they may argue with you upon it before your Lord? Do ye not therefore understand?' Do they not then know that God knoweth what they keep secret and what they make known abroad?

And some of them there are, illiterate folk, that know not the Book, but only idle tales; for they do but fancy. But woe to those who write out the Book with their hands and say 'this is from' God; to buy therewith a little price! and woe to them for what their hands have written, and woe to them for what they gain!

And then they say, 'Hell fire shall not touch us save for a number of days[2].' Say, 'Have ye taken a covenant with God?' but God breaks not His

[1] A constant charge against the Jews is that of having corrupted the Scriptures.

[2] A superstition of certain Jews.

covenant. Or do ye say of God that which ye do not know?

[75] Yea! whoso gains an evil gain, and is encompassed by his sins, those are the fellows of the Fire, and they shall dwell therein for aye! But such as act aright, those are the fellows of Paradise, and they shall dwell therein for aye!

And when we took from the children of Israel a covenant, saying, 'Serve ye none but God, and to your two parents show kindness, and to your kindred and the orphans and the poor, and speak to men kindly, and be steadfast in prayer, and give alms;' and then ye turned back, save a few of you, and swerved aside.

And when we took a covenant from you; 'shed ye not your kinsman's blood, nor turn your kinsmen out of their homes[1]:' then did ye confirm it and were witnesses thereto. Yet ye were those who slay your kinsmen and turn a party out of their homes, and back each other up against them with sin and enmity. But if they come to you as captives ye ransom them!—and yet it is as unlawful for you to turn them out. Do ye then believe in part of the Book and disbelieve in part? But the reward of such among you as do that shall be nought else but disgrace in this worldly life, and on the day of the resurrection shall they be driven to the most grievous torment, for God is not unmindful of what ye do.

[80] Those who have bought this worldly life with the Future, the torment shall not be lightened from them nor shall they be helped.

---

[1] Alluding to some quarrels among the Jewish Arabs.

We gave Moses the Book and we followed him up with other apostles, and we gave Jesus the son of Mary manifest signs and aided him with the Holy Spirit. Do ye then, every time an apostle comes to you with what your souls love not, proudly scorn him, and charge a part with lying and slay a part?

They say, 'Our hearts are uncircumcised;' nay, God has cursed them in their unbelief, and few it is who do believe. And when a book came down from God confirming what they had with them, though they had before prayed for victory over those who misbelieve, yet when that came to them[1] which they knew, then they disbelieved it,—God's curse be on the misbelievers.

For a bad bargain have they sold their souls, not to believe in what God has revealed, grudging because God sends down of His grace on whomsoever of His servants He will; and they have brought on themselves wrath after wrath and for the misbelievers is there shameful woe.

[85] And when they are told to believe in what God has revealed, they say, 'We believe in what has been revealed to us;' but they disbelieve in all beside, although it is the truth confirming what they have. Say, 'Wherefore did ye kill God's prophets of yore if ye were true believers?'

Moses came to you with manifest signs, then ye took up with the calf when he had gone and did so wrong. And when we took a covenant with you and raised the mountain over you, 'Take what we have given you with resolution and hear;'

[1] The Qur'ân.

they said, 'We hear but disobey;' and they were made to drink the calf down into their hearts for their unbelief[1]. Say, 'An evil thing is it which your belief bids you do, if ye be true believers.' Say, 'If the abode of the future with God is yours alone and not mankind's: long for death then if ye speak the truth.' But they will never long for it because of what their hands have sent on before; but God is knowing as to the wrong doers.

[90] Why, thou wilt find them the greediest of men for life; and of those who associate others with God one would fain live for a thousand years,—but he will not be reprieved from punishment by being let live, for God seeth what they do.

Say, 'Who is an enemy to Gabriel[2]?' for he hath revealed to thy heart, with God's permission, confirmation of what had been before, and a guidance and glad tidings to believers. Who is an enemy to God and His angels and His apostles and Gabriel and Michael?—Verily, God is an enemy to the unbelievers. We have sent down to thee conspicuous signs, and none will disbelieve therein except the evildoers. Or every time they make a covenant, will a part of them repudiate it? Nay, most of them do not believe.

[95] And when there comes to them an apostle confirming what they have, a part of those who have received the Book repudiate God's book, casting it behind their backs as though they did not

[1] Exodus xxxii. 20.

[2] The Jews objected to Mohammed's assertion that the archangel Gabriel revealed the Qur'ân to him, saying that he was an avenging angel, and that had it been Michael, their own guardian angel (Dan. xii. 1), they would have believed.

know. And they follow that which the devils recited against Solomon's kingdom;—it was not Solomon who misbelieved[1], but the devils who misbelieved, teaching men sorcery,—and what has been revealed to the two angels at Babylon, Hârût and Mârût[2]; yet these taught no one until they said, 'We are but a temptation, so do not misbelieve.' Men learn from them only that by which they may part man and wife; but they can harm no one therewith, unless with the permission of God, and they learn what hurts them and profits them not. And yet they knew that he who purchased it would have no portion in the future; but sad is the price at which they have sold their souls, had they but known. But had they believed and feared, a reward from God were better, had they but known.

O ye who believe! say not 'râ'hinâ,' but say 'un*th*urnâ[3],' and hearken; for unto misbelievers shall be grievous woe.

They who misbelieve, whether of those who have the Book or of the idolaters, would fain that no good were sent down to you from your Lord; but God specially favours with His mercy whom He will, for God is Lord of mighty grace.

[100] Whatever verse we may annul or cause thee

---

[1] Solomon's acts of disobedience and idolatry are attributed by Muslim tradition to the tricks of devils, who assumed his form.

[2] Two angels who having fallen in love with daughters of men (Gen. vi. 2) were condemned to hang in chains in a pit at Babylon, where they teach men magic.

[3] The Jewish Arabs used the first of these two words derisively. In Arabic it merely means 'observe us,' but the Jews connected it with the Hebrew root rû'há, 'to be mischievous.' Un*th*urnâ signifies 'behold us.'

to forget, we will bring a better one than it, or one like it; dost thou not know that God is mighty over all? Dost thou not know that God's is the kingdom of the heavens and the earth? nor have ye besides God a patron or a help.

Do ye wish to question your apostle as Moses was questioned aforetime? but whoso takes misbelief in exchange for faith has erred from the level road.

Many of those who have the Book would fain turn you back into misbelievers after ye have once believed, through envy from themselves, after the truth has been made manifest to them; but pardon and shun them till God brings His command; verily, God is mighty over all.

Be ye steadfast in prayer, and give alms; and whatsoever good ye send before for your own souls, ye shall find it with God, for God in all ye do doth see.

[105] They say, 'None shall enter Paradise save such as be Jews or Christians;' that is their faith. Say thou, 'Bring your proofs, if ye be speaking truth.'

Aye, he who resigns[1] his face to God, and who is kind, he shall have his reward from his Lord, and no fear shall be on them, and they shall not grieve.

The Jews say, 'The Christians rest on nought;' and the Christians say, 'The Jews rest on nought;' and yet they read the Book. So, too, say those who know not, like to what these say; but God shall judge between them on the resurrection day concerning that whereon they do dispute.

---

[1] The word resignation (Islâm) is that by which Mohammed's religion is known and by which it is spoken of in the Qur'ân.

But who is more unjust than he who prohibits God's mosques[1], that His name should not be mentioned there, and who strives to ruin them? 'Tis not for such to enter into them except in fear, for them is disgrace in this world, and in the future mighty woe.

God's is the east and the west, and wherever ye turn there is God's face; verily, God comprehends and knows.

[110] They say, 'God takes unto Himself a son.' Celebrated be His praise[2]! Nay, His is what is in the heavens and the earth, and Him all things obey. The Originator of the heavens and the earth, when He decrees a matter He doth but say unto it, 'BE,' and it is.

And those who do not know (the Scriptures) say, 'Unless God speak to us, or there comes a sign.' So spake those before them like unto their speech. Their hearts are all alike. We have made manifest the signs unto a people that are sure.

We have sent thee with the truth, a bearer of good tidings and of warning, and thou shalt not be questioned as to the fellows of hell.

The Jews will not be satisfied with thee, nor yet the Christians, until thou followest their creed. Say, 'God's guidance is the guidance;' and if thou followest their lusts after the knowledge that has come to thee, thou hast not then from God a patron or a help.

[115] They to whom we have brought the Book

[1] Probably alluding to the occasion on which the Meccans prevented Mohammed from using the Kaabah, in the sixth year of the Higrah.

[2] I.e. God forbid!

and who read it as it should be read, believe therein; and whoso disbelieve therein, 'tis they who lose thereby.

O children of Israel! remember my favours with which I favoured you, and that I have preferred you over the worlds. And fear the day when no soul shall pay a recompense for a soul, nor shall an equivalent be received therefrom, nor any intercession avail; and they shall not be helped.

And when his Lord tried Abraham with words, and he fulfilled them, He said, 'Verily, I will set thee as a high priest [1] for men.' Said he, 'And of my seed?' God said, 'My covenant touches not the evildoers.'

And when we made the House [2] a place of resort unto men, and a sanctuary, and (said) take the station of Abraham [3] for a place of prayer; and covenanted with Abraham and Ishmael, saying, 'Do ye two cleanse my house for those who make the circuit, for those who pay devotions there, for those who bow down, and for those too who adore.'

[120] When Abraham said, 'Lord, make this a town of safety, and provide the dwellers there with fruits, such as believe in God and the last day!' (God) said, 'And he who misbelieves, I will give him but little to enjoy, then will I drive him to the torment of the fire, an evil journey will it be.'

---

[1] Imâm, the name given to the priest who leads the prayer, it is equivalent to Antistes.

[2] The Kaabah or square temple at Mecca is spoken of as Bâit Allâh=Bethel, 'the house of God.'

[3] The Muqâm Ibrahîm, in the Kaabah enclosure, where a so-called footprint of the patriarch is shown.

And when Abraham raised up the foundations of the House with Ishmael, 'Lord! receive it from us, verily, thou art hearing and dost know. Lord! and make us too resigned[1] unto Thee, and of our seed also a nation resigned unto Thee, and show us our rites, and turn towards us, verily, Thou art easy to be turned and merciful. Lord! and send them an apostle from amongst themselves, to read to them Thy signs and teach them the Book and wisdom, and to purify them; verily, Thou art the mighty and the wise.'

Who is averse from the faith of Abraham save one who is foolish of soul? for we have chosen him in this world, and in the future he is surely of the righteous.

[125] When his Lord said to him, 'Be resigned,' he said, 'I am resigned[1] unto the Lord of the worlds.'

And Abraham instructed his sons therein, and Jacob (saying), 'O my sons! verily, God has chosen for you a religion, do not therefore die unless ye be resigned[1].'

Were ye then witnesses when Jacob was facing death, when he said to his sons, 'What will ye serve when I am gone?' They said, 'We will serve thy God, the God of thy fathers Abraham, and Ishmael, and Isaac, one God; and we are unto Him resigned.'

That is a nation that has passed away, theirs is what they gained; and yours shall be what ye have gained; ye shall not be questioned as to that which they have done.

---

[1] See note, p. 15. The last sentence might be rendered 'until ye become Muslims.'

They say, 'Be ye Jews or Christians so shall ye be guided.' Say, 'Not so! but the faith of Abraham the 'Hanîf[1], he was not of the idolaters.'

[130] Say ye, 'We believe in God, and what has been revealed to us, and what has been revealed to Abraham, and Ishmael, and Isaac, and Jacob, and the Tribes, and what was brought to Moses and Jesus, and what was brought unto the Prophets from their Lord; we will not distinguish between any one of them, and unto Him are we resigned.'

If they believe in that in which ye believe, then are they guided; but if they turn back, then are they only in a schism, and God will suffice thee against them, for He both hears and knows.

The dye[2] of God! and who is better than God at dyeing? and we are worshippers of Him.

Say, 'Do ye dispute with us concerning God, and He is our Lord and your Lord? Ye have your works and we have ours, and unto Him are we sincere.'

Do ye say that Abraham, and Ishmael, and Isaac, and Jacob, and the Tribes were Jews or Christians? Say, 'Are ye more knowing than God? Who is more unjust than one who conceals a testimony that he has from God?' But God is not careless of what ye do.

[135] That is a nation that has passed away; theirs is what they gained, and yours shall be what ye have gained; ye shall not be questioned as to that which they have done.

---

[1] The word means in Arabic 'inclining to what is right;' it is often used technically for one who professes El Islâm.

[2] The metaphor is derived from dyeing cloth, and must not be translated by the technical word baptism, as in Sale's version.

The fools among men will say, 'What has turned them from their qiblah[1], on which they were agreed?'

Say, 'God's is the east and the west, He guides whom He will unto the right path[2].' Thus have we made you a middle nation, to be witnesses against men, and that the Apostle may be a witness against you.

We have not appointed the qiblah on which thou wert agreed, save that we might know who follows the Apostle from him who turns upon his heels; although it is a great thing save to those whom God doth guide. But God will not waste your faith, for verily, God with men is kind and merciful.

We see thee often turn about thy face in the heavens, but we will surely turn thee to a qiblah thou shalt like. Turn then thy face towards the Sacred Mosque[3]; wherever ye be, turn your faces towards it; for verily, those who have the Book know that it is the truth from their Lord;—God is not careless of that which ye do.

[140] And if thou shouldst bring to those who have been given the Book every sign, they would not follow your qiblah; and thou art not to follow their qiblah; nor do some of them follow the qiblah of the others: and if thou followest their lusts after the knowledge that has come to thee then art thou of the evildoers.

---

[1] The point to which they turn in prayer, from qabala, 'to be before.'

[2] At first Mohammed and his followers adopted no point of adoration. After the higrah, or flight from Mecca to Medina, however, he bade them turn their face, as did the Jews, to the temple at Jerusalem; but in the second year of the higrah he resumed the ancient Arab plan, and turned to the Kaabah at Mecca when he prayed.

[3] I.e. at Mecca.

Those whom we have given the Book know him[1] as they know their sons, although a sect of them do surely hide the truth, the while they know.

The truth (is) from thy Lord; be not therefore one of those who doubt thereof.

Every sect has some one side to which they turn (in prayer); but do ye hasten onwards to good works; wherever ye are God will bring you all together[2]; verily, God is mighty over all.

From whencesoever thou comest forth, there turn thy face towards the Sacred Mosque, for it is surely truth from thy Lord; God is not careless about what ye do. [145] And from whencesoever thou comest forth, there turn thy face towards the Sacred Mosque, and wheresoever ye are, turn your faces towards it, that men may have no argument against you, save only those of them who are unjust; and fear them not, but fear me and I will fulfil my favours to you, perchance ye may be guided yet.

Thus have we sent amongst you an apostle of yourselves, to recite to you our signs, to purify you and teach you the Book and wisdom, and to teach you what ye did not know; remember me, then, and I will remember you; thank me, and do not misbelieve[3].

O ye who do believe! seek aid from patience and from prayer, verily, God is with the patient. And say not of those who are slain in God's way[4] (that they are) dead, but rather living; but ye do not perceive.

---

[1] I. e. know Mohammed from the prophecies the Scriptures are alleged to contain about him. See Introduction.

[2] On the last day.

[3] Or rather be not ungrateful, the word Kufr implying negation of benefits received as well as of faith.

[4] I. e. in the cause of religion.

[150] We will try you with something of fear, and hunger and loss of wealth, and souls and fruit; but give good tidings to the patient, who when there falls on them a calamity say, 'Verily, we are God's and, verily, to Him do we return[1].' These, on them are blessings from their Lord and mercy, and they it is who are guided.

Verily, Zafâ and Merwah[2] are of the beacons of God, and he who makes the pilgrimage unto the House, or visits it, it is no crime for him to compass them both about; and he who obeys his own impulse to a good work,—God is grateful and doth know.

Verily, those who hide what we have revealed of manifest signs and of guidance after we have manifested it to men in the Book, them God shall curse, and those who curse shall curse them too. [155] Save those who turn and do right and make (the signs) manifest; these will I turn to again, for I am easy to be turned and merciful.

Verily, those who misbelieve and die while still in misbelief, on them is the curse of God, and of the angels, and of mankind altogether; to dwell therein for aye; the torment shall not be lightened for them, nor shall they be looked upon[3].

Your God is one God; there is no God but He, the merciful, the compassionate.

Verily, in the creation of the heavens and the earth, and the alternation of night and day, and in the ship that runneth in the sea with that which profits man, and in what water God sends down from heaven and

---

[1] This formula is always used by Mohammedans in any danger and sudden calamity, especially in the presence of death.

[2] Two mountains near Mecca, where two idols used to stand.

[3] Or, 'respited,' as some interpret it.

quickens therewith the earth after its death, and spreads abroad therein all kinds of cattle, and in the shifting of the winds, and in the clouds that are pressed into service betwixt heaven and earth, are signs to people who can understand.

[160] Yet are there some amongst mankind who take to themselves peers[1] other than God; they love them as they should love God; while those who believe love God more. O that those who are unjust could only see, when they see the torment, that power is altogether God's! Verily, God is keen to torment.

When those who are followed[2] clear themselves of those who followed them, and see the torment, and the cords[3] are cut asunder, those who followed shall say, 'Had we but another turn[4], then would we clear ourselves of them as they have cleared themselves of us.' So will God show them their works; for them are sighs, and they shall not come forth from out the fire.

O ye folk! eat of what is in the earth, things lawful and things good, and follow not the footsteps of Satan, verily, to you he is an open foe. He does but bid you evil and sin, and that ye should speak against God what ye do not know.

[165] When it is said to them, 'Follow what God has revealed,' they say, 'Nay, we will follow what we found our fathers agreed upon.' What! and though their fathers had no sense at all or guidance—?

The likeness of those who misbelieve is as the likeness of him who shouts to that which hears him

[1] Variously interpreted 'idols' and 'chiefs.'

[2] Chiefs of sects and founders of false religions.

[3] I.e. their mutual relations.

[4] I.e. on earth.

not, save only a call and a cry[1]; deafness, dumbness, blindness, and they shall not understand.

O ye who do believe! eat of the good things wherewith we have provided you, and give thanks unto God if it be Him ye serve. He has only forbidden for you what is dead, and blood, and flesh of swine, and whatsoever has been consecrated to other than God[2]; but he who is forced, neither revolting nor transgressing, it is in no sin for him; verily, God is forgiving and merciful.

Verily, those who hide what God has revealed of the Book, and sell it for a little price, they shall eat nothing in their bellies save fire; and God will not speak to them on the day of resurrection, nor will He purify them, but for them is grievous woe.

[170] They who sell guidance for error, and pardon for torment, how patient must they be of fire!

That (is), because God has revealed the Book with truth, and verily those who disagree about the Book are in a wide schism.

Righteousness is not that ye turn your faces towards the east or the west, but righteousness is, one who believes in God, and the last day, and the angels, and the Book, and the prophets, and who gives wealth for His love to kindred, and orphans, and the poor, and the son of the road[3], and beggars, and those in captivity; and who is steadfast in prayer, and gives alms; and those who are sure of

---

[1] I. e. as cattle hear the sound of the drover without understanding the meaning of his words, so the infidels fail to comprehend the meaning and importance of the words that are preached to them.

[2] At the time of slaughtering an animal the Muslims always repeat the formula bismi'llâh, in the name of God.

[3] I. e. the wayfarer.

their covenant when they make a covenant; and the patient in poverty, and distress, and in time of violence; these are they who are true, and these are those who fear.

O ye who believe! Retaliation is prescribed for you for the slain: the free for the free, the slave for the slave, the female for the female; yet he who is pardoned at all by his brother, must be prosecuted in reason, and made to pay with kindness [1].

That is an alleviation from your Lord, and a mercy; and he who transgresses after that for him is grievous woe.

[175] For you in retaliation is there life, O ye possessors of minds! it may be ye will fear.

It is prescribed for you that when one of you is face to face with death, if he leave (any) goods, the legacy is to his parents, and to his kinsmen, in reason. A duty this upon all those that fear.

But he who alters it [2] after that he has heard it,—the sin thereof is only upon those who alter it; verily, God doth hear and know.

And he who fears from the testator a wrong intention, or a crime, and doth make up the matter between the parties, it is no sin to him; verily, God is forgiving and merciful.

O ye who believe! There is prescribed for you the fast as it was prescribed for those before you; haply ye may fear. [180] A certain number of days, but he amongst you who is ill or on a journey, then (let him fast) another number of days. And

[1] The relations of a murdered man are always allowed to choose the fine instead of the blood revenge.

[2] The legacy.

those who are fit to fast [1] may redeem it by feeding a poor man; but he who follows an impulse to a good work it is better for him; and if ye fast it is better for you, if ye did but know.

The month of Rama*dh*ân, wherein was revealed the Qur'ân, for a guidance to men, and for manifestations of guidance, and for a Discrimination. And he amongst you who beholds this month [2] then let him fast it; but he who is sick or on a journey, then another number of days;—God desires for you what is easy, and desires not for you what is difficult,—that ye may complete the number, and say, 'Great is God,' for that He has guided you; haply ye may give thanks.

When my servants ask thee concerning me, then, verily, I am near; I answer the prayer's prayer whene'er he prays to me. So let them ask me for an answer, and let them believe in me; haply they may be directed aright.

Lawful for you on the night of the fast is commerce with your wives; they are a garment unto you, and ye a garment unto them. God knows that ye did defraud yourselves, wherefore He has turned towards you and forgiven you; so now go in unto them and crave what God has prescribed for you, and eat and drink until a white thread can be distinguished by you from a black one at the dawn. Then fulfil the fast until the night, and go not in unto them, and ye at your devotions in the mosques the while. These are the bounds that God has set, so draw not near thereto. Thus does God make

[1] I. e. able to fast but do not.

[2] I. e. who is at home during the month Rama*dh*ân and not on a journey, or in a place where it is impossible to keep the fast.

manifest His signs to men, that haply they may fear.

Devour not your wealth among yourselves vainly, nor present it to the judges that ye may devour a part of the wealth of men sinfully, the while ye know.

[185] They will ask thee about the phases of the moon; say, 'They are indications of time for men and for the pilgrimage.' And it is not righteousness that ye should enter into your houses from behind them [1], but righteousness is he who fears; so enter into your houses by the doors thereof and fear God; haply ye may prosper yet.

Fight in God's way [2] with those who fight with you, but transgress [3] not; verily, God loves not those who do transgress.

Kill them wherever ye find them, and drive them out from whence they drive you out; for sedition is worse than slaughter; but fight them not by the Sacred Mosque until they fight you there; then kill them, for such is the recompense of those that misbelieve.

But if they desist, then, verily, God is forgiving and merciful.

But fight them that there be no sedition and that the religion may be God's; but, if they desist, then let there be no hostility save against the unjust.

[190] The sacred month for the sacred month [4];

---

[1] The Arabs before Mohammed's time had a superstition that it was unlucky to enter their houses by the doors on their return from Mecca, so they made holes in the hinder walls to enter in by instead.

[2] Or, 'cause,' see note 4, p. 21.

[3] By beginning the fight yourselves.

[4] The other Arabs had, attacked them during the month

for all sacred things demand retaliation[1]; and whoso transgresses against you, transgress against him like as he transgressed against you; but fear ye God, and know that God is with those who fear.

Expend in alms in God's way and be not cast by your own hands into perdition; but do good, for God loves those who do good.

And fulfil the pilgrimage and the visitation to God; but if ye be besieged, then what is easiest for you by way of gift. But shave not your heads until your gift shall reach its destination; and he amongst you who is sick or has a hurt upon his head, then the redemption is by fasting or by alms or by an offering. But when ye are safe again, then let him who would enjoy the visitation until the pilgrimage[2] (bring) what is easiest as a gift. And he who cannot find (anything to bring), then let him fast three days on the pilgrimage and seven when ye return; these make ten days complete. That is, for him whose family are not present in the Sacred Mosque; and fear God and know that God is keen to punish.

The pilgrimage is (in) well-known months: whosoever then makes it incumbent on himself (let him have neither) commerce with women, nor fornication, nor a quarrel on the pilgrimage; and whatsoever of good ye do, God knoweth it; then provide yourself for your journey; but the best provision is piety. Fear ye me ye who possess minds.

DHu'lqa'hdah, which was one of their sacred months; the Moslems therefore are bidden to attack them if necessary in the sacred month of Rama*dh*ân.

[1] If a breach of their sanctity be committed.

[2] I.e. going to the visitation at once without waiting for the month of the pilgrimage to come round.

It is no crime to you that ye seek good[1] from your Lord; but when ye pour forth from 'Arafât, remember God by the sacred beacon[2]. Remember Him how He guided you, although ye were surely before of those who err.

[195] Then pour ye forth from whence men do pour forth and ask pardon of God; verily, God is forgiving and merciful.

And when ye have performed your rites, remember God as ye remember your fathers, or with a keener memory still.

There is among men such as says, 'Our Lord! give us in this world;' but of the future life no portion shall he have.

And some there be who say, 'Our Lord! give us in this world good and in the future good; and keep us from the torment of the fire!'

These,—they have their portion from what they have earned; for God is swift at reckoning up.

Remember God for a certain number of days; but whoso hastens off in two days, it is no sin to him, and he who lingers on it is no sin to him,—for him who fears. So fear ye God and know that unto Him shall ye be gathered.

[200] There is among men one[3] whose speech about the life of this world pleases thee, and he calls on God to witness what is in his heart; yet is he most fierce in opposition unto thee. And when he turns away, he strives upon the earth to do evil therein, and

---

[1] By trading during the 'Ha*gg*.

[2] On the rites and stations of the 'Ha*gg* pilgrimage, see Introduction.

[3] A'*h*nas ibn *S*urâiq eth Thaqafî, a fair spoken man of pleasant appearance, who pretended to believe in Mohammed.

to destroy the tilth and the stock; verily, God loves not evil doing. And when it is said to him, 'Fear God,' then pride takes hold upon him in sin; but hell is enough for him! surely an evil couch is that.

And there is among men one who selleth his soul[1], craving those things that are pleasing unto God; and God is kind unto His servants.

O ye who believe! enter ye into the peace[2], one and all, and follow not the footsteps of Satan; verily, to you he is an open foe. [205] And if ye slip after that the manifest signs have come to you, then know that God is the mighty, the wise.

What can they expect but that God should come unto them in the shadow of a cloud, and the angels too? But the thing is decreed, and unto God do things return.

Ask the children of Israel how many a manifest sign we gave to them; and whoso alters God's favours after that they have come to him, then God is keen at following up.

Made fair to those who misbelieve is this world's life; they jest at those who do believe. But those who fear shall be above them on the resurrection day. God gives provision unto whom He will without account.

Men were one nation once, and God sent prophets with good tidings and with warnings, and sent

---

[1] Zuhâib ibn Sinân er Rûmî, who being threatened at Mecca with death unless he apostatized from Islâm, said, 'I am an old man, who cannot profit you if he be with you, nor hurt you if he be against you,' and was allowed to escape to Medina.

[2] Here used as a synonym for resignation, i. e. Islâm.

down with them the Book in truth, to judge between men in that wherein they disagreed; but none did disagree therein save those who had been given it after that manifest signs had come to them, through greed amongst themselves; and God guided those who did believe to that truth concerning which they disagreed by His permission, for God guides whom He will unto the right path.

[210] Did ye count to enter Paradise, while there had nothing come to you like those who passed away before you; there touched them violence and harm, and they were made to quake, until the Apostle and those who believed with him said, 'When (comes) God's help? Is not God's help then surely nigh?'

They will ask thee what they are to expend in alms: say, 'Whatsoever good ye expend it should be for parents and kinsmen, and the orphan and the poor, and the son of the road; and whatsoever good ye do, verily, of it God knows.'

Prescribed for you is fighting, but it is hateful to you. Yet peradventure that ye hate a thing while it is good for you, and peradventure that ye love a thing while it is bad for you; God knows, and ye,—ye do not know!

They will ask thee of the sacred month,—of fighting therein. Say, 'Fighting therein is a great sin; but turning folks off God's way, and misbelief in Him and in the Sacred Mosque, and turning His people out therefrom, is a greater in God's sight; and sedition is a greater sin than slaughter.'

They will not cease from fighting you until they turn you from your religion if they can; but whosoever of you is turned from his religion and dies while still a misbeliever; these are those whose works are vain in this world and the next; they are the fellows of the Fire, and they shall dwell therein for aye.

[215] Verily, those who believe, and those who flee[1], and those who wage war[2] in God's way; these may hope for God's mercy, for God is forgiving and merciful.

They will ask thee about wine[3] and el mâisar[4], say, 'In them both is sin and profit to men; but the sin of both is greater than the profit of the same.'

They will ask thee what they shall expend in alms: say, 'The surplus.' Thus does God manifest to you His signs; haply ye may reflect on this world and the next! They will ask thee about orphans: say, 'To do good to them is best.' But if ye interfere with them—they are your brethren, and God knows the evildoer from the well doer; and if God will He will surely trouble you[5]. Verily, God is mighty, wise.

[1] In the Arabic hâ*g*arû, i. e. who fled with Mohammed in his hi*g*rah or expatriation to Medina, from which the Muslim era dates.

[2] The *g*ihâd, or general war of extermination against infidels, to threaten or preach which is a favourite diplomatic weapon with Mohammedan nations.

[3] '*H*amr, which is rendered 'wine,' includes all alcoholic and intoxicating drinks.

[4] El mâisar was a game of chance, played with arrows, the prize being a young camel, which was slaughtered and given to the poor, the price of it being paid by the losers. This distribution to the poor Mohammed speaks of as useful, but the quarrels and extravagance to which the game gave rise, he considers, overbalanced the profit.

[5] I. e. if ye wrong orphans.

[220] Wed not with idolatrous women until they believe, for surely a believing handmaid is better than an idolatrous woman, even though she please you. And wed not to idolatrous men until they believe, for a believing slave is better than an idolater, even though he please you.

Those invite you to the fire, but God invites you to paradise and pardon by His permission, and makes clear His signs to men; haply they may remember.

They will ask thee about menstruation: say, 'It is a hurt.' So keep apart from women in their menstruation, and go not near them till they be cleansed; but when they are cleansed come in to them by where God has ordered you; verily, God loves those who turn to Him, and those who keep themselves clean.

Your women are your tilth, so come into your tillage how you choose; but do a previous good act for yourselves [1], and fear God, and know that ye are going to meet Him; and give good tidings unto those who do believe.

Make not God the butt of your oaths, that ye will keep clear and fear and make peace amongst men, for God both hears and knows.

[225] He will not catch you up [2] for a casual word in your oaths, but He will catch you up for what your hearts have earned; but God is forgiving and clement.

Those who swear off [2] from their women, they must wait four months; but if they break their vow God is forgiving and merciful.

---

[1] Either wishing for a child, or saying, 'in the name of God,' Bâi*dh*âvî.

[2] See note 1, p. 1.

And if they intend to divorce them, verily, God hears and knows.

Divorced women must wait for themselves three courses; and it is not lawful to them that they hide what God has created in their wombs, if they believe in God and in the last day. Their husbands will do better to take them back in that (case) if they wish for reconciliation; for, the same is due to them as from them; but the men should have precedence over them. God is mighty and wise.

Divorce (may happen) twice; then keep them in reason, or let them go with kindness. It is not lawful for you to take from them anything of what you have given them, unless both fear that they cannot keep within God's bounds. So if ye fear that ye cannot keep within God's bounds there is no crime in you both about what she ransoms herself with [1]. These are God's bounds, do not transgress them; and whoso transgresses God's bounds, they it is who are unjust.

[230] But if he divorce her (a third time) she shall not be lawful to him after that, until she marry another husband; but, if he divorce her too, it is no crime in them both to come together again, if they think that they can keep within God's bounds. These are God's bounds which He explains to a people who know.

[1] The confusion of numbers and persons is in the original. The meaning of the passage is that 'divorce is allowed twice only, and that on each occasion the man may take the woman back if pregnant during the next four months; that if a woman be retained after divorce she is to be treated kindly, but if she be sent away she is not to be deprived of her dowry. If, however, they feel that they cannot live together, the woman may give up a part of her dowry to induce her husband to part with her.'

When ye divorce women, and they have reached the prescribed time, then keep them kindly, or let them go in reason, but do not keep them by force to transgress; for whoso does that, he is unjust to his own soul: and do not take God's signs in jest; and remember God's favours to you, and what He has sent down to you of the Book and wisdom, to admonish you thereby; and fear God, and know that God doth all things know.

When ye divorce women, and they have reached their prescribed term, do not prevent them from marrying their (fresh) husbands, when they have agreed with each other reasonably. That is what he is admonished with who amongst you believes in God and in the last day. That is more pure for you and cleaner. But God knows, and ye know not.

Mothers must suckle their children two whole years for one who wishes to complete the time of suckling; and on him to whom it is born its sustenance and clothing are incumbent; but in reason, for no soul shall be obliged beyond its capacity. A mother shall not be forced for her child; nor he to whom it is born for his child. And the same (is incumbent) on the heir (of the father). But if both parties wish to wean, by mutual consent and counsel, then it is no crime in them. And if ye wish to provide a wet-nurse for your children, it is no crime in you when you pay what you have promised her, in reason. Fear God, and know that God on what ye do doth look.

Those of you who die and leave wives behind, let these wait by themselves for four months and ten days; and when they have reached their prescribed time, there is no crime in them for what they do with themselves in reason; for God of what ye do is well aware.

[235] Nor is there any crime in you for that ye make them an offer of marriage, or that ye keep it secret, in your minds. God knows that ye will remember them; but do not propose to them in secret, unless ye speak a reasonable[1] speech; and resolve not on the marriage tie until the Book shall reach its time[2]; but know that God knows what is in your souls; so beware! and know that God is forgiving and clement.

It is no crime in you if ye divorce your women ere you have yet touched them, or settled for them a settlement. But provide maintenance for them; the wealthy according to his power, and the straitened in circumstances according to his power, must provide, in reason;—a duty this upon the kind.

And if ye divorce them before ye have touched them, but have already settled for them a settlement; the half of what ye have settled, unless they remit it, or he in whose hand is the marriage tie remits it[3]; and that ye should remit is nearer to piety, and forget not liberality between you. Verily, God on what ye do doth look.

Observe the prayers[4], and the middle prayer[5], and stand ye attent before God.

---

[1] I. e. with honest intentions.

[2] Until the time prescribed by the Qur'ân be fulfilled,

[3] That is, unless the wife choose to give up a part of the half which she could claim, or the husband do the same on his part, in which case an unequal partition is lawful.

[4] See excursus on the Rites and Ceremonies of Islâm.

[5] Interpreted to mean either the middle or the odd one of the five.

[240] And if ye fear, then afoot[1] or on horseback; but when ye are in safety remember God, how He taught you while yet ye did not know.

Those of you who die and leave wives, should bequeath to their wives maintenance for a year, without expulsion (from their home); but if they go out, there is no crime in you for what they do of themselves, in reason; but God is mighty and wise.

And divorced women should have a maintenance in reason,—a duty this on those that fear. Thus does God explain to you His signs; haply ye may understand.

Dost thou not look at those who left their homes by thousands, for fear of death; and God said to them 'Die,' and then He quickened them again[2]? Verily, God is Lord of grace to men, but most men give no thanks.

[245] Fight then in God's way, and know that God both hears and knows.

Who is there that will lend to God a good loan? He will redouble it many a double; God closes His hand and holds it out, and unto Him shall ye return.

Dost thou not look at the crowd of the children of Israel after Moses' time, when they said to a prophet of theirs[3], 'Raise up for us a king, and we will fight

[1] That is, if ye are in danger, say your prayers, as best you can, on foot or horseback, not staying so as to endanger your lives.

[2] The legend to which this alludes is variously told, but the most usually accepted version is that a number of the Israelites fled from their homes to avoid a *g*ihâd or 'religious war,' and were struck dead, and afterwards revived by the prophet Ezekiel's intervention. The story is apparently a distorted version of Ezekiel's vision of the dry bones. Ezek. xxxvii. 1–10.

[3] Samuel.

in God's way?' He said, 'Will ye perhaps, if it be written down for you to fight, refuse to fight?' They said, 'And why should we not fight in God's way, now that we are dispossessed of our homes and sons?' But when it was written down for them to fight they turned back, save a few of them, and God knows who are evildoers. Then their prophet said to them, 'Verily, God has raised up for you *T*âlût[1] as a king;' they said, 'How can the kingdom be his over us; we have more right to the kingdom than he, for he has not an amplitude of wealth?' He said, 'Verily, God has chosen him over you, and has provided him with an extent of knowledge and of form. God gives the kingdom unto whom He will; God comprehends and knows.

Then said to them their prophet, 'The sign of his kingdom is that there shall come to you the ark with the shechina[2] in it from your Lord, and the relics of what the family of Moses and the family of Aaron left; the angels shall bear it.' In that is surely a sign to you if ye believe[3].

[250] And when *T*âlût set out with his soldiery, he said, 'God will try you with a river, and he who drinks therefrom, he is not of mine; but whoso tastes it not, he is of mine, save he who laps it lapping with his hand[4].'

And they drank from it save a few of them, and

---

[1] Saul.

[2] The commentators do not understand that the word sakînah, which is in the original, is identical with the Hebrew shechina, and render it 'repose' or 'tranquillity.'

[3] 1 Samuel iv, v, vi.

[4] Gideon and Saul are here confused; this portion of the story is taken from Judges vi.

when he crossed it, he and those who believed with him, they said, 'We have no power this day against *G*âlût [1] and his soldiery,' those who thought that they should meet their Lord said, 'How many a small division of men have conquered a numerous division, by the permission of God, for God is with the patient.'

And when they went out against *G*âlût and his soldiery, they said, 'Lord, pour out patience over us, and make firm our steps, and help us against the misbelieving people!'

And they put them to flight by the permission of God, and David killed *G*âlût, and God gave him the kingdom and wisdom, and taught him of what He willed. And were it not for God's repelling men one with another the earth would become spoiled; but God is Lord of grace over the worlds.

These are the signs of God, we recite them to thee in truth, for, verily, thou art of those who are sent.

These apostles have we preferred one of them above another. Of them is one to whom God spake [2]; and we have raised some of them degrees; and we have given Jesus the son of Mary manifest signs, and strengthened him by the Holy Spirit. And, did God please, those who came after them would not have fought after there came to them manifest signs. But they did disagree, and of them are some who believe, and of them some who misbelieve, but, did God please, they would not have fought, for God does what He will.

[255] O ye who believe! expend in alms of what

---

[1] Goliath.

[2] Moses, called Kalîmu 'llâh, 'He with whom God spake.'

we have bestowed upon you, before the day comes in which is no barter, and no friendship, and no intercession; and the misbelievers, they are the unjust.

God[1], there is no god but He, the living, the self-subsistent. Slumber takes Him not, nor sleep. His is what is in the heavens and what is in the earth. Who is it that intercedes with Him save by His permission? He knows what is before them and what behind them, and they comprehend not aught of His knowledge but of what He pleases. His throne extends over the heavens and the earth, and it tires Him not to guard them both, for He is high and grand.

There is no compulsion in religion; the right way has been distinguished from the wrong, and whoso disbelieves in *Tâghût*[2] and believes in God, he has got hold of the firm handle in which is no breaking off; but God both hears and knows.

God is the patron of those who believe, He brings them forth from darkness into light. But those who misbelieve, their patrons are *Tâghût*, these bring them forth from light to darkness,—fellows of the Fire, they dwell therein for aye.

[260] Do you not look at him who disputed with Abraham about his Lord, that God had given him the kingdom[3]? When Abraham said, 'My Lord is He who giveth life and death,' he said, 'I give life

---

[1] This is the famous âyatu 'l kursîy, or 'verse of the throne,' considered as one of the finest passages in the Qur'ân, and frequently found inscribed in mosques and the like.

[2] The idols and demons of the ancient Arabs are so called.

[3] Nimrod, who persecuted Abraham, according to the eastern legend; see Chapter XXI, verses 52-69.

and death.' Abraham said, 'But verily, God brings the sun from the east, do thou then bring it from the west?' And he who misbelieved was dumbfounded, for God does not guide unjust folk.

Or like him who passed by a village [1], when it was desolate and turned over on its roofs, and said, 'How will God revive this after its death?' And God made him die for a hundred years, then He raised him, and said, 'How long hast thou tarried?' Said he, 'I have tarried a day, or some part of a day.' He said, 'Nay, thou hast tarried a hundred years; look at thy food and drink, they are not spoiled, and look at thine ass; for we will make thee a sign to men. And look at the bones how we scatter them and then clothe them with flesh.' And when it was made manifest to him, he said, 'I know that God is mighty over all.'

And when Abraham said, 'Lord, show me how thou wilt revive the dead,' He said, 'What, dost thou not yet believe?' Said he, 'Yea, but that my heart may be quieted.' He said, 'Then take four birds, and take them close to thyself; then put a part of them on every mountain; then call them, and they will come to thee in haste; and know that God is mighty, wise [2].'

The likeness of those who expend their wealth in God's way is as the likeness of a grain that grows to seven ears, in every ear a hundred grains, for God will double unto whom He pleases; for God both embraces and knows.

---

[1] According to the Arabic commentators, 'Huzair (Esdras) ibn *S*ara'hyâ or Al '*H*iẓr (Elias) is the person alluded to; and the 'village' Jerusalem after its destruction by Ba'*h*tnazr, Nebuchadnezzar. The legend probably refers to Nehemiah ii. 13.

[2] Cf. Genesis xv. 9.

Those who expend their wealth in God's way, then do not follow up what they expend by taunting with it and by annoyance, these have their hire with their Lord, and no fear is on them, neither shall they grieve.

[265] Kind speech and pardon are better than almsgiving followed by annoyance, and God is rich and clement.

O ye who believe! make not your almsgiving vain by taunts and annoyance, like him who expends what he has for the sake of appearances before men, and believes not in God and the last day; for his likeness is as the likeness of a flint with soil upon it, and a heavy shower falls on it and leaves it bare rock; they can do nought with what they earn, for God guides not the misbelieving folk.

But the likeness of those who expend their wealth craving the goodwill of God, and as an insurance for their souls, is as the likeness of a garden on a hill. A heavy shower falls on it, and it brings forth its eatables twofold; and if no heavy shower falls on it, the dew does; and God on what ye do doth look.

Would one of you fain have a garden of palms and vines, with rivers flowing beneath it, in which is every fruit; and when old age shall reach him, have weak seed, and there fall on it a storm wind with fire therein, and it gets burnt?

Thus does God manifest to you His signs, mayhap ye will reflect.

O ye who believe! expend in alms of the good things that ye have earned, and of what we have brought forth for you out of the earth, and do not take the vile thereof to spend in alms,—[270] what you would not take yourselves save by connivance at it[1]; but know that God is rich and to be praised.

The devil promises you poverty and bids you sin, but God promises you pardon from Him and grace, for God both embraces and knows. He bringeth wisdom unto whom He will, and he who is brought wisdom[2] is brought much good; but none will remember save those endowed with minds.

Whatever expense ye expend, or vow ye vow, God knows it; but the unjust have no helpers. If ye display your almsgiving, then well is it; but if ye hide it and bring it to the poor, then is it better for you, and will expiate for you your evil deeds; for God of what ye do is well aware.

Thou[3] art not bound to guide them; but God guides whom He will; and whatever good ye expend it is for yourselves, and do not expend save craving for God's face.

And what ye expend of good, it shall be repaid you, and ye shall not be wronged,—unto the poor who are straitened in God's way, and cannot knock about[4] in the earth. The ignorant think them to be rich because of their modesty; you will know them

---

[1] I. e. by a mutual understanding between seller and buyer.

[2] See note 2, p. 1.

[3] I. e. Mohammed.

[4] I must again remind the reader of the remarks made in the Introduction that the language of the Qur'ân is really rude and rugged, and that although the expressions employed in it are now considered as refined and elegant, it is only because all literary Arabic has been modelled on the style of the Qur'ân. The word which I have ventured to translate by this somewhat inelegant phrase (*dh*arban) means literally, 'to beat or knock about,' and as colloquial English affords an exact equivalent I have not hesitated to use it.

by their mark, they do not beg from men importunately; but what ye spend of good God knows.

[275] Those who expend their wealth by night and day, secretly and openly, they shall have their hire with their Lord. No fear shall come on them, nor shall they grieve.

Those who devour usury shall not rise again, save as he riseth whom Satan hath paralysed with a touch; and that is because they say 'selling is only like usury,' but God has made selling lawful and usury unlawful; and he to whom the admonition from his Lord has come, if he desists, what has gone before is his[1]: his matter is in God's hands. But whosoever returns (to usury) these are the fellows of the Fire, and they shall dwell therein for aye. God shall blot out usury, but shall make almsgiving profitable, for God loves not any sinful misbeliever.

Verily, those who believe, and act righteously, and are steadfast in prayer, and give alms, theirs is their hire with their Lord; there is no fear on them, nor shall they grieve.

O ye who believe! fear God, and remit the balance of usury, if ye be believers; and if ye will not do it, then hearken to the proclamation of war from God and His Apostle; but if ye repent, your capital is yours. Ye shall not wrong, nor shall ye be wronged.

[280] And if it be one in difficulties, then wait for easy circumstances; but that ye remit it as alms is better for you, if ye did but know.

Fear the day wherein ye shall return to God; then shall each soul be paid what it has earned, and they shall not be wronged.

[1] I. e. his former conduct shall be pardoned.

O ye who believe! if ye engage to one another in a debt for a stated time, then write it down, and let a scribe write it down between you faithfully; nor let a scribe refuse to write as God taught him, but let him write, and let him who owes dictate; but let him fear God his Lord, and not diminish therefrom aught; but if he who owes be a fool, or weak, or cannot dictate himself, then let his agent dictate faithfully, and let them call two witnesses out from amongst their men; or if there be not two men, then a man and two women, from those whom he chooses for witnesses, so that if one of the two should err, the second of the two may remind the other; and let not the witnesses refuse when they are summoned; and let them not tire of writing it, be it small or great, with its time of payment. That is more just in the sight of God, and more upright for testimony, and brings you nearer to not doubting. Unless, indeed, it be a ready-money transaction between you, which ye arrange between yourselves, then it is no crime against you that ye do not write it down; but bring witnesses to what ye sell one to another, and let not either scribe or witness come to harm, for if ye do it will be abomination in you; but fear God, for God teaches you, and God knows all things. But if ye be upon a journey, and ye cannot find a scribe, then let a pledge be taken. But if one of you trust another, then let him who is trusted surrender his trust, and let him fear God his Lord, and conceal not testimony, for he who conceals it, verily, sinful is his heart: God knows what ye do.

God's is what is in heaven and in the earth, and if ye show what is in your souls, or hide it, God will call you to account; and He forgives whom He will, and punishes whom He will, for God is mighty over all.

[285] The Apostle believes in what is sent down to him from his Lord, and the believers all believe on God, and His angels, and His Books, and His apostles,—we make no difference between any of His apostles,—they say, 'We hear and obey, Thy pardon, O Lord! for to Thee our journey tends. God will not require of the soul save its capacity. It shall have what it has earned, and it shall owe what has been earned from it. Lord, catch us not up, if we forget or make mistake; Lord, load us not with a burden, as Thou hast loaded those who were before us. Lord, make us not to carry what we have not strength for, but forgive us, and pardon us, and have mercy on us. Thou art our Sovereign, then help us against the people who do not believe!'

The Chapter of Imrân's Family.

(III. Medina.)

In the name of the merciful and compassionate God.

A. L. M. God, there is no god but He, the living, the self-subsistent. He has sent down to thee the Book in truth, confirming what was before it, and has revealed the law, and the gospel before for the guidance of men, and has revealed the Discrimination.

Verily, those who disbelieve in the signs of God, for them is severe torment, for God is mighty and avenging.

Verily, God, there is nothing hidden from Him in the earth, nor in the heaven; He it is who fashions you in the womb as He pleases. There is no God but He, the mighty, the wise.

[5] He it is who has revealed to thee the Book, of which there are some verses that are decisive, they are the mother[1] of the Book; and others ambiguous; but as for those in whose hearts is perversity, they follow what is ambiguous, and do crave for sedition, craving for (their own) interpretation of it; but none know the interpretation of it except God. But those who are well grounded in knowledge say, 'We believe in it; it is all from our Lord; but none will remember save those who possess minds.

'O Lord! pervert not our hearts again when Thou hast guided them, and grant us mercy from Thee, for Thou art He who grants. O Lord! Thou shalt gather together men unto the day wherein is no doubt. Verily, God will not depart from His promise.'

Verily, those who misbelieve, their wealth shall not help them, nor their children, against God at all; and they it is who are the fuel of the fire.

As was the wont of Pharaoh's people, and those before them, they said our signs were lies, and God caught them up in their sins, for God is severe to punish.

[10] Say to those who misbelieve, 'Ye shall be overcome and driven together to hell, an ill couch will it be.

'Ye have had a sign in the two parties who met; one party fighting in the way of God, the other misbelieving; these saw twice the same number as themselves to the eye-sight[2], for God aids

---

[1] I.e. the fundamental part of it.

[2] On the occasion of the battle of Bedr. See Introduction.

with His help those whom He pleases.' Verily, in that is a lesson for those who have perception. Seemly unto men is a life of lusts, of women, and children, and hoarded talents of gold and silver, and of horses well-bred, and cattle, and tilth;—that is the provision for the life of this world; but God, with Him is the best resort.

Say, 'But shall we tell you of a better thing than this?' For those who fear are gardens with their Lord, beneath which rivers flow; they shall dwell therein for aye, and pure wives and grace from God; the Lord looks on His servants, who say, 'Lord, we believe, pardon Thou our sins and keep us from the torment of the fire,' [15]—upon the patient, the truthful, the devout, and those who ask for pardon at the dawn.

God bears witness that there is no god but He, and the angels, and those possessed of knowledge standing up for justice. There is no God but He, the mighty, the wise.

Verily, (the true) religion in God's sight is Islâm, and those to whom the Book was given disagreed not until after that there was given to them knowledge, through mutual envy. But whoso disbelieves in God's signs, truly God is quick at reckoning up.

And if they would dispute with thee, then say, 'I turn my face with resignation unto God, and whoso follows me.'

And say to those who have been given the Book, unto the Gentiles[1], 'Are ye, too, resigned[2]?' and

---

[1] The word also means 'illiterate,' and refers here to the Pagan Arabs in Mohammed's time. He seems to have borrowed the expression from the Jews, ummîyûn having the same signification as the Hebrew goyîm.

[2] See note, p. 15.

if they are resigned, then are they guided. But if they turn their backs, then thou hast only to preach, and God looks on his servants.

[20] Verily, those who disbelieve in God's signs, and kill the prophets without right, and kill those from among men, who bid what is just,—to them give the glad tidings of grievous woe! These are they whose works are void in this world and the next, and helpers have they none.

Did ye not see those who have been given a portion of the Book? they were called unto the Book of God to decide between them; and then a sect of them turned their backs and turned away;—that is because they say the fire shall not touch us save for a certain number of days. But that deceived them in their religion which they had invented. How will it be when we have gathered them together for a day whereof there is no doubt, when each soul shall be paid what it has earned, and they shall not be wronged?

[25] Say, 'O God, Lord of the kingdom! Thou givest the kingdom to whomsoever Thou pleasest, and strippest the kingdom from whomsoever Thou pleasest; Thou honourest whom Thou pleasest, and abasest whom Thou pleasest; in Thy hand is good. Verily, Thou art mighty over all. Thou dost turn night to day, and dost turn day to night, and dost bring forth the living from the dead, and dost provide for whom Thou pleasest without taking count.'

Those who believe shall not take misbelievers for their patrons, rather than believers, and he who does this has no part with God at all, unless, indeed, ye fear some danger from them. But God bids you beware of Himself, for unto Him your journey is.

Say, 'If ye hide that which is in your breasts, or if ye show it, God knows it: He knows what is in the heavens and what is in the earth, for God is mighty over all.'

The day that every soul shall find what it has done of good present before it; and what it has done of evil, it would fain that there were between itself and that a wide interval. 'God bids you beware of Himself, but God is gentle with His servants.'

Say, 'If ye would love God then follow me, and God will love you and forgive you your sins, for God is forgiving and merciful.'

Say, 'Obey God and the Apostle; but if ye turn your backs God loves not misbelievers.'

[30] Verily, God has chosen Adam, and Noah, and Abraham's people, and Imrân's [1] people above the world,—a seed, of which one succeeds the other, but God both hears and knows.

When Imrân's wife said, 'Lord! I have vowed to Thee what is within my womb, to be dedicated unto Thee, receive it then from me. Verily, Thou dost hear and know.' And when she brought it forth she said, 'Verily, I have brought it forth a female'—but God knew best what she brought forth; and a male is not like a female—'I have called her Mary, and I seek a refuge in Thee for her and for her seed from Satan the pelted [2].'

---

[1] Amram, who, according to the Mohammedans, was the father of the Virgin Mary, (Miriam.) A confusion seems to have existed in the mind of Mohammed between Miriam 'the Virgin Mary,' and Miriam the sister of Moses.

[2] The Mohammedan superstition is that the devils listen at the

And her Lord received her with a good reception, and made her grow up with a good growth, and Zachariah took care of her. Whenever Zachariah entered the chamber to her he found beside her a provision, and said, 'O Mary, how hast thou this?' She said, 'It is from God, for God provides for whom He pleases without count.' Therefore prayed Zachariah to his Lord, and said, 'Lord, grant me from Thee a good seed. Verily, Thou hearest prayer.' And an angel cried out to him as he was standing praying in the chamber (and said) that 'God gives thee the glad tidings of John, to confirm the Word from God,—of a chief and a chaste one, and a prophet from amongst the righteous.'

[35] He said, 'My Lord, how can there be to me a boy when old age has reached me, and my wife is barren?' Said he, 'Thus God does what He pleaseth.' He said, 'My Lord, make for me a sign.' He said, 'Thy sign is that thou shalt not speak to men for three days, save by gesture; but remember thy Lord much, and celebrate His praises in the evening and the morning.'

And when the angels said, 'O Mary! verily, God has chosen thee, and has purified thee, and has chosen thee above the women of the world. O Mary! be devout unto thy Lord, and adore and bow down with those who bow. That is (one) of the declarations of the unseen world which we reveal to

---

gate of heaven for scraps of the knowledge of futurity, and when detected by the angels are pelted with shooting stars. The expression may also refer to the ceremony of 'pelting the devil,' as performed by '*Hagg* pilgrims at Minâ, in memory, it is said, of Abraham's having driven Iblîs away with stones when tempted by him to disobey God and refuse to sacrifice Isaac.

thee, though thou wert not by them when they threw their lots[1] which of them should take care of Mary, nor were ye by them when they did dispute.'

[40] When the angel said, 'O Mary! verily, God gives thee the glad tidings of a Word from Him; his name shall be the Messiah Jesus the son of Mary, regarded in this world and the next and of those whose place is nigh to God. And he shall speak to people in his cradle, and when grown up, and shall be among the righteous.' She said, 'Lord! how can I have a son, when man has not yet touched me?' He said, 'Thus God creates what He pleaseth. When He decrees a matter He only says BE and it is; and He will teach him the Book, and wisdom, and the law, and the gospel, and he shall be a prophet to the people of Israel (saying), that I have come to you, with a sign from God, namely, that I will create for you out of clay as though it were the form of a bird, and I will blow thereon and it shall become a bird by God's permission; and I will heal the blind from birth, and lepers; and I will bring the dead to life by God's permission; and I will tell you what you eat and what ye store up in your houses. Verily, in that is a sign for you if ye be believers. And I will confirm what is before you of the law, and will surely make lawful for you some of that which was pro hibited from you. I have come to you with a sign from your Lord, so fear God and follow me, for

[1] The legend is, that the priests threw lots by casting arrows into the river Jordan. The word used for arrows means simply unfeathered and unpointed arrows, and is the same as that used in the Arab game mâisar, referred to in page 32.

God is my Lord, and your Lord, so worship Him:—this is the right path.'

[45] And when Jesus perceived their unbelief, He said, 'Who are my helpers for God?' Said the apostles[1], 'We are God's helpers. We believe in God, so bear witness that we are resigned[2]. Lord, we have believed in what Thou hast revealed, and we have followed the Apostle, so write us down with those which bear witness.' But they (the Jews) were crafty, and God was crafty, for God is the best of crafty ones!

When God said, 'O Jesus! I will make Thee die and take Thee up again to me[3] and will clear thee of those who misbelieve, and will make those who follow thee above those who misbelieve, at the day of judgment, then to me is your return. I will decide between you concerning that wherein ye disagree. And as for those who misbelieve, I will punish them with grievous punishment in this world and the next, and they shall have none to help them.' [50] But as for those who believe and do what is right, He will pay them their reward, for God loves not the unjust.

That is what we recite to thee of the signs and of the wise reminder[4]. Verily, the likeness of Jesus

---

[1] The Arabic expression is 'Havârîyûn, which means 'fullers,' and is explained by the commentators either as referring to their 'trade' or to their 'sincerity and candour.' The word is really derived from an Ethiopic root signifying 'to send.'

[2] See note 1, page 15.

[3] The Mohammedans believe that it was an eidolon and not Jesus himself who was crucified.

[4] This word dhikr is used by Mohammedans for the recitation of the Qur'ân, and is also applied to the religious celebrations of the dervishes.

with God is as the likeness of Adam. He created him from earth, then He said to him BE, and he was;—the truth from thy Lord, so be thou not of those who are in doubt. And whoso disputeth with thee after what has come to thee of knowledge, say, 'Come, let us call our sons and your sons, and our women and your women, and ourselves and yourselves: then we will imprecate and put God's curse on those who lie.'

[55] Verily, those are the true stories, and there is no god but God, and, verily, God He is the mighty, the wise; but if they turn back, God knows the evildoers.

Say, 'O ye people of the Book, come to a word laid down plainly between us and you, that we will not serve other than God, nor associate aught with him, nor take each other for lords rather than God.' But if they turn back then say, 'Bear witness that we are resigned.'

O people of the Book, why do ye dispute about Abraham, when the law and the gospel were not revealed until after him? What! do ye not understand? Here ye are, disputing about what ye have some knowledge of; why then do ye dispute about what ye have no knowledge of? God knows and ye know not.

[60] Abraham was not a Jew, nor yet a Christian, but he was a 'Hanîf[1] resigned, and not of the idolaters. Verily, the people most worthy of Abraham are those who follow him and his prophets, and those who believe;—God is the patron of the believers.

[1] See note 1, p. 19.

A sect of the people of the Book would fain they could lead you astray, but they only lead themselves astray, and they do not perceive.

O people of the Book! why do ye disbelieve in the signs of God, the while ye witness them? O people of the Book! why do ye clothe the truth with falsehood and hide the truth the while ye know? [65] A sect of the people of the Book say, 'Believe in what was revealed to those who believed at the first appearance of the day, and disbelieve it at the end thereof,'—that (others) may perchance go back (from their faith)[1]—'do not believe save one who followeth your religion.'

Say, 'Verily, the (true) guidance is the guidance of God, that one should be given like what ye are given.' Or would they dispute with you before your Lord, say, 'Grace is in the hand of God, He gives it to whom he pleases, for God both comprehends and knows. He specially favours with his mercy whom he pleases, for God is Lord of mighty grace.'

And of the people of the Book, there are some of them who, if thou entrust them with a talent[2] give it back to you; and some of them, if thou entrust them with a dînâr[2], he will not give it back to thee except so long as thou dost stand over him. That is because they say, 'We owe no duty

---

[1] This is said to allude to some Jews who professed Islâm in the morning and recanted at night, saying that they had in the meantime consulted their books and found nothing to confirm it, hoping by this stratagem to raise doubts in the believers' minds.

[2] A 'talent,' qin*t*âr, is used for any very large sum, a dînâr ('denarius') was a gold coin worth about 10 s.

to the Gentiles;' but they tell a lie against God, the while they know.

[70] Yea, whoso fulfils his covenant and fears,—verily, God loves those who fear. Those who sell God's covenant and their oaths for a little price, these have no portion in the future life. God will not speak to them, and will not look upon them on the resurrection day, and will not purify them; but for them is grievous woe.

And, verily, amongst them is a sect who twist their tongues[1] concerning the Book, that ye may reckon it to be from the Book, but it is not from the Book. They say, 'It is from God,' but it is not from God, and they tell a lie against God, the while they know.

It is not right for a man that God should give him a Book, and judgment, and prophecy, and that then he should say to men, 'Be ye servants of mine rather than of God;' but be ye rather masters[2] of teaching the Book and of what ye learn.

He does not bid you take the angels and the prophets for your lords; shall He bid you misbelieve again when you are once resigned?

[75] And when God took the compact from the prophets '(this is) surely what we have given you of the Book and wisdom. Then shall come to you the Apostle confirming what is with you. Ye must believe in him and help him.' He said, moreover, 'Are ye resolved and have ye taken my compact on that (condition)?' They say, 'We are resolved.'

---

[1] I.e. pervert it.

[2] In the original Rabbânîyîn, an expression identical with Rabboni, cf. John xx. 16.

He said, 'Then bear witness, for I am witness with you; but he who turns back after that, these are sinners[1].'

What is it other than God's religion that they crave? when to Him is resigned whosoever is in the heavens and the earth, will he or nill he, and to him shall they return!

Say, 'We believe in God, and what has been revealed to thee, and what was revealed to Abraham, and Ishmael, and Isaac, and Jacob, and the tribes, and what was given to Moses, and Jesus, and the prophets from their Lord,—we will make no distinction between any of them,—and we are unto Him resigned. Whosoever craves other than Islam for a religion, it shall surely not be accepted from him, and he shall, in the next world, be of those who lose.'

[80] How shall God guide people who have disbelieved after believing and bearing witness that the Apostle is true, and after there come to them manifest signs? God guides the unjust folk.

These, their reward is, that on them is the curse of God, and of the angels, and of men together; they shall dwell therein for aye—the torment shall not be alleviated from them, nor shall they be respited; save those who repent after that, and act aright, for verily, God is forgiving and merciful.

Verily, those who misbelieve after believing, and then increase in misbelief, their repentance shall not be accepted; these are those who err.

[85] Verily, those who misbelieve and die in mis-

---

[1] The legend, borrowed from Talmudic sources, is that God assembled all past, present, and future prophets on Mount Sinai and entered into the compact mentioned in the text.

belief, there shall not be accepted from any one of them the earth-full of gold, though he should give it as a ransom. For them is grievous woe, and helpers have they none.

Ye cannot attain to righteousness until ye expend in alms of what ye love. But what ye expend in alms, that God knows.

All food was lawful to the children of Israel save what Israel made unlawful to himself before that the law was revealed. Say, 'Bring the law and recite it, if ye speak the truth.' But whoso forges against God a lie, after that, they are the unjust. Say, 'God speaks the truth, then follow the faith of Abraham, a 'hanîf, who was not of the idolaters.'

[90] Verily, the first House founded for men was surely that at Bekkah[1], for a blessing and a guidance to the worlds. Therein are manifest signs,—Abraham's station, and whosoever enters in is safe. There is due to God from man a pilgrimage unto the House, for whosoever can find his way there. But whoso misbelieves—God is independent of the worlds.

Say, 'O people of the Book! why do ye misbelieve in God's signs, while God is witness of what ye do?'

Say, 'O people of the Book! why do ye turn from the way of God him who believes, craving to make it crooked, while ye are witnesses? But God is not careless of what ye do.'

[95] O ye who believe! if ye obey the sect of those to whom the Book was brought, they will turn you, after your faith, to unbelievers again. How can ye

[1] Another name of Mecca.

misbelieve while unto you are recited the signs of God, and among you is His Apostle? But whoso takes tight hold on God, he is guided into the right way.

O ye who believe! fear God with the fear that He deserves, and die not save ye be resigned.

Take tight hold of God's rope altogether, and do not part in sects; but remember the favours of God towards you, when ye were enemies and He made friendship between your hearts, and on the morrow ye were, by His favour, brothers. Ye were on the edge of a pit of fire, but he rescued you therefrom[1]. Thus does God show to you His signs, perchance ye may be guided; [100] and that there may be of you a nation who shall invite to good, and bid what is reasonable, and forbid what is wrong; these are the prosperous.

Be not like those who parted in sects and disagreed after there came to them manifest signs; for them is mighty woe, on the day when faces shall be whitened and faces shall be blackened. As for those whose faces are blackened,—'Did ye misbelieve after your faith, then taste the torment for your misbelief!' But as for those whose faces are whitened, they are in God's mercy, and they shall dwell therein for aye.

These are the signs of God. We recite them to you in truth, for God desires not wrong unto the worlds.

[105] God's is what is in the heavens and what is in the earth, and unto God affairs return.

---

[1] Alluding to an occasion in which the ancient rivalry between the two tribes of El Aus and El '*H*azra*g*, which had been reconciled by Islâm, was on the point of breaking out again.

Ye were the best of nations brought forth unto man. Ye bid what is reasonable, and forbid what is wrong, believing in God. Had the people of the Book believed, it would have been better for them. There are believers among them, though most of them are sinners.

They shall surely not harm you save a hurt[1]; and if they fight you, they shall show you their backs, then they shall not be helped.

They are smitten with abasement wherever they be found, save for the rope of God and the rope of man[2]; and they draw on themselves wrath from God. They are smitten, too, with poverty; that is because they did disbelieve in God's signs, and kill the prophets undeservedly. That is because they did rebel and did transgress.

They are not all alike. Of the people of the Book there is a nation upright, reciting God's signs throughout the night, as they adore the while.
[110] They believe in God, and in the last day, and bid what is reasonable, and forbid what is wrong, and vie in charity; these are among the righteous.

What ye do of good surely God will not deny, for God knows those who fear.

Verily, those who misbelieve, their wealth is of no service to them, nor their children either, against God; they are the fellows of the Fire, and they shall dwell therein for aye.

The likeness of what they expend in this life of the world, is as the likeness of wind wherein is a

---

[1] I.e. only a slight hurt.

[2] That is, unless they enter into either the spiritual or temporal dominion of Islâm, by professing the Mohammedan creed, or by paying a tribute.

cold blast that falls upon a people's tilth who have wronged themselves and destroys it. It is not God who wrongs them, but it is themselves they wrong.

O ye who believe! take not to intimacy with others than yourselves; they will not fail to spoil you; they would fain ye came to trouble,—hatred is shown by their mouths; but what their breasts conceal is greater still. We have made manifest to you our signs, did ye but understand.

[115] Ye it is who love them, but they love not you; and ye believe in the Book, all of it. But when they meet you they say, 'We believe;' and when they go aside they bite their finger tips at you through rage. Say, 'Die in your rage, for God doth know the nature of men's breasts.'

If good luck touch you it is bad for them, but if bad luck befal you they rejoice therein; yet if ye are patient and fear, their tricks shall not harm you, for what they do God comprehends.

When thou didst set forth early[1] from thy people to settle for the believers a camp to fight;—but God both hears and knows;—when two companies of you were on the point of showing cowardice; but God was their guardian, for on God surely the believers do rely. Why! God gave you victory at Bedr when ye were in a poor way; fear God, then, haply ye may give thanks. [120] When thou didst say unto the believers, 'Is it not enough for you that your Lord assists you with three thousand of the angels

[1] This refers to the battle of Ohod, when Mohammed experienced a severe check, and lost two teeth by a shot from an arrow.

sent down from on high? Yea, if ye are patient and fear God, and they come upon you on a sudden, now, your Lord will assist you with five thousand of His angels, (angels) of mark. God only made this as glad tidings for you to comfort your hearts withal,—for victory is but from God, the mighty, the wise; —to cut off the flank of those who misbelieve, or make them downcast, that they may retire disappointed.'

Thou hast nothing to do with the affair at all, whether He turn towards them again or punish them; for, verily, they are unjust.

God's is what is in the heavens and in the earth. He forgives whom He pleases, and punishes whom He pleases; for God is forgiving and merciful.

[125] O ye who believe! devour not usury doubly doubled, but fear God, perchance ye may be prosperous; fear the fire which is prepared for the unbelievers, and obey God and His Apostle, perchance ye may get mercy. And vie with one another for pardon from your Lord, and for Paradise, the breadth of which is as the heaven and the earth, prepared for those who fear;—for those who expend in alms, in prosperity and adversity, for those who repress their rage, and those who pardon men; God loves the kind. Those who when they do a crime, or wrong themselves, remember God, and ask forgiveness for their sins,—and who forgives sins save God?—and do not persevere in what they did, the while they know;—[130]—these have their reward: —pardon from their Lord, and gardens beneath which rivers flow, dwelling therein for aye; for pleasant is the hire of those who act like this.

Incidents have passed before your time, go on

then in the earth, and see what was the end of those who called (the prophets) liars.

This is an explanation unto men, and a guidance and a warning unto those who fear. Do not give way nor grieve, for ye shall have the upper hand if ye but be believers.

If a sore touch you, a sore like it has touched people: these are days[1] which we make to alternate amongst mankind that God may know who it is that believe, and may take from you witnesses[2], for God loves not the unjust; [135] and that God may assay those who believe, and blot out the misbelievers. Do ye think that ye can enter Paradise and God not know those of you who have fought well, or know the patient? Why, ye longed for death before ye met it! Now ye have looked upon it and ye halt!

Mohammed is but an apostle; apostles have passed away before his time; what if he die or is killed, will ye retreat upon your heels? He who retreats upon his heels does no harm to God at all; but God will recompense the thankful. It is not for any soul to die, save by God's permission written down for an appointed time; but he who wishes for the reward of this world we will give him of it, and he who wishes for the reward of the future we will give him of it, and we will recompense the grateful.

[140] How many prophets have myriads fought against! yet they did not give way at what befel them in God's way! Nor were they weak, nor did they demean themselves:—God loves the patient. And their word was only to say, 'Lord, forgive us

---

[1] Or 'battles.' [2] Or 'martyrs.'

our sins and our extravagance in our affairs; and make firm our footing, and help us against the misbelieving folk!' and God gave them the reward of this world, and good reward for the future too, for God doth love the kind.

O ye who believe! if ye obey those who misbelieve, they will turn you back upon your heels, and ye will retreat the losers. Nay, God is your Lord, He is the best of helpers. We will throw dread into the hearts of those who misbelieve, for that they associate that with God which He has sent down no power for; but their resort is fire, and evil is the resort of the unjust.

[145] God has truly kept His promise, when ye knocked them senseless by His permission, until ye showed cowardice, and wrangled, and rebelled, after he had shown you what ye loved. Amongst you are those who love this world, and amongst you are those who love the next. Then He turned you away from them to try you; but He has pardoned you, for God is Lord of grace unto believers,—when ye went up and looked not round upon any one, although the Apostle was calling you from your rear. Therefore did God reward you with trouble on trouble that ye should not grieve after what ye had missed [1], nor for what befel you, for God is well aware of what ye do. Then He sent down upon you after trouble safety,—drowsiness creeping over one company of you, and one company of you getting anxious about themselves, suspecting about God other than the truth, with the suspicion of the ignorant [2], and saying, 'Have we any chance in

[1] Plunder.

[2] This word is always used for the pagan Arabs.

the affair?' Say, 'Verily, the affair is God's.' They conceal in themselves what they will not show to thee, and say, 'If we had any chance in the affair we should not be killed here.' Say, 'If ye were in your houses, surely those against whom slaughter was written down, would have gone forth to fight even to where they are lying now; that God may try what is in your breasts and assay what is in your hearts, for God doth know the nature of men's breasts.'

Verily, those of you who turned your backs on that day when the two armies met, it was but Satan who made them slip for something they had earned. But God has now pardoned them; verily, God is forgiving and clement.

[150] O ye who believe! be not like those who misbelieve, and say unto their brethren when they knock about in the earth, or are upon a raid, 'Had they but been at home, they had not died and had not been killed.' It was that God might make a sighing in their hearts, for God gives life and death; and God on what ye do doth look.

And if, indeed, ye be killed in God's way or die, surely forgiveness from God and mercy is better than what ye gather; and if ye die or be killed it is to God ye shall be assembled. It was by a sort of mercy from God thou didst deal gently with them, for hadst thou been rough and rude of heart they had dispersed from around thee. But pardon them, and ask forgiveness for them, and take counsel with them in the affair. As for what thou hast resolved, rely upon God; verily, God loves those who do rely. If God help you, there is none can overcome you; but if He leave you in the lurch, who is there can help you after Him? Upon God then let believers rely.

[155] It is not for the prophet to cheat; and he who cheats shall bring what he has cheated on the resurrection day. Then shall each soul be paid what it has earned, and they shall not be wronged. Is he who follows the pleasure of God, like him who has drawn on himself anger from God, whose resort is hell? An evil journey shall it be! These are degrees with God, and God sees what ye do.

God was surely very gracious to the believers, when He sent amongst them an apostle from themselves, to recite to them His signs, and purify them, and teach them the Book and wisdom, although they surely were before his time in manifest error. Or when an accident befals you, and ye have fallen on twice as much, ye say, 'How is this[1]?' Say, 'It is from yourselves. Verily, God is mighty over all.'

[160] And what befel you the day when the two armies met, it was by God's permission; that He might know the believers, and might know those who behaved hypocritically; for it was said to them, 'Come, fight in God's way,' or 'repel (the foe);' they said, 'If we knew how to fight we would surely follow you.' They were that day far nigher unto misbelief than they were to faith. They say with their mouths what is not in their hearts, but God doth know best what they hid. Those who said of their brethren, whilst they themselves stayed at home, 'Had they obeyed us they would not have

[1] He means that the loss at Ohod was more than counterbalanced by their previous success at Bedr. For an account of these engagements see Introduction.

been killed.' Say, 'Ward off from yourselves death, if ye do speak the truth.'

Count not those who are killed in the way of God as dead, but living with their Lord;—provided for, rejoicing in what God has brought them of His grace, and being glad for those who have not reached them yet,—those left behind them; there is no fear for them, and they shall not be grieved; [165] glad at favour from God and grace, and that God wasteth not the hire of the believers. Whoso answered to the call of God and of His prophet after sorrow had befallen them, for those, if they do good and fear God, is a mighty hire. To whom when men said, 'Verily, men have gathered round you, fear then them,' it only increased their faith, and they said, 'God is enough for us, a good guardian is He.' Then they retired in favour from God and grace; no evil touched them; they followed the pleasure of God, and God is Lord of mighty grace.

It is only that Satan who frightens his friends. Do not ye fear them, but fear me, if ye be believers.

[170] Let them not grieve thee who vie with each other in misbelief. Verily, they cannot hurt God at all. God wills not to make for them a portion in the future life; but for them is mighty woe.

Verily, those who purchase misbelief for faith, they do not hurt God at all, and for them is grievous woe.

Let not those who misbelieve reckon that our letting them range is good for themselves. We only let them have their range that they may increase in sin. And for them is shameful woe. God would not leave believers in the state which ye are in, until He discerns the vile from the good. And God would not inform you of the unseen, but God chooses of His apostles whom He pleases. Wherefore believe ye in God and His Apostle; and if ye believe and fear, for you is mighty hire.

[175] And let not those who are niggard of what God has given them of His grace, count that it is best for them;—nay, it is worse for them. What they have been niggard of shall be a collar round their necks upon the resurrection day. And God's is the heritage of the heavens and the earth, and God of what ye do is well aware.

God heard the speech of those who said, 'Verily, God is poor [1] and we are rich.' We will write down what they said, and how they killed the prophets undeservedly, and say, 'Taste ye the torment of burning;' this shall they suffer for what their hands have sent on before;—for, verily, God is no unjust one to His servants,—who say, 'Verily, God has covenanted with us that we should not believe in an apostle until he gives us a sacrifice which fire devours [2].'

[180] Say, 'There have come to you apostles before me with manifest signs, and with what ye

[1] Mohammed, in his message to the Jewish tribe of Kainûka, used the words of the Qur'ân, and bade them 'lend to God at good interest,' when Phineas Ibn Azûra mockingly said, 'Surely, God is poor since they try to borrow for him!' Whereupon Abu Bekr, who had brought the letter, smote him on the face and said, that, but for the truce between them, he would have smitten off his head. On complaint being made of this conduct to Mohammed the above verse was revealed.

[2] The commentators say that the Jewish Rabbis demanded of Mohammed this proof of his prophetic mission, having regard, probably, to the contest between Elijah and the priests of Baal on Mount Carmel.

talk about; why then did ye kill them, if ye speak the truth?'

And if they did call thee a liar, apostles before thee have been called liars too, who came with manifest signs, and with scriptures, and with the illuminating Book.

Every soul must taste of death; and ye shall only be paid your hire upon the resurrection day. But he who is forced away from the fire and brought into Paradise is indeed happy; but the life of this world is but a possession of deceit. Ye shall surely be tried in your wealth, and in your persons, and ye shall surely hear from those who have had the Book brought them before you, and from those who associate others with God, much harm. But if ye be patient and fear,—verily, that is one of the determined affairs.

When God took the compact from those who have had the Book brought them that 'Ye shall of a surety manifest it unto men, and not hide it,' they cast it behind their backs, and bought therewith a little price,—but evil is what they buy.

[185] Count not that those who rejoice in what they have produced, and love to be praised for what they have not done,—think not that they are in safety from woe,—for them is grievous woe!

God's is the kingdom of the heavens and the earth, and God is mighty over all!

Verily, in the creation of the heavens and the earth, and in the succession of night and day, are signs to those possessed of minds; who remember God standing and sitting or lying on their sides, and reflect on the creation of the heavens and the earth. 'O Lord! thou hast not created this in vain. We celebrate Thy praise; then keep us from the torment of the fire! Lord! verily, whomsoever Thou hast made to enter the fire, Thou hast disgraced him; and the unjust shall have none to help them.

[190] 'Lord! verily, we heard a crier calling to the faith, "Believe in your Lord," and we did believe. Lord! forgive us our sins and cover our offences, and let us die with the righteous. Lord! and bring us what Thou hast promised us by Thy apostles, and disgrace us not upon the resurrection day; for, verily, Thou dost not break Thy promises!' And the Lord shall answer them, 'I waste not the works of a worker amongst you, be it male or female,—one of you is from the other[1].

'Those who fled, and were turned out of their houses, and were harmed in my way, and who fought and were killed, I will cover their offences, and I will make them enter into gardens beneath which rivers flow.' [195] A reward from God; for God, with Him are the best of rewards.

Let it not deceive you that those who misbelieve go to and fro in the earth. It is a slight possession, and then their resort is Hell; an evil couch shall it be. But those who fear their Lord, for them are gardens beneath which rivers flow, and they shall dwell therein for aye,—an entertainment from God; and that which is with God is best for the righteous.

Verily, of the people of the Book are some who do believe in God, and in what has been revealed to

[1] This passage was revealed in answer to the objection of Umm Salmâ, one of Mohammed's wives, when the women who fled with him were not mentioned as well as the men in the promised reward of the future life.

you, and what was revealed to them, humbling themselves before God, and selling not the signs of God for a little price. These shall have their reward with their Lord; verily, God is quick at reckoning up.

[200] O ye who believe! be patient and vie in being patient[1], and be on the alert, and fear God, that haply ye may prosper.

The Chapter of Women.

(IV. Medînah.)

In the name of the merciful and compassionate God.

O ye folk! fear your Lord, who created you from one soul, and created therefrom its mate, and diffused from them twain many men and women. And fear God, in whose name ye beg of one another, and the wombs; verily, God over you doth watch[2].

And give unto the orphans their property, and give them not the vile in exchange for the good, and devour not their property to your own property; verily, that were a great sin. But if ye fear that ye cannot do justice between orphans, then marry what seems good to you of women, by twos, or threes, or fours; and if ye fear that ye cannot be equitable, then only one, or what your right hands possess[3]. That keeps you nearer to not being partial.

And give women their dowries freely; and if they

---

[1] That is, with their enemies.

[2] That is, fear God, and pay respect to your mothers and wives.

[3] That is, female slaves.

are good enough to remit any of it of themselves, then devour it with good digestion and appetite[1].

But do not give up to fools[2] their property which God has made you to stand by; but maintain them from it, and clothe them, and speak to them with a reasonable speech. [5] Prove orphans until they reach a marriageable age, and if ye perceive in them right management, then hand over to them their property, and do not devour it extravagantly in anticipation of their growing up. And he who is rich, let him abstain; but he who is poor, let him devour in reason, and when ye hand over to them their property, then take witnesses against them; but God sufficeth for taking account.

Men should have a portion of what their parents and kindred leave, and women should have a portion of what their parents and kindred leave, whether it be little or much, a determined portion. And when the next of kin and the orphans and the poor are present at the division, then maintain them out of it, and speak to them a reasonable speech. [10] And let these fear lest they leave behind them a weak seed, for whom they would be afraid; and let them fear God, and speak a straightforward speech. Verily, those who devour the property of orphans unjustly, only devour into their bellies fire, and they shall broil in flames.

[1] The Arabic idiom for the enjoyment of property being to eat it up, Mohammed here gives the men permission to enjoy such portion of their wives' dowries as the latter might be pleased to remit, and adds, with a sort of humour, the colloquial expression used by the Arabs when any one is eating. The sentence might be paraphrased 'and if they are kind enough to remit any portion of it of their own accord, then enjoy it, and much good may it do you!'

[2] To idiots or persons of weak intellect.

God instructs you concerning your children; for a male the like of the portion of two females, and if there be women above two, then let them have two-thirds of what (the deceased) leaves; and if there be but one, then let her have a half; and as to the parents, to each of them a sixth of what he leaves, if he has a son; but if he have no son, and his parents inherit, then let his mother have a third, and if he have brethren, let his mother have a sixth after payment of the bequest he bequeaths and of his debt.

Your parents or your children, ye know not which of them is nearest to you in usefulness:—an ordinance this from God; verily, God is knowing and wise! And ye shall have half of what your wives leave, if they have no son; but if they have a son, then ye shall have a fourth of what they leave, after payment of the bequests they bequeath or of their debts. And they shall have a fourth of what ye leave, if ye have no son; but if ye have a son, then let them have an eighth of what ye leave, after payment of the bequest ye bequeath and of your debts.

[15] And if the man's or the woman's (property) be inherited by a kinsman who is neither parent nor child[1], and he have a brother or sister, then let each of these two have a sixth; but if they are more than that, let them share in a third after payment of the bequest he bequeaths and of his debts, without prejudice[2],—an ordinance this from God, and God is knowing and clement!

---

[1] The word in the original is that always used to express this relationship.

[2] I. e. to the heirs.

These be God's bounds, and whoso obeys God and the Apostle He will make him enter into gardens beneath which rivers flow, and they shall dwell therein for aye;—that is the mighty happiness.

But whoso rebels against God and His Apostle, and transgresses His bounds, He will make him enter into fire, and dwell therein for aye; and for him is shameful woe.

Against those of your women who commit adultery, call witnesses four in number from among yourselves; and if these bear witness, then keep the women in houses[1] until death release them, or God shall make for them a way.

[20] And if two of you commit it, then hurt them both[2]; but if they turn again and amend, leave them alone, verily, God is easily turned, compassionate.

God is only bound to turn again towards those who do evil through ignorance and then turn again. Surely, these will God turn again to, for God is knowing, wise. His turning again is not for those who do evil, until, when death comes before one of them, he says, 'Now I turn again;' nor yet for those who die in misbelief. For such as these have we prepared a grievous woe.

O ye who believe! it is not lawful for you to inherit women's estates against their will; nor to

---

[1] Women taken in adultery or fornication were at the beginning of Islâm literally immured.

[2] The commentators are not agreed as to the nature of the offence here referred to. The text, however, speaks of two of the masculine gender. The punishment to be inflicted is also the subject of dispute, the original merely saying, as I have translated it, 'hurt them.'

hinder them[1], that ye may go off with part of what ye brought them, unless they commit fornication manifestly; but associate with them in reason, for if ye are averse from them, it may be that ye are averse from something wherein God has put much good for you.

But if ye wish to exchange one wife for another, and have given one of them a talent[2], then take not from it anything. What! would you take it for a calumny and a manifest crime[3]?

[25] How can ye take it when one of you has gone in unto the other, and they have taken from you a rigid compact?

And do not marry women your fathers married,—except bygones,—for it is abominable and hateful, and an evil way; unlawful for you are your mothers, and your daughters, and your sisters, and your paternal aunts and maternal aunts, and your brother's daughters, and your sister's daughters, and your foster mothers, and your foster sisters, and your wives' mothers, and your step daughters who are your wards, born of your wives to whom ye have gone in; but if ye have not gone in unto them, then it is no crime in you; and the lawful spouses of your sons from your own loins, and that ye form a connexion between two sisters,—except bygones,—verily, God is forgiving, merciful; and married women, save such as your right hands possess,—God's Book against you!—but lawful for you is

---

[1] That is, from marrying again.

[2] That is, a large dowry.

[3] This question is ironical, and intended as a warning against bringing a false accusation of infidelity against a wife for the sake of keeping her dowry when divorced.

all besides this, for you to seek them with your wealth, marrying them and not fornicating; but such of them as ye have enjoyed, give them their hire as a lawful due; for there is no crime in you about what ye agree between you after such lawful due, verily, God is knowing and wise.

But whosoever of you cannot go the length of marrying marriageable women who believe, then take of what your right hands possess, of your maidens who believe;—though God knows best about your faith. Ye come one from the other; then marry them with the permission of their people, and give them their hire in reason, they being chaste and not fornicating, and not receivers of paramours.

[30] But when they are married, if they commit fornication, then inflict upon them half the penalty for married women; that is for whomsoever of you fears wrong; but that ye should have patience is better for you, and God is forgiving and merciful.

God wishes to explain to you and to guide you into the ordinances of those who were before you, and to turn towards you, for God is knowing, wise. God wishes to turn towards you, but those who follow their lusts wish that ye should swerve with a mighty swerving! God wishes to make it light for you, for man was created weak.

O ye who believe! devour not your property amongst yourselves vainly, unless it be a merchandise by mutual consent. And do not kill yourselves; verily, God is compassionate unto you.

But whoso does that maliciously and unjustly, we will broil him with fire; for that is easy with God.

[35] If ye avoid great sins from which ye are for-

bidden, we will cover your offences and make you enter with a noble entrance.

And do not covet that by which God has preferred one of you over another. The men shall have a portion of what they earn, and the women a portion of what they earn; ask God for His grace, verily, God knows all.

To every one have we appointed kinsfolk as heirs of what parents and relatives and those with whom ye have joined right hands leave; so give them their portion, for, verily, God is over all a witness.

Men stand superior to women in that God hath preferred some of them over others, and in that they expend of their wealth: and the virtuous women, devoted, careful (in their husbands') absence, as God has cared for them. But those whose perverseness ye fear, admonish them and remove them into bed-chambers and beat them; but if they submit to you, then do not seek a way against them; verily, God is high and great.

And if ye fear a breach between the two [1], then send a judge from his people and a judge from her people. If they wish for reconciliation, God will arrange between them; verily, God is knowing and aware.

[40] And serve God, and do not associate aught with Him; and to your parents show kindness, and to kindred, and orphans, and the poor, and the neighbour who is akin, and the neighbour who is a stranger, and the companion who is strange, and the son of the road, and what your right hands possess [2], verily, God loves not him who is proud and boastful;

---

[1] Man and wife. [2] I.e. slaves.

who are miserly and bid men be miserly too, and who hide what God has given them of His grace;—but we have prepared for the misbelievers shameful woe.

And those who expend their wealth in alms for appearance sake before men, and who believe not in God nor in the last day;—but whosoever has Satan for his mate, an evil mate has he.

What harm would it do them if they believed in God and in the last day, and expended in alms of what God has provided them with? but God knows about them.

Verily, God would not wrong by the weight of an atom; and if it's[1] a good work, He will double it and bring from Himself a mighty hire.

[45] How then when we bring from every nation a witness, and bring thee as a witness against these on the day when those who misbelieve and rebel against the Apostle would fain that the earth were levelled with them? but they cannot hide the news from God.

O ye who believe! approach not prayer while ye are drunk, until ye well know what ye say; nor yet while polluted,—unless ye be passing by the way,—until ye have washed yourselves. But if ye are sick, or on a journey, or one of you come from the privy, or if ye have touched a woman, and ye cannot find water, then use good surface sand and wipe your faces and your hands therewith; verily, God pardons and forgives.

Do ye not see those who have been given a portion of the Book? they buy error, and they

---

[1] The abbreviated form taku (for takun) is used in the Arabic.

wish that ye may err from the way! But God knows best who your enemies are, and God suffices as a patron, and sufficient is God as a help.

And those who are Jews, and those who pervert the words from their places, and say, 'We hear but we rebel, and do thou listen without hearing,' and (who say) 'râ'hinâ[1],' distorting it with their tongues and taunting about religion. But had they said, 'We hear and we obey, so listen and look upon us,' it would have been better for them and more upright;—but may God curse them in their misbelief, for they will not believe except a few.

[50] O ye who have been given the Book! believe in what we have revealed, confirming what ye had before; ere we deface your faces and turn them into hinder parts, or curse you as we cursed the fellows of the Sabbath[2] when God's command was done.

Verily, God pardons not associating aught with Him, but He pardons anything short of that to whomsoever He pleases; but he who associates aught with God, he hath devised a mighty sin.

Do ye not see those who purify themselves? nay, God purifies whom He will, and they shall not be wronged a straw[3].

Behold, how they devise against God a lie, and that is manifest sin enough.

Do ye not see those to whom a portion of the Book has been given? They believe in *G*ibt[4] and *Tâgh*ût[4], and they say of those who misbelieve,

[1] See note 3, p. 14.

[2] See Chapter II, verse 61.

[3] The word in the original means a fibre in the cleft of a date stone, or the rush wick of a candle.

[4] Idols of the ancient Arabs; see p. 40.

'These are better guided in the way than those who believe.'
[55] These are those whom God has cursed,
and whom God has cursed no helper shall he find.

Shall they have a portion of the kingdom? Why even then they would not give to men a jot[1].

Do they envy man for what God has given of His grace? We have given to Abraham's people the Book and wisdom, and we have given them a mighty kingdom. And of them are some who believe therein, and of them are some who turn from it, but Hell is flaming enough for them.

Verily, those who disbelieve in our signs, we will broil them with fire; whenever their skins are well done, then we will change them for other skins, that they may taste the torment. Verily, God is glorious and wise.

[60] But those who believe and do aright, we will make them enter gardens beneath which rivers flow, and they shall dwell therein for ever and aye, for them therein are pure wives, and we will make them enter into a shady shade. Verily, God bids you pay your trusts to their owners, and when ye judge between men to judge with justice. Verily, God, excellent is what He admonishes you with; verily, God both hears and sees.

O ye who believe! obey God, and obey the Apostle and those in authority amongst you; and if ye quarrel about anything, refer to God and the Apostle, if ye believe in God and the last day; that is better and fairer as a settlement.

Do ye not see those who pretend that they believe in what has been revealed to them, and what was

[1] Literally, a dent or cleft in a date stone.

revealed before thee; they wish to refer their judgment to *Tâgh*ût[1], but they are bidden to disbelieve therein, and Satan wishes to lead them into a remote error. And when it is said to them, 'Come round to what God has sent down and unto the Apostle,' thou seest the hypocrites turning from thee, turning away.

[65] How then when there befalls them a mischance through what their hands have sent on before? then will they come to you, and swear by God, 'We meant naught but good and concord.' These, God knows what is in their hearts. Turn thou away from them and admonish them, and speak to them into their souls with a searching word.

We have never sent an apostle save that he should be obeyed by the permission of God; and if they, when they have wronged themselves, come to thee and ask pardon of God, and the Apostle asks pardon for them, then they will find God easy to be turned, compassionate.

But no! by thy Lord! they will not believe, until they have made thee judge of what they differ on; then they will not find in themselves aught to hinder what thou hast decreed, and they will submit with submission. But had we prescribed for them, 'Kill yourselves, or go ye forth out of your houses,' they would not have done it, save only a few of them; but had they done what they are admonished, then it would have been better for them, and a more firm assurance.

[70] And then we would surely have brought them from ourselves a mighty hire, and would have guided them into a right path.

Whoso obeys God and the Apostle, these are

[1] See note 2, p. 40.

with those God has been pleased with, of prophets and confessors and martyrs and the righteous;—a fair company are they.

That is grace from God, and God knows well enough.

O ye who believe! take your precautions and sally in detachments or altogether. Verily, there is of you who tarries behind, and, if a mischance befalls you, says, 'God has been gracious to me, since I am not with them a martyr.'

[75] But if there befalls you grace from God, he would say—as though there were no friendship between you and him—'O would that I had been with thee to attain this mighty happiness!' Let those then fight in God's way who sell this life of the world for the next; and whoso fights in God's way, then, be he killed or be he victorious, we will give him a mighty hire.

What ails you that ye do not fight in God's way, and for the weak men and women and children, who say, 'Lord, bring us out of this town[1] of oppressive folk, and make for us from Thee a patron, and make for us from Thee a help?'

Those who believe fight in the way of God; and those who disbelieve fight in the way of *Tâgh*ût; fight ye then against the friends of Satan, verily, Satan's tricks are weak.

Do ye not see those to whom it is said, 'Restrain your hands, and be steadfast in prayer and give alms;' and when it is prescribed for them to fight then a band of them fear men, as though it were the fear of God or a still stronger fear, and they say, 'O our Lord! why hast thou prescribed for us to fight,

[1] Mecca.

couldst thou not let us abide till our near appointed time?' Say, 'The enjoyment of this world is but slight, and the next is better for him who fears;'—but they shall not be wronged a straw.

[80] Wheresoe'er ye be death will overtake you, though ye were in lofty towers. And if a good thing befall them, they say, 'This is from God,' but if a bad thing, they say, 'This is from thee.' Say, 'It is all from God.' What ails these people? they can hardly understand a tale.

What befalls thee of good it is from God; and what befalls thee of bad it is from thyself. We have sent thee to mankind as an apostle, and God sufficeth for a witness.

Whoso obeys the prophet he has obeyed God; and he who turns back—we have not sent thee to watch over them.

They say, 'Obedience!' but when they sally forth from you, a company of them brood by night over something else than that which thou hast said; but God writes down that over which they brood. Turn then from them and rely on God, for God sufficeth for a guardian. Do they not meditate on the Qur'ân? if it were from other than God they would find in it many a discrepancy.

[85] And when there comes to them a matter of security or fear they publish it; but if they were to report it to the Apostle and to those in authority amongst them, then those of them who would elicit it from them would know it; but were it not for God's grace upon you and His mercy ye had followed Satan, save a few.

Fight, then, in the way of God; impose not aught on any but thyself, and urge on the believers; it may be that God will restrain the violence of those who misbelieve, for God is more violent and more severe to punish.

Whoso intercedes with a good intercession shall have a portion therefrom; but he who intercedes with a bad intercession shall have the like thereof, for God keeps watch over all things.

And when ye are saluted with a salutation, salute with a better than it, or return it;—verily, God of all things takes account.

God, there is no God but He! He will surely assemble you on the resurrection day, there is no doubt therein; who is truer than God in his discourse?

[90] Why are ye two parties about the hypocrites, when God hath overturned them for what they earned? Do ye wish to guide those whom God hath led astray? Whoso God hath led astray ye shall not surely find for him a path. They would fain that ye misbelieve as they misbelieve, that ye might be alike; take ye not patrons from among them until they too flee in God's way; but if they turn their backs, then seize them and kill them wheresoever ye find them, and take from them neither patron nor help,—save those who reach a people betwixt whom and you is an alliance—or who come to you while their bosoms prevent them from fighting you or fighting their own people. But had God pleased He would have given you dominion over them, and they would surely have fought you. But if they retire from you and do not fight you, and offer you peace,—then God hath given you no way against them.

Ye will find others who seek for quarter from

you, and quarter from their own people; whenever they return to sedition they shall be overturned therein: but if they retire not from you, nor offer you peace, nor restrain their hands, then seize them and kill them wheresoever ye find them;—over these we have made for you manifest power.

It is not for a believer to kill a believer save by mistake; and whosoever kills a believer by mistake then let him free a believing neck[1]; and the blood-money must be paid to his people save what they shall remit as alms. But if he be from a tribe hostile to you and yet a believer, then let him free a believing neck. And if it be a tribe betwixt whom and you there is an alliance, then let the blood-money be paid to his friends, and let him free a believing neck; but he who cannot find the means, then let him fast for two consecutive months—a penance this from God, for God is knowing, wise.

[95] And whoso kills a believer purposely, his reward is hell, to dwell therein for aye; and God will be wrath with him, and curse him, and prepare for him a mighty woe.

O ye who believe! when ye are knocking about in the way of God be discerning, and do not say to him who offers you a salutation, 'Thou art no believer,' craving after the chances of this world's life[2], for with God are many spoils! So were ye aforetime, but God was gracious to you, be ye then discerning; verily, God of what ye do is well aware.

---

[1] Captive.

[2] Because a believer might not be attacked and plundered as an infidel might be.

Not alike are those of the believers who sit at home without harm, and those who are strenuous in God's way with their wealth and their persons. God hath preferred those who are strenuous with their wealth and their persons to those who sit still, by many degrees, and to each hath God promised good, but God hath preferred the strenuous for a mighty hire over those who sit still,—degrees from him, and pardon and mercy, for God is forgiving and merciful.

Verily, the angels when they took the souls of those who had wronged themselves[1], said, 'What state were ye in?' they say, 'We were but weak in the earth;' they said, 'Was not God's earth wide enough for you to flee away therein?' These are those whose resort is hell, and a bad journey shall it be!

[100] Save for the weak men, and women, and children, who could not compass any stratagem, and were not guided to a way; these it may be God will pardon, for God both pardons and forgives.

Whosoever flees in the way of God shall find in the earth many a spacious refuge; and he who goes forth from his house, fleeing unto God and His prophet, and then death catches him up,—his hire devolves on God, and God is forgiving and merciful.

And when ye knock about in the earth, it is no crime to you that ye come short in prayer, if ye fear that those who disbelieve will set upon you; verily, the misbelievers are your obvious foes.

---

[1] Alluding to some half-hearted Muslims, slain at Bedr.

When thou art amongst them, and standest up to pray with them, then let a party of them stand up with thee, and let them take their arms; and when they adore, let them go behind you, and let another party who have not yet prayed come forward and pray with thee; and let them take their precautions and their arms.

Fain would those who misbelieve that ye were careless of your arms and your baggage, that they might turn upon you with a single turning. And it is no crime to you if ye be annoyed with rain or be sick, that ye lay down your arms; but take your precautions,—verily, God has prepared for those who misbelieve a shameful woe.

But when ye have fulfilled your prayer, remember God standing and sitting and lying on your sides; and when ye are in safety then be steadfast in prayer; verily, prayer is for the believers prescribed and timed!

[105] And do not give way in pursuit of the people; if ye suffer they shall surely suffer too, even as ye suffer; and ye hope from God, but they hope not! and God is knowing, wise.

Verily, we have revealed to thee the Book in truth that thou mayest judge between men of what God has shown thee; so be not with the treacherous a disputant; but ask God's pardon: verily, God is forgiving, merciful.

And wrangle not for those who defraud themselves; for God loves not him who is a fraudulent sinner. They hide themselves from men; but they cannot hide themselves from God, for He is with them while they brood at night over speeches that please Him not;—but God doth compass what they do!

Here are ye, wrangling for them about this world's life;—but who shall wrangle with God for them on the day of judgment, or who shall be a guardian over them?

[110] Yet whoso does evil and wrongs himself, and then asks pardon of God, shall find God forgiving and merciful; and whoso commits a crime, he only commits it against himself, for God is knowing, wise.

And whoso commits a fault or a sin and throws it on the innocent, he hath to bear a calumny and a manifest sin.

Were it not for God's grace upon thee, and His mercy, a party of them would have tried to lead thee astray; but they only lead themselves astray; they shall not hurt you in aught: for God hath sent down upon thee the Book and the wisdom, and taught thee what thou didst not know, for God's grace was mighty on thee.

There is no good in most of what they talk in private; save in his who bids almsgiving, or kindness, or reconciliation between men; and whoso does this, craving the good pleasure of God, we will give to him a mighty hire.

[115] But he who severs himself from the prophet after that we have made manifest to him the guidance, and follows other than the way of the believers, we will turn our backs on him as he hath turned his back; and we will make him reach hell, and a bad journey shall it be.

Verily, God forgives not associating aught with Him, but He pardons anything short of that, to whomsoever He will; but whoso associates aught with God, he hath erred a wide error.

Verily, they call not beside Him on aught save females; and they do not call on aught save a rebellious devil.

God curse him! for he said, 'I will take from thy servants a portion due to me; and I will lead them astray; and I will stir up vain desires within them; and I will order them and they shall surely crop the ears of cattle; and I will order them and they shall surely alter God's creation[1];' but he who takes the devil for his patron instead of God, he loses with a manifest loss. He promises them, and stirs up vain desires within them; but the devil promises only to deceive.

[120] These, their resort is hell; they shall not find an escape therefrom! But those who believe, and do what is right, we will make them enter into gardens beneath which rivers flow, to dwell therein for aye,—God's promise in truth; and who is truer than God in speech? Not for your vain desires, nor the vain desires of the people of the Book. He who doeth evil shall be recompensed therewith, and shall not find for him beside God a patron, or a help. But he who doeth good works,—be it male or female,—and believes, they shall enter into Paradise, and they shall not be wronged a jot.

Who has a better religion than he who resigns his face to God, and does good, and follows the faith of

[1] The pagan Arabs used to cut off the ears of cattle, and mutilate their slaves by branding, and filing their teeth, partly that they might recognise them and partly as a superstitious ceremony. See p. 112, note 1.

Abraham, as a 'Hanîf?—for God took Abraham as a friend.

[125] And God's is what is in the heavens and in the earth, and God encompasses all things!

They will ask thee a decision about women; say, 'God decides for you about them, and that which is rehearsed to you in the Book; about orphan women to whom ye do not give what is prescribed for them, and whom ye are averse from marrying; and about weak children; and that ye stand fairly by orphans;—and what ye do of good, verily, that God knows.'

And if a woman fears from her husband perverseness or aversion, it is no crime in them both that they should be reconciled to each other, for reconciliation is best. For souls are prone to avarice; but if ye act kindly and fear God, of what ye do He is aware.

Ye are not able, it may be, to act equitably to your wives, even though ye covet it; do not however be quite partial, and leave one as it were in suspense; but if ye be reconciled and fear, then God is forgiving and merciful; but if they separate, God can make both independent out of His abundance; for God is abundant, wise.

[130] God's is what is in the heavens and what is in the earth! We have ordained to those who have been given the Book before you, and to you too that ye fear God;—but if ye misbelieve, verily, God's is what is in the heavens and what is in the earth, and God is rich and to be praised!

God's is what is in the heavens and what is in the earth! and God sufficeth for a guardian!

If He will He can make ye pass away, O men! and can bring others;— God is able to do all that.

He who wishes for a reward in this world,—with God is the reward of this world and of the next, and God both hears and sees.

O ye who believe! be ye steadfast in justice, witnessing before God though it be against yourselves, or your parents, or your kindred, be it rich or poor, for God is nearer akin than either.

Follow not, then, lusts, so as to act partially; but if ye swerve or turn aside, God of what ye do is well aware.

[135] O ye who believe! believe in God and His apostles, and the Book which He hath revealed to His Apostle, and the Book which He sent down before; for whoso disbelieves in God, and His angels, and His Apostle, and the last day, has erred a wide error.

Verily, those who believe and then misbelieve, and then believe and then misbelieve, and then increase in misbelief, God will never pardon them, nor will He guide them in the path.

Give to the hypocrites the glad tidings that for them is grievous woe!

Those who take the misbelievers for their patrons rather than believers,—do they crave honour from them? Verily, honour is altogether God's!

He hath revealed this to you in the Book[1], that when ye hear the signs of God disbelieved in and mocked at, then sit ye not down with them until they plunge into another discourse, for verily, then ye would be like them. Verily, God will gather the hypocrites and misbelievers into hell together.

---

[1] Chap. VI, v. 67, which chronologically precedes the present; see Introduction.

[140] Those who lie in wait for you, and if the victory be yours from God, say, 'Were we not with you?' and if the misbelievers have a chance, they say, 'Did we not get the mastery over you, and defend you from the believers?' But God shall judge between you on the resurrection day; for God will not give the misbelievers a way against believers.

Verily, the hypocrites seek to deceive God, but He deceives them; and when they rise up to pray, they rise up lazily to be seen of men, and do not remember God, except a few; wavering between the two, neither to these nor yet to those! but whomsoever God doth lead astray thou shall not find for him a way.

O ye who believe! take not misbelievers for patrons rather than believers; do ye wish to make for God a power against you?

Verily, the hypocrites are in the lowest depths of hell-fire, and thou shalt not find for them a help.

[145] Save those who turn again, and do right, and take tight hold on God, and are sincere in religion to God; these are with the believers, and God will give to the believers mighty hire.

Why should God punish you, if ye are grateful and believe? for God is grateful and knowing.

God loves not publicity of evil speech, unless one has been wronged; for God both hears and knows.

If ye display good or hide it, or pardon evil, verily, God is pardoning and powerful!

Verily, those who disbelieve in God and His apostles desire to make a distinction between God and His apostles, and say, 'We believe in part and disbelieve in part, and desire to take a midway course between the two:' [150] these are the misbelievers, and we have prepared for misbelievers shameful woe! But those who believe in God and His apostles, and who do not make a distinction between any one of them,—to these we will give their hire, for God is forgiving and merciful!

The people of the Book will ask thee to bring down for them a book from heaven; but they asked Moses a greater thing than that, for they said, 'Show us God openly;' but the thunderbolt caught them in their injustice. Then they took the calf, after what had come to them of manifest signs; but we pardoned that, and gave Moses obvious authority. And we held over them the mountain[1] at their compact, and said to them, 'Enter ye the door adoring;' and we said to them, 'Transgress not on the Sabbath day,' and we took from them a rigid compact.

But for that they broke their compact, and for their misbelief in God's signs, and for their killing the prophets undeservedly, and for their saying, 'Our hearts are uncircumcised,'—nay, God hath stamped on them their misbelief, so that they cannot believe except a few,—[155] and for their misbelief, and for their saying about Mary a mighty calumny, and for their saying, 'Verily, we have killed the Messiah, Jesus the son of Mary, the apostle of God,' . . . . but they did not kill him, and they did not crucify him, but a similitude was made for them. And verily, those who differ about him are in doubt concerning him; they have no knowledge concerning him, but only follow an opinion. They did not kill

[1] See note, p. 8.

him, for sure! nay, God raised him up unto Himself; for God is mighty and wise[1]!

And there shall not be one of the people of the Book but shall believe in him before his death[2]; and on the day of judgment he shall be a witness against them.

And for the injustice of those who are Jews have we forbidden them good things which we had made lawful for them, and for their obstructing so much the way of God, and for their taking usury when we had forbidden it, and for their devouring the wealth of people in vain,—but we have prepared for those of them who misbelieve a grievous woe.

[160] But those amongst them who are firm in knowledge, and the believers who believe in what is revealed to thee, let what is revealed before thee, and the steadfast in prayer, and the givers of alms, and the believers in God and the last day,—unto these we will give a mighty hire.

Verily, we have inspired thee as we inspired Noah and the prophets after him, and as we inspired Abraham, and Ishmael, and Jacob, and the tribes, and Jesus, and Job, and Jonas, and Aaron, and Solomon; and to David did we give Psalms.

Of apostles we have already told thee of some before; and of apostles some we have not told thee of;—

But Moses did God speak to, speaking;—apostles giving glad tidings and warning, that men should have no argument against God, after the apostles, for God is mighty, wise!

---

[1] See p. 53, note 3.

[2] This may allude to the time of his death after his second advent, when he shall slay the antichrist.

But God bears witness to what He has revealed to thee: He revealed it in His knowledge, and the angels bear witness too; though God is witness enough.

[165] Verily, those who misbelieve and obstruct the way of God, have erred a wide error.

Verily, those who misbelieve and are unjust, God will not pardon them, nor will He guide them on the road—save the road to hell, to dwell therein for aye;—that is easy enough to God!

O ye folk! the Apostle has come to you with truth from your Lord: believe then, for it is better for you. But if ye misbelieve, then God's is what is in the heavens and the earth, and God is knowing, wise.

O ye people of the Book! do not exceed in your religion, nor say against God aught save the truth. The Messiah, Jesus the son of Mary, is but the apostle of God and His Word, which He cast into Mary and a spirit from Him; believe then in God and His apostles, and say not 'Three.' Have done! it were better for you. God is only one God, celebrated be His praise that He should beget a Son! His is what is in the heavens and what is in the earth; and God sufficeth for a guardian.

[170] The Messiah doth surely not disdain to be a servant of God, nor do the angels who are nigh to Him; and whosoever disdains His service and is too proud, He will gather them altogether to Himself.

But as for those who believe and do what is right, He will pay their hire and will give increase to them of His grace. But as for those who disdain and are too proud, He will punish them with a grievous woe, and they shall not find for them other than God a patron or a help.

O ye folk! proof has come to you from your Lord, and we have sent down to you manifest light. As for those who believe in God, and take tight hold of Him, He will make them enter into mercy from Him and grace; and He will guide them to Himself by a right way.

[175] They will ask thee for a decision; say, 'God will give you a decision concerning remote kinship[1].'

If a man perish and have no child, but have a sister, let her have half of what he leaves; and he shall be her heir, if she have no son. But if there be two sisters, let them both have two thirds of what he leaves; and if there be brethren, both men and women, let the male have like the portion of two females. God makes this manifest to you lest ye err; for God all things doth know.

The Chapter of the Table.

(V. Medînah.)

In the name of the merciful and compassionate God.

O ye who believe! fulfil your compacts.—Lawful for you are brute beasts, save what is here recited to you, not allowing you the chase while ye are on pilgrimage; verily, God ordaineth what He will.

O ye who believe! do not deem the monuments of God to be lawful, nor the sacred month[2], nor the offering, nor its neck garlands, nor those who sojourn at the sacred house, craving grace from their Lord and His pleasure.

---

[1] See note 1, p. 73.

[2] Mu'harram.

But when ye are in lawful state again, then chase; and let not ill-will against the people who turned you from the Sacred Mosque[1] make you transgress; but help one another in righteousness and piety, and do not help one another to sin and enmity; but fear God,—verily, God is keen to punish.

Forbidden to you is that which dies of itself, and blood, and the flesh of swine, and that which is devoted to other than God, and the strangled and the knocked down, and that which falls down, and the gored, and what wild beasts have eaten—except what ye slaughter in time—and what is sacrificed to idols[2], and dividing carcases by arrows[3].

To-day shall those who disbelieve in your religion despair; do ye not then fear them, but fear me—
[5] To-day is perfected for you your religion, and fulfilled upon you is my favour, and I am pleased for you to have Islâm for a religion. But he who is forced by hunger, not inclined wilfully to sin, verily, God is forgiving, compassionate.

They will ask thee what is lawful for them? say, 'Lawful for you are good things and what ye have taught beasts of prey (to catch), training them like dogs;—ye teach them as God taught you;—so eat of what they catch for you, and mention the name of God over it, and fear God, for verily, God is swift in reckoning up.'

Lawful for you to-day are good things, and the food of those to whom the Book has been given is

[1] The Qurâish, who sent to meet Mohammed with 1400 men at 'Hudâibîyeh to prevent him from approaching Mecca, A. H. 6.

[2] Literally, 'stones set up,' Dolmens and the like, which are so common throughout Arabia.

[3] By the game of mâisar, see p. 32.

lawful for you, and your food is lawful for them; and chaste women of those who believe, and chaste women of those to whom the Book has been given before you,—when you have given them their hire, living chastely and not fornicating, and not taking paramours. But whoso disbelieves in the faith, of a truth his work is vain, and he shall be in the next life of those who lose.

O ye who believe! when ye rise up to prayer wash your faces, and your hands as far as the elbows, and wipe your heads, and your feet down to the ankles. And if ye are polluted, then purify yourselves. But if ye are sick, or on a journey, or if one of you comes from the privy, or if ye have touched women and cannot find water, then take fine surface sand and wipe your faces and your hands therewith. God does not wish to make any hindrance for you; but he wishes to purify you and to fulfil his favour upon you; haply ye may give thanks.

[10] Remember the favour of God to you and His covenant which He covenanted with you, when ye said, 'We hear and we obey[1];' and fear God, verily, God knows the nature of men's breasts.

O ye who believe! stand steadfast to God as witnesses with justice; and let not ill-will towards people make you sin by not acting with equity. Act with equity, that is nearer to piety, and fear God; for God is aware of what ye do.

God has promised to those who believe and work righteousness, that for them is pardon and a mighty hire. But those who disbelieve and call our signs lies, these are the fellows of hell.

---

[1] Referring to the oath of fidelity which Mohammed's adherents took at 'Akabah.

O ye who believe! remember God's favour towards you, when a people intended to stretch their hands against you, but He withheld their hands from you[1]; and upon God let believers rely.

[15] God did take a compact from the children of Israel, and raised up of them twelve wardens; and God said, 'Verily, I am with you, if ye be steadfast in prayer, and give alms, and believe in my apostles, and assist them, and lend to God a goodly loan; then will I cover your offences and make you enter gardens beneath which rivers flow: and whoso disbelieves after that, he hath erred from the level way.'

And for that they broke their compact, we cursed them, and placed in their hearts hardness, so that they perverted the words from their places, and forgot a portion of what they were reminded of[2].

But thou wilt not cease to light upon treachery amongst them, save a few of them; but pardon them and shun them; verily, God loves the kind.

And of those who say, 'Verily, we are Christians,' we have taken a compact; but they have forgotten a portion of what they were reminded of; wherefore have we excited amongst them enmity and hatred till the resurrection day; but God will tell them of what they have done.

O ye people of the Book! our Apostle has come to you to explain to you much of what ye had hidden of the Book, and to pardon much. There has come to you from God a light, and a perspicuous

---

[1] Various stories are told in explanation of this passage, but they are all obviously apocryphal, the angel Gabriel intervening to prevent some mischief either to the Apostle or his followers.

[2] That is, the text foretelling the coming of Mohammed; see Introduction.

Book; God guides thereby those who follow His pleasure to the way of peace, and brings them into a right way.

They misbelieve who say, 'Verily, God is the Messiah the son of Mary;' say, 'Who has any hold on God, if he wished to destroy the Messiah the son of Mary, and his mother, and those who are on earth altogether?'

[20] God's is the kingdom of the heavens and the earth and what is between the two; He createth what He will, for God is mighty over all!

But the Jews and the Christians say, 'We are the sons of God and His beloved.' Say, 'Why then does He punish you for your sins? nay, ye are mortals of those whom He has created! He pardons whom He pleases, and punishes whom He pleases; for God's is the kingdom of the heavens and the earth, and what is between the two, and unto Him the journey is.'

O people of the Book! our Apostle has come to you, explaining to you the interval of apostles; lest ye say, 'There came not to us a herald of glad tidings nor a warner.' But there has come to you now a herald of glad tidings and a warner, and God is mighty over all!

When Moses said to his people, 'O my people! remember the favour of God towards you when He made amongst you prophets, and made for you kings, and brought you what never was brought to anybody in the worlds. O my people! enter the Holy Land which God has prescribed for you; and be ye not thrust back upon your hinder parts and retreat losers:' [25] They said, 'O Moses! verily, therein is a people, giants; and we will surely not enter therein until they go out from thence; but if they go out then we will enter in.' Then said two men of those who fear,—God had been gracious to them both,—'Enter ye upon them by the door, and when ye have entered it, verily, ye shall be victorious; and upon God do ye rely if ye be believers.' They said, 'O Moses! we shall never enter it so long as they are therein; so, go thou and thy Lord and fight ye twain; verily, we will sit down here.' Said he, 'My Lord, verily, I can control only myself and my brother; therefore part us from these sinful people.' He said, 'Then, verily, it is forbidden them; for forty years shall they wander about in the earth; so vex not thyself for the sinful people.'

[30] Recite to them the story of the two sons of Adam; truly when they offered an offering and it was accepted from one of them, and was not accepted from the other, that one said, 'I will surely kill thee;' he said, 'God only accepts from those who fear. If thou dost stretch forth to me thine hand to kill me, I will not stretch forth mine hand to kill thee; verily, I fear God the Lord of the worlds; verily, I wish that thou mayest draw upon thee my sin and thy sin, and be of the fellows of the Fire, for that is the reward of the unjust.' But his soul allowed him to slay his brother, and he slew him, and in the morning he was of those who lose. And God sent a crow to scratch in the earth and show him how he might hide his brother's shame, he said, 'Alas, for me! Am I too helpless to become like this crow and hide my brother's shame?' and in the morning he was of those who did repent.

[35] For this cause have we prescribed to the children of Israel that whoso kills a soul, unless it

be for another soul or for violence in the land, it is as though he had killed men altogether; but whoso saves one, it is as though he saved men altogether.

Our apostles came to them with manifest signs; then, verily, many of them did after that commit excesses in the earth.

The reward of those who make war against God and His Apostle, and strive after violence in the earth, is only that they shall be slaughtered or crucified, or their hands cut off and their feet on alternate sides, or that they shall be banished from the land;—that is a disgrace for them in this world, and for them in the next is mighty woe; save for those who repent before ye have them in your power, for know ye that God is forgiving, merciful.

O ye who believe! fear God and crave the means to approach Him, and be strenuous in His way, haply ye will prosper then.

[40] Verily, those who disbelieve, even though they had what is in the earth, all of it, and the like thereof with it, to offer as a ransom from the punishment of the resurrection day, it would not be accepted from them; but for them is grievous woe. They may wish to go forth from the Fire, but they shall not go forth therefrom, for them is lasting woe.

The man thief and the woman thief, cut off the hands of both as a punishment, for that they have erred;—an example from God, for God is mighty, wise.

But whoso turns again after his injustice and acts aright, verily, God will turn to him, for, verily, God is forgiving, merciful.

Do ye not know that God, His is the kingdom of

the heavens and the earth; He punishes whom He pleases, and forgives whom He pleases, for God is mighty over all?

[45] O thou Apostle! let not those grieve thee who vie in misbelief; or those who say with their mouths 'We believe,' but their hearts do not believe; or of those who are Jews, listeners to a lie,—listeners to other people, but who come not to thee. They pervert the words from their places and say, 'If this is what ye are given, take it; but if ye are not given it, then beware!' but he whom God wishes to mislead, thou canst do nothing with God for him; these are those whose hearts God wishes not to purify, for them in this world is disgrace, and for them in the next is mighty woe,—listeners to a lie, eaters of unlawful things!

But if they come to thee, then judge between them or turn aside from them; but if thou turnest aside from them they shall not harm thee at all, but if thou judgest, then judge between them with justice, verily, God loves the just. But how should they make thee their judge, when they have the law wherein is God's judgment? Yet they turn back after that, for they do not believe.

Verily, we have revealed the law in which is guidance and light; the prophets who were resigned did judge thereby those who were Jews, as did the masters[1] and doctors by what they remembered of the Book of God and by what they were witnesses of. Fear not men, but fear me, and sell not my signs for a little price; for whoso will not judge by what God has revealed, these be the misbelievers.

---

[1] See note 2, p. 56.

We have prescribed for thee therein 'a life for a life, and an eye for an eye, and a nose for a nose, and an ear for an ear, and a tooth for a tooth, and for wounds retaliation;' but whoso remits it, it is an expiation for him, but he whoso will not judge by what God has revealed, these be the unjust.

[50] And we followed up the footsteps of these (prophets) with Jesus the son of Mary, confirming that which was before him and the law, and we brought him the gospel, wherein is guidance and light, verifying what was before it of the law, and a guidance and an admonition unto those who fear.

Then let the people of the gospel judge by that which is revealed therein, for whoso will not judge by what God has revealed, these be the evildoers.

We have revealed to thee the Book in truth verifying what was before it, and preserving it; judge then between them by what God has revealed, and follow not their lusts, turning away from what is given to thee of the truth.

For each one of you have we made a law and a pathway; and had God pleased He would have made you one nation, but He will surely try you concerning that which He has brought you. Be ye therefore emulous in good deeds; to God is your return altogether, and He will let you know concerning that wherein ye do dispute.

Wherefore judge thou between them by what God has revealed, and follow not their lusts; but beware lest they mislead thee from part of what God has revealed to thee; yet if they turn back, then know that God wishes to fall on them for some sins of theirs,—verily, many men are evildoers.

[55] Is it the judgment of the Ignorance they

crave[1]? but who is better than God to judge for people who are sure?

O ye who believe! take not the Jews and Christians for your patrons: they are patrons of each other; but whoso amongst you takes them for patrons, verily, he is of them, and, verily, God guides not an unjust people.

Thou wilt see those in whose hearts is a sickness vieing with them; they say, 'We fear lest there befall us a reverse.' It may be God will give the victory, or an order from Himself, and they may awake repenting of what they thought in secret to themselves.

Those who believe say, 'Are these they who swore by God with their most strenuous oath that they were surely with you?'—their works are in vain and they shall wake the losers.

O ye who believe! whoso is turned away from his religion—God will bring (instead) a people[2] whom He loves and who love Him, lowly to believers, lofty to unbelievers, strenuous in the way of God, fearing not the blame of him who blames. That is God's grace! He gives it unto whom He pleases, for God both comprehends and knows.

[60] God only is your patron, and His Apostle and those who believe, who are steadfast in prayer and give alms, bowing down. Whoso taketh as patrons God and His apostles and those who believe;—verily, God's crew, they are victorious!

O ye who believe! take not for patrons those who

---

[1] The time before the Mohammedan dispensation is always so called.

[2] I. e. to take his place.

take your religion for a jest or a sport, from amongst those who have been given the Book before and the misbelievers; but fear God if ye be believers. Nor those who, when ye call to prayer, take it for a jest and a sport; that is because they are a people who do not understand.

Say, 'O people of the Book! do ye disavow us, for aught but that we believe in God, and what was revealed to us before, and for that most of you are evildoers?'

[65] Say, 'Can I declare unto you something worse than retribution from God?' Whomsoever God has cursed and been wroth with—and he has made of them apes and swine—and who worship *Tâghût*, they are in a worse plight and are more erring from the level path. When they come to you they say, 'We believe;' but they entered in with unbelief, and they went out therewith, and God knows best what they did hide.

Thou wilt see many of them vieing in sin and enmity, and in eating unlawful things,—evil is it that they have done. The masters and their doctors prohibit them from speaking sin and eating unlawful things,—evil is what they have performed.

The Jews say, 'God's hand is fettered;' their hands are fettered and they are cursed for what they said; nay! His hands are outspread, He expends how He pleases! and that which has been sent down to thee from thy Lord will surely increase many of them in their rebellion and misbelief, for we have cast amongst them enmity and hatred till the resurrection day. Whenever they light a fire[1] for war,

[1] The ancient Arabs always lit a beacon-fire as a proclamation of war, or a notice of the approach of an enemy.

God puts it out; they strive for corruption in the earth, but God loves not the corrupt.

[70] But did the people of the Book believe and fear, we would cover their offences, and we would make them enter into gardens of pleasure; and were they steadfast in the law and the gospel, and what has been sent down to them from their Lord, they should eat from above them and below them. Amongst them are a nation who are moderate, but many of them—bad is what they do.

O thou Apostle! preach what has been revealed to thee from thy Lord; if thou do it not thou hast not preached His message, and God will not hold thee free from men; for God guides not people who misbelieve.

Say, 'O people of the Book! ye rest on naught until ye stand fast by the law and the gospel, and what is revealed to you from your Lord.' But what has been revealed to thee from thy Lord will of a surety increase many of them in rebellion and misbelief, vex not thyself then for a people who misbelieve.

Verily, those who believe and those who are Jews, and the Sabæans, and the Christians, whosoever believes in God and the last day, and does what is right, there is no fear for them, nor shall they grieve.

We took a compact of the children of Israel, and we sent to them apostles; every time there came to them an apostle with what their souls loved not, a part of them they did call liars and a part of them they slew.

[75] And they reckoned that there would be no disturbance; but they were blind and deaf! and then

God turned again towards them: and then many amongst them were blind and deaf! but God saw what they did.

They misbelieve who say, 'Verily, God is the Messiah the son of Mary;' but the Messiah said, 'O children of Israel! worship God, my Lord and your Lord;' verily, he who associates aught with God, God hath forbidden him Paradise, and his resort is the Fire, and the unjust shall have none to help them.

They misbelieve who say, 'Verily, God is the third of three;' for there is no God but one, and if they do not desist from what they say, there shall touch those who misbelieve amongst them grievous woe.

Will they not turn again towards God and ask pardon of Him? for God is forgiving and merciful.

The Messiah the son of Mary is only a prophet: prophets before him have passed away; and his mother was a confessor; they used both to eat food.—See how we explain to them the signs, yet see how they turn aside!

[80] Say, 'Will ye serve, other than God, what can neither hurt you nor profit you?' but God, He both hears and knows.

Say, 'O people of the Book! exceed not the truth in your religion, and follow not the lusts of a people who have erred before, and who lead many astray, and who go away from the level path.'

Those of the children of Israel who disbelieved were cursed by the tongue of David and Jesus the son of Mary; that is because they rebelled and did transgress; they would not desist from the wrong they did; evil is that which they did. Thou wilt see many of them taking those who disbelieve for their patrons; evil is that which their souls have sent before them, for God's wrath is on them, and in the torment shall they dwell for aye. But had they believed in God and the prophet, and what was revealed to him, they had not taken these for their patrons; but many of them are evildoers.

[85] Thou wilt surely find that the strongest in enmity against those who believe are the Jews and the idolaters; and thou wilt find the nearest in love to those who believe to be those who say, 'We are Christians;' that is because there are amongst them priests and monks, and because they are not proud.

And when they hear what has been revealed to the prophet, you will see their eyes gush with tears at what they recognise as truth therein; and they will say, 'O our Lord! we believe, so write us down amongst the witnesses. Why should we not believe in God and the truth that is given to us, nor desire that our Lord should make us enter with the upright people?'

Therefore has God rewarded them, for what they said, with gardens beneath which rivers flow, to dwell therein for aye; that is the reward of those who do good; but those who disbelieve and say our signs are lies, they are the fellows of hell.

O ye who believe! forbid not the good things which God has made lawful for you, nor transgress; verily, God loves not the transgressors.

[90] But eat of what God has provided you lawfully of good things; and fear God, in whom ye believe.

God will not catch you up for a casual word in your oaths, but He will catch you up for having what ye make deliberate oaths about; and the expiation thereof is to feed ten poor men with the middling food ye feed your families withal, or to clothe them, or to free a neck[1]; but he who has not the means, then let him fast three days. That is the expiation of your oaths, when ye have sworn to keep your oaths; thus does God explain to you His signs,—haply ye may be grateful.

O ye who believe! verily, wine, and el mâisar[2], and statues[3], and divining (arrows) are only an abomination of Satan's work; avoid them then that haply ye may prosper. Satan only desires to place enmity and hatred between you by wine and mâisar, and to turn you from the remembrance of God and from prayer; but will ye not desist, and obey God, and obey the apostles, and beware, for if ye turn back then know that our Apostle has only his message to preach?

There is no crime in those who believe and do right, for having tasted food, when they fear God, and believe, and do what is right, and then fear Him, and believe, and then fear, and do good, for God loves those who do good.

[95] O ye who believe! God will try you with something of the game that your hands and your lances take, that God may know who fears Him in secret; and whoso transgresses after that, for him is grievous woe.

O ye who believe! kill not game while ye are on

[1] I. e. from the yoke of captivity.

[2] See note 4, p. 32.

[3] This has been thought by strict Musselmans to exclude the game of chess. Sunnîs, however, play the game with plain pieces like drafts, though Persians and Indians are not so scrupulous.

pilgrimage. But he amongst you who kills it purposely, his compensation is the like of that which he has killed, in sheep—of which two equitable persons amongst you shall be judge—an offering brought to the Kaabah; or as an expiation, the food of poor persons, or an equivalent thereof in fasting, that he may taste the evil result of his deed. God pardons bygones; but whoso returns, God will take vengeance on him, for God is mighty and the avenger.

Lawful for you is the game of the sea, and to eat thereof; a provision for you and for travellers; but forbidden you is the game of the land while ye are on pilgrimage; so fear God to whom ye shall be gathered.

God has made the Kaabah, the sacred House, to be a station for men, and the sacred month, and the offering and its neck garland; this is that ye may know that God knows what is in the heavens and what is in the earth, and that God knows all things. Know that God is keen to punish, but that God is forgiving, merciful.

The Apostle has only to preach his message, but God knows what ye show and what ye hide.

[100] Say, 'The vile shall not be deemed equal with the good, although the abundance of the vile please thee.' Fear God then, O ye who have minds! haply ye may prosper.

O ye who believe! ask not about things which if they be shown to you will pain you; but if ye ask about them when the (whole) Qur'ân is revealed, they shall be shown to you. God pardons that, for God is forgiving and clement. People before you have asked about that, yet on the morrow did they disbelieve therein.

And God has not ordained any Ba'hîrah or Sâibah, nor Wazîlah nor 'Hâmî[1], but those who misbelieve invent a lie against God, for most of them do not understand.

And when it is said to them, 'Come round to what God has revealed unto His Apostle,' they say, 'Enough for us is what we found our fathers agreed upon.' What! though their fathers knew nothing and were not guided.

O ye who believe! mind yourselves; he who errs can do you no hurt when ye are guided: unto God is your return altogether, and He will declare to you that which ye do not know.

[105] O ye who believe! let there be a testimony between you when any one of you is on the point of death—at the time he makes his will—two equitable persons from amongst you; or two others from some other folk, if ye be knocking about in the land, and the calamity of death befall you; ye shall shut them both up after prayer, and they shall both swear by

[1] These were the names given to certain animals which were marked and allowed to graze at liberty. Ba'hîrah was the name given to a camel which had had ten young ones; her ear was then slit and she was turned loose to feed. When she died her flesh was eaten by the men only, the women being forbidden to touch it. There were, however, cases in which any she-camel was so called and treated. Sâïbah signifies merely a camel turned loose, her being so turned out was generally in fulfilment of a vow. Wazîlah was a term applied to any cattle, including sheep and goats, and generally meant a beast who had brought forth a male and female at the seventh parturition. 'Hâmî was a stallion camel which, after begetting ten young ones, was turned loose. As all these customs were connected with the idolatrous superstitions of the pagan Arabs, and tended to keep alive the rites and beliefs of paganism, Mohammed forbade them, with other similar superstitions.

God, if ye doubt them, (saying), 'We will not sell (our testimony) for a price, though it were to a relative, nor will we hide God's testimony, verily, then, we should be among sinners.' But if it shall be lit upon that they too have deserved the imputation of sin, then let two others stand up in their place with those who think them deserving of the imputation, the nearest two in kin, and they shall both swear by God, 'Indeed, our testimony is truer than the testimony of those two, and we have not transgressed, for then we should surely be of the unjust:' thus is it easier for men to bear testimony according to the purport thereof, else must they fear lest an oath be given to rebut their own oath; but let them fear God and listen, for God guides not the people who do ill.

On the day when God shall assemble the apostles and shall say, 'How were ye answered?' they will say, 'We have no knowledge; verily, thou art He who knoweth the unseen.'

When God said, 'O Jesus, son of Mary! remember my favours towards thee and towards thy mother, when I aided thee with the Holy Ghost, till thou didst speak to men in the cradle and when grown up.

[110] 'And when I taught thee the Book and wisdom and the law and the gospel; when thou didst create of clay, as it were, the likeness of a bird, by my power, and didst blow thereon, it became a bird; and thou didst heal the blind from birth, and the leprous by my permission; and when thou didst bring forth the dead by my permission; and when I did ward off the children of Israel from thee, when thou didst come to them with manifest signs, and those who

misbelieved amongst them said, "This is naught but obvious magic."

'And when I inspired the apostles that they should believe in him and in my Apostle, they said, "We believe; do thou bear witness that we are resigned."'

When the apostles said, 'O Jesus, son of Mary! is thy Lord able to send down to us a table from heaven?' he said, 'Fear God, if ye be believers;' and they said, 'We desire to eat therefrom that our hearts may be at rest, and that we may know that what thou hast told us is the truth, and that we may be thereby amongst the witnesses.' Said Jesus the son of Mary, 'O God, our Lord! send down to us a table from heaven to be to us as a festival,—to the first of us and to the last, and a sign from Thee,—and grant us provision, for Thou art the best of providers.'

[115] God said, 'Verily, I am about to send it down to you; but whoso disbelieves amongst you after that, verily, I will torment him with the torment which I have not tormented any one with in all the worlds.'

And when God said, 'O Jesus, son of Mary! is it thou who didst say to men, take me and my mother for two gods, beside God?' He said, 'I celebrate Thy praise! what ails me that I should say what I have no right to? If I had said it, Thou wouldst have known it; Thou knowest what is in my soul, but I know not what is in Thy soul; verily, Thou art one who knoweth the unseen. I never told them save what Thou didst bid me,—"Worship God, my Lord and your Lord," and I was a witness against them so long as I was amongst them; but when Thou didst take me away to thyself Thou wert the watcher over them, for Thou art witness over all. If

Thou shouldst punish them, verily, they are Thy servants; if Thou shouldst forgive them, verily, Thou art the mighty and the wise.' God said, 'This is the day when their confession shall profit the confessors, for them are gardens beneath which rivers flow, to dwell therein for ever and for aye.'

God is well pleased with them, and they well pleased with Him; that is the mighty happiness.

[120] God's is the kingdom of the heavens, and the earth, and all that is therein, and He is mighty over all.

The Chapter of Cattle[1].

(VI. Mecca.)

In the name of the merciful and compassionate God!

Praise belongs to God who created the heavens and the earth, and brought into being the darkness and the light[2]. Yet do those who misbelieve hold Him to have peers.

He it is who created you from clay; then He decreed a term,—a term[3] ordained with Him. And yet ye doubt thereof.

He is God in the heavens and the earth. He knows your secret conduct and your plain, and He knows what ye earn[4].

---

[1] So called from the mention which it contains of the superstitious customs of the Arabs with regard to their cattle.

[2] Said to be a protest against the dualistic doctrine that Light and Darkness were two co-eternal principles.

[3] I. e. a term for your life and another for your resurrection.

[4] By good or evil works.

There came not to them any sign of the signs of their Lord, but they turned away; [5] and they have called the truth a lie now that it has come to them, but there shall come to them the message of that at which they mocked.

Do not they see how many a generation we have destroyed before them, whom we had settled in the earth as we have not settled for you, and sent the rain of heaven upon them in copious showers, and made the waters flow beneath them? Then we destroyed them in their sins, and raised up other generations after them.

Had we sent down to thee a book on paper, and they had touched it with their hands, still those who misbelieve would have said, 'This is naught but obvious magic.' They say, 'Why has not an angel been sent down to him?' but if we had sent down an angel, the affair would have been decided, and then they would have had no respite.

And had we made him[1] an angel, we should have made him as a man too; and we would have made perplexing for them that which they deem perplexing now.

[10] There have been prophets before thee mocked at, but that encompassed them which the scoffers among them mocked at.

Say, 'Go about in the earth, then wilt thou see how has been the end of those who called them liars.'

Say, 'Whose is what is in the heavens and the earth?'

Say, 'God's, who has imposed mercy on himself.'

[1] I. e. the prophet.

He will surely gather you together for the resurrection day. There is no doubt in that, but those who waste their souls [1] will not believe.

His is whatsoever dwells in the night or in the day, He both hears and knows.

Say, 'Other than God shall I take for a patron, the Originator of the heavens and the earth? He feedeth men, but is not fed.' Say, 'I am bidden to be the first of those resigned;' and it was said to me, 'Be not thou of the idolaters.' [15] Say, 'I fear, if I rebel against my Lord, the torment of the mighty day.'

Whomsoever it is averted from on that day, God will have had mercy on; and that is obvious happiness.

And if God touch thee with harm, there is none to take it off but He; and if He touch thee with good, He is mighty over all. He is sovereign over His servants, He is the wise, the aware!

Say, 'What is the greatest witness?' Say, 'God is witness between you and me.' This Qur'ân was inspired to me to warn you and those it reaches. Do ye really bear witness that with God are other gods? Say, 'I bear not witness thereto:' say, 'He is but one God, and I am clear of your associating (gods with him).'

[20] Those to whom we have brought the Book know him [2] as they know their sons;—those who lose their souls do not believe.

Who is more unjust than he who forges against God a lie, or says His signs are lies? verily, the unjust shall not prosper.

[1] I. e. their innate propensities to good and their reason.

[2] Mohammed.

On the day when we shall gather them all together, then shall we say to those who have associated others with ourself, 'Where are your associates whom ye did pretend?' Then they will have no excuse but to say, 'By God our Lord, we did not associate (others with thee)!' See how they lie against themselves, and how what they did forge deserts them!
[25] And they are some who listen unto thee, but we have placed a veil upon their hearts lest they should understand it, and in their ears is dulness of hearing; and though they saw each sign they would not believe therein; until when they come to thee to wrangle with thee, the unbelievers say, 'These are but old folks' tales.'

They forbid it and they avoid it;—but they destroy none but themselves; yet they do not perceive.

But couldst thou see when they are set over the fire and say, 'Would that we were sent back! we would not call our Lord's signs lies, but we would be of the believers?' Nay! now is shown to them what they did hide before; and could they be sent back, they would return to that they were forbidden, for they are very liars.

They say there is naught but this life of ours
in the world and we shall not be raised. [30] But
couldst thou see when they are set before their Lord; he says, 'Is not this the truth?' They say, 'Yea, by our Lord!' he says, 'Then taste the torment, for that ye did misbelieve!'

Losers are they who disbelieved in meeting God, until when the hour comes suddenly upon them they say, 'Woe is us for our neglect thereof!' for they shall bear their burdens on their backs, evil is what they bear.

The life of this world is nothing but a game and a sport, and surely the next abode were better for those who fear. What! do they not understand?

Full well we know that verily that which they say grieves thee; but they do not call thee only a liar, for the unjust gainsay the signs of God. Called liars too were apostles before thee; but they were patient of being called liars and of being hurt until our help came to them; for there is none to change the words of God—now has there come to thee the story of those He sent.

[35] And if their turning from thee be hard for thee, and if thou canst seek for a shaft down into the earth, or a ladder up into the sky, to bring them a sign—but if God pleased He would bring them all to guidance, be thou not then of the ignorant.

He only answers the prayer of those who listen; but the dead will God raise up, then unto Him shall they return. They say, 'Unless there be sent down some sign from his Lord'—say, 'Verily, God is able to send down a sign, but most of them do not know.'

There is not a beast upon the earth nor a bird that flies with both its wings, but is a nation like to you; we have omitted nothing from the Book; then to their Lord shall they be gathered. Those who say our signs are lies—deafness, dumbness, in the dark! whom He pleases does God lead astray, and whom He pleases He places on the right way.

[40] Say, 'Look you now! if there should come God's torment, or there should come to you the hour, on other than God would ye call, if ye do tell the truth?' Nay, it is on Him that ye would call,

and He will avert that which ye call upon Him for if He but please; and ye shall forget that which ye did associate with Him.

Ere this we sent unto nations before thee, and we caught them in distress and trouble that haply they might humble themselves. And do they not, when our violence falls upon them, humble themselves?—but their hearts were hard, and Satan made seemly to them that which they had done.

And when they forgot what they were reminded of, we opened for them the gates of everything, until when they rejoiced at what they had, we caught them up suddenly, and lo! they were in despair.

[45] And the uttermost part of the people who did wrong were cut off; praise be to God, Lord of the worlds!

Say, 'Look you now! if God should catch your hearing and your sight, and should set a seal upon your hearts—who is god but God to bring you it again?'

Say, 'Look you now! if God's torment should come upon you suddenly or openly, would any perish save the people who do wrong?'

We do not send our messengers save as heralds of glad tidings and of warning, and whoso believes and acts aright, there is no fear for them, and they shall not be grieved, but those who say our signs are lies, torment shall touch them, for that they have done so wrong.

[50] Say, 'I do not say to you, mine are the treasuries of God, nor that I know the unseen; I do not say to you, I am an angel—if I follow aught but what I am inspired with—:' say, 'Is the blind equal to him who sees—?' what! do ye not reflect?

Admonish therewith those who fear that they shall be gathered unto their Lord; there is no patron for them but Him, and no intercessor; haply they may fear.

Repulse not those who call upon their Lord in the morning and in the evening, desiring His face; they have no reckoning against thee at all, and thou hast no reckoning against them at all;—repulse them and thou wilt be of the unjust.

So have we tried some of them by others, that they may say, 'Are these those unto whom God has been gracious amongst ourselves?' Does not God know those who give thanks?

And when those who believe in our signs come to thee, say, 'Peace be on you! God hath prescribed for Himself mercy; verily, he of you who does evil in ignorance, and then turns again and does right,—verily, He is forgiving and merciful.'

[55] Thus do we detail our signs, that the way of the sinners may be made plain.

Say, 'I am forbidden to worship those ye call upon beside God;' say, 'I will not follow your lusts, for then should I err and not be of the guided.'

Say, 'I stand on a manifestation from my Lord, which ye call a lie. I have not with me what ye fain would hasten on, that the matter might be settled between me and you; but God knows best who are the unjust.'

With Him are the keys[1] of the unseen. None knows them save He; He knows what is in the

[1] Most of the Mohammedan commentators say this word means 'treasuries.' The allusion, however, is obviously to the Rabbinical tradition of the three keys, in the hands of God.

land and in the sea; and there falls not a leaf save that He knows it; nor a grain in the darkness of the earth, nor aught that is moist, nor aught that is dry, save that is in His perspicuous Book.

[60] He it is who takes you to Himself at night[1], and knows what ye have gained in the day; then He raises you up again, that your appointed time may be fulfilled; then unto Him is your return, and then will He inform you of what ye have done.

He triumphs over His servants; He sends to them guardian angels, until, when death comes to any one of you, our messengers take him away; they pass not over any one, and then are they returned to God, their true sovereign.

Is not His the rule? but He is very quick at reckoning up.

Say, 'Who rescues you from the darkness of the land and of the sea?' ye call upon Him in humility and in secret, 'Indeed, if He would rescue us from this, we will surely be of those who give Him thanks.' Say, 'God rescues from the darkness thereof, and from every trouble, yet ye associate others with Him.'

[65] Say, 'He is able to send torment on you from above you and from beneath your feet, and to confuse you in sects, and to make some of you taste the violence of others.'

See how we turn about the signs, that haply they may discriminate. Thy people called it a lie, and yet it is the truth. Say, 'I have not charge over you; to every prophecy is a set time, and in the end ye shall know.'

[1] In sleep.

When thou dost see those who plunge deeply into the discussion of our signs, turn from them until they plunge deeply into some other discourse; for it may be that Satan may make thee forget; but sit not, after thou hast remembered, with the unjust people.

Those who fear are not bound to take account of them at all, but mind!—haply they may fear.

Leave those who have taken their religion for a play and a sport, whom this world's life hath deceived, and remind them thereby that a soul shall be given up for what it has earned; nor has it, beside God, patron or intercessor; and though it should compensate with the fullest compensation, it would not be accepted. Those who are given up for what they have gained, for them is a drink of boiling water, and grievous woe for that they have misbelieved.

[70] Say, 'Shall we call on what neither profits us nor harms us, and be thrown back upon our heels after God has guided us, like him whom Satan hath led away bewildered in the earth, who has companions who call him to guidance, "Come to us?"' Say, 'Verily, God's guidance is the guidance, and we are bidden to resign ourselves unto the Lord of the worlds, and be ye steadfast in prayer and fear Him, for He it is to whom we shall be gathered.'

He it is who has created the heavens and the earth in truth; and on the day when He says, 'BE,' then it is. His word is truth; to Him is the kingdom on the day when the trumpets shall be blown; the knower of the unseen and of the evident; He is wise and well aware.

When Abraham said to his father Âzar[1], 'Dost thou take idols for gods? verily, I see thee and thy people in obvious error.' [75] Thus did we show Abraham the kingdom of heaven and of the earth, that he should be of those who are sure. And when the night overshadowed him he saw a star and said, 'This is my Lord;' but when it set he said, 'I love not those that set.' And when he saw the moon beginning to rise he said, 'This is my Lord;' but when it set he said, 'If God my Lord guides me not I shall surely be of the people who err.' And when he saw the sun beginning to rise he said, 'This is my Lord, this is greatest of all;' but when it set he said, 'O my people! verily, I am clear of what ye associate with God; verily, I have turned my face to him who originated the heaven and the earth, as a 'Hanîf, and I am not of the idolaters.' [80] And his people disputed with him;—he said, 'Do ye dispute with me concerning God, when He has guided me? but I fear not what ye associate with Him unless my Lord should wish for anything. My Lord doth comprehend all things in His knowledge, will ye not then remember? How should I fear what ye associate with Him, when ye yourselves fear not to associate with God what He has sent down to you no power to do? Which then of the two sects is worthier of belief, if indeed ye know?'

Those who believe and do not obscure their faith with wrong, they are those who shall have security, and they are guided.

---

[1] The Hebrew Terah is in Arabic Târah. Eusebius gives the form Athar, which may in some measure account for the name here given.

These are our arguments which we gave to Abraham against his people;—we raise the rank of whom we will; verily, thy Lord is wise and knowing. And we gave to him Isaac and Jacob, each did we guide. And Noah we guided before and all his seed,—David and Solomon and Job and Joseph and Moses and Aaron,—for thus do we reward those who do good. [85] And Zachariah and John and Jesus and Elias, all righteous ones; and Ishmael and Elisha and Jonas and Lot, each one have we preferred above the worlds; and of their fathers and their seed and brethren; we have chosen them and guided them into a right way.

That is God's guidance; He guides those whom He will of His servants; and if they associate aught with Him,—vain is that which they have worked.

It is to these we give the Book and judgment and prophecy; and if these disbelieve therein we have given them in charge to a people who shall not disbelieve.

[90] It is these that God hath guided, and by their guidance be thou led.

Say, 'I will not ask you for it a hire: it is naught save a reminder to the worlds.'

They do not prize God at His true worth when they say, 'God has never revealed to mortal anything.' Say, 'Who revealed the Book wherewith Moses came, a light and a guidance unto men? Ye put it on papers which ye show, though ye hide much[1];

[1] The Jews are here, as frequently in the Qur'ân, accused of suppressing and altering those parts of their scriptures which referred, according to the Mussulman theory, to the mission of Mohammed.

and ye are taught what ye knew not, neither you nor your fathers.' Say, 'God,' then leave them in their discussion to play.

This is the Book which we have revealed, a blessing and a confirmation to those which were before it, and that the mother of cities [1] may be warned, with those who are round about her. Those who believe in the last day believe therein, and they unto their prayers will keep.

Who is more unjust than he who devises against God a lie, or says, 'I am inspired [2],' when he was not inspired at all? and who says, 'I will bring down the like of what God has sent down;' but didst thou see when the unjust are in the floods of death, and the angels stretch forth their hands, 'Give ye forth your souls; to-day shall ye be recompensed with the torment of disgrace, for that ye did say against God what was not true, and were too proud to hear His signs [3]. And ye come now single-handed as we created you at first, and ye have left behind your backs that which we granted you; and we see not with you your intercessors whom ye pretended were partners [4] amongst you; betwixt you have the ties

---

[1] Mecca.

[2] This refers to Abdallah ibn Sa'hd ibn Abî Sar'h, who acted as amanuensis to Mohammed, and when he came to the words 'We have created man from an extract of clay . . . . , then we produced it another creation,' he said, 'and blessed be God, best of creators,' and Mohammed told him to write that down too; whereupon he boasted that he also had been inspired with this sentence which Mohammed acknowledged to be part of the Qur'ân.

[3] This word is nearly always used for the verses of the Qur'ân.

[4] That is, partners with God, idols; to associate being the usual phrase in the Qur'ân for idolatry.

been cut asunder; and strayed away from you is what ye did pretend.'

[95] Verily, God it is who cleaves out the grain and the date-stone; He brings forth the living from the dead, and it is He who brings the dead from the living. There is God! how then can ye be beguiled?

He it is who cleaves out the morning, and makes night a repose, and the sun and the moon two reckonings—that is the decree of the mighty, the wise!

He it is who made for you stars that ye might be guided thereby in the darkness of the land and of the sea. Now have we detailed the signs unto a people who do know.

He it is who made you spring from one soul, and gave you a settlement and a depository[1]. Now have we detailed the signs unto a people who discern.

He it is who sends down from the heavens water; and we bring forth therewith growths of everything; and we bring forth therefrom green things, wherefrom we bring forth grain in full ear; and the palm, from its spathe come clusters within reach; and gardens of grapes and olives and pomegranates, alike and unlike;—behold its fruit when it fruits and ripens! verily, in that ye have a sign for the people who believe.

[100] Yet they made the *g*inn[2] partners with

---

[1] In the womb.

[2] Supernatural beings created, like the devils, of fire instead of clay, and possessed of miraculous powers. They are devoutly believed in by Muslims, and are supposed to be subject to the same controlling laws as mankind, and to have also had prophets sent to them. They are probably a survival of some old worship

God, though He created them! and they ascribed to Him sons and daughters, though they have no knowledge; celebrated be His praise! and exalted be He above what they attribute to Him! The inventor of the heavens and the earth! how can He have a son, when He has no female companion, and when He has created everything, and everything He knows?

There is God for you,—your Lord! There is no god but He, the Creator of everything; then worship Him, for He o'er everything keeps guard!

Sight perceives Him not, but He perceives men's sights; for He is the subtle, the aware.

Now has an insight from your Lord come unto you, and he who looks therewith it is for himself; but he who is blind thereto, it is against his soul; and I am not your keeper.

[105] Thus do we turn about the signs, that they may say, 'Thou hast studied,' and that we may explain to those who know.

Follow what is revealed to thee from thy Lord; there is no god but He, and shun the idolaters.

But had God pleased, they would not have associated aught with Him; but we have not made thee a keeper over them, nor art thou for them a warder.

Do not abuse those who call on other than God, for then they may abuse God openly in their ignorance. So do we make seemly to every nation their work, then unto their Lord is their return, and He will inform them of what they have done.

---

of the powers of nature. The word *ginn* is the same as that which in the old translation of the Arabian Nights is rendered 'genie.'

They swore by God with their most strenuous oath, that if there come to them a sign they will indeed believe therein. Say, 'Signs are only in God's hands;—but what will make you understand that even when one has come, they will not believe?'

[110] We will overturn their hearts and their eyesights, even as they believed not at first; and we will leave them, in their rebellion, blindly wandering on.

And had we sent down unto them the angels, or the dead had spoken to them, or we had gathered everything unto them in hosts [1], they would not have believed unless that God pleased—but most of them are ignorant.

So have we made for every prophet an enemy,—devils of men and *g*inns; some of them inspire others with specious speech to lead astray; but had thy Lord pleased they would not have done it; so leave them with what they do devise.

And let the hearts of those who believe not in the hereafter listen to it; and let them be well pleased with it; and let them gain what they may gain!

Of other than God shall I crave a decree, when it is He who has sent down to you the Book in detail, and those to whom we gave the Book know that it is sent down from thy Lord, in truth? be thou not then of those who doubt.

[115] The words of thy Lord are fulfilled in truth and justice; there is none to change His words, for He both hears and knows.

But if thou followest most of those who are in the

---

[1] This word may also be rendered 'before them' or 'a surety' (for the truth of the revelation).

land, they will lead thee astray from the path of God; they only follow suspicion and they only (rest on) conjecture.

Thy Lord, He knows best who errs from His path, and He knows best the guided.

Eat then cf what God's name has been pronounced over, if ye believe in His signs. What ails you that ye do not eat from what God's name is pronounced over, when He has detailed to you what is unlawful for you? Save what ye are forced to; but, verily, many will lead you astray by their fancies, without knowledge. Verily, thy Lord knows best the transgressors.

[120] Leave alone the outside of sin and the inside thereof; verily, those who earn sin shall be recompensed for what they have gained.

But eat not of what the name of God has not been pronounced over, for, verily, it is an abomination. Verily, the devils inspire their friends that they may wrangle with you; but if ye obey them, verily, ye are idolaters.

Is he who was dead and we have quickened him, and made for him a light, that he might walk therein amongst men, like him whose likeness is in the darkness whence he cannot come forth? Thus is made seemly to the misbelievers what they have done.

And thus have we placed in every town the great sinners thereof, that they may use craft therein; but they use not craft except against themselves, although they do not understand.

And when there comes to them a sign, they say, 'We will not believe until we are brought like what the apostles were brought;' God knows best where to put His message. There shall befall those who sin, meanness in God's eyes, and grievous torment for the craft they used.

[125] Whomsoever God wishes to guide, He expands his breast to Islâm; but whomsoever He wishes to lead astray, He makes his breast tight and straight, as though he would mount up into heaven[1]; thus does God set His horror on those who do not believe.

This is the way of thy Lord—straight. We have detailed the signs unto a mindful people; for them is an abode of peace; and their Lord, He is their patron for what they have done.

And on the day when He shall gather them all together, 'O assembly of the *g*inns! ye have got much out of mankind.' And their clients from among mankind shall say, 'O our Lord! much advantage had we one from another;' but we reached our appointed time which thou hadst appointed for us. Says He, 'The fire is your resort, to dwell therein for aye! save what God pleases; verily, thy Lord is wise and knowing.'

Thus do we make some of the unjust patrons of the others, for that which they have earned.

[130] O assembly of *g*inns and men! did there not come to you apostles from among yourselves, relating to you our signs, and warning you of the meeting of this very day of yours? They say, 'We bear witness against ourselves.' The life of this world deceived them, and they bear witness against themselves that they were unbelievers.

---

[1] That is, makes him appear as one who would attempt some great but impossible thing and fails therein.

That is because thy Lord would never destroy towns unjustly while their people are careless; but for every one are degrees of what they have done; and thy Lord is not careless of that which they do.

Thy Lord is rich, merciful; if He pleases He will take you off, and will cause what He pleases to succeed you; even as He raised you up from the seed of other people.

Verily, what ye are promised will surely come, nor can ye frustrate it.

[135] Say, 'O my people! act according to your power, verily, I am acting too; and soon shall ye know whose is the future of the abode!' verily, the unjust shall not prosper.

They set apart for God, from what He raises of tilth and of cattle, a portion, and they say, 'This is God's;'—as they pretend—'and this is for our associates [1];' but that which is for their associates reaches not to God, and that which was for God does reach to their associates;—evil is it what they judge [2].

Thus too have their associates made seemly to many of the idolaters the killing of their children [3],

---

[1] I.e. the idols.

[2] The pagan Arabs used to set apart certain of the produce of their fields to Allah the chief God, and other portions to minor deities of their pantheon. The fruits of the portion of the latter were reserved for the priests, who were careful to restore to their lot anything that might have fallen into that of Allah, but seldom troubled themselves to do the converse. This custom survives to a certain extent in the desert to the present day, where one tree in every district is devoted to patron saints, and allowed to grow untouched, although the others in the neighbourhood are hacked to pieces as food for camels.

[3] Alluding both to human sacrifices to idols and the cruel custom of burying female children alive. See Introduction.

to destroy them, and to obscure for them their religion [1]; but had God pleased they would not have done it, leave them alone and that which they have forged.

And they say, 'These cattle and tilth are inviolable; none shall taste thereof, save such as we please'—as they pretend—and there are cattle whose backs are prohibited, and cattle over whom God's name is not pronounced,—forging a lie against Him! He shall reward them for what they have forged.

[140] And they say, 'What is in the wombs of these cattle is unlawful for our wives, but if it be (born) dead, then are they partners therein.' He will reward them for their attribution; verily, He is wise and knowing.

Losers are they who kill their children foolishly, without knowledge, and who prohibit what God has bestowed upon them, forging a lie against God; they have erred and are not guided.

He it is who brought forth gardens with trailed [2] and untrailed vines, and the palms and corn land, with various food, and olives, and pomegranates, alike and unlike. Eat from the fruit thereof whene'er it fruits, and bring the dues thereof on the day of harvest, and be not extravagant; verily, He loves not the extravagant.

Of cattle are there some to ride on and to spread [3]. Eat of what God has bestowed upon you, and follow

---

[1] That is, to obscure what little trace it had of the original faith of Abraham the 'Hanîf.

[2] Trailed over an 'Arîsh, that is, a sort of hut made of boughs.

[3] That is, spread out when slaughtered, or from the hides and wool, &c., of which a bed (farsh) is made.

not the footsteps of Satan; verily, he is to you an open foe.

Eight pairs,—of sheep two, and of goats two; say, 'Are the two males unlawful, or the two females, or what the wombs of the two females contain? inform me with knowledge if ye tell the truth.' [145] And of camels two, and cows two; say, 'Are the two males unlawful, or the two females, or what the wombs of the two females contain? Were ye witnesses when God ordained for you these?—Then who is more unjust than he who devises a lie against God, to lead men astray without knowledge? verily, God guides not the unjust people[1].'

Say, 'I cannot find in what I am inspired with anything unlawful for the taster to taste; unless it be dead (of itself), or blood that has been shed, or the flesh of swine,—for that is a horror—or an abomination that is consecrated to other than God. But he who is forced, not wilfully nor transgressing,—then, verily, thy Lord is forgiving and merciful.'

To those who were Jews did we prohibit everything that hath a solid hoof; and of oxen and sheep did we prohibit to them the fat, save what the backs of both do bear, or the inwards, or what is mixed with bone; with that did we recompense them for their rebellion, for, verily, we are true.

And if they give thee the lie, say, 'Your Lord is of ample mercy, nor shall His violence be turned back from the sinful people.'

---

[1] The Arabs alternately made it unlawful to eat the males, and then the young of these four kinds of cattle. Mohammed in this passage shows the absurdity of their custom by pointing out the difficulty of deciding which is lawful and unlawful in the case of eight pairs.

Those who associate others with God will say, 'Had God pleased, we had not so associated, nor our fathers; nor should we have forbidden aught.' Thus did they give the lie to those who came before them, until they tasted of our violence! Say, 'Have ye any knowledge? if so, bring it forth to us: ye only follow suspicion, and ye do but conjecture.'

[150] Say, 'God's is the searching argument; and had He pleased He would have guided you all.'

Say, 'Come on then with your witnesses, who bear witness that God has prohibited these!' but if they do bear witness, bear thou not witness with them; nor follow the lust of those who say our signs are lies, and those who do not believe in the last day, or those who for their Lord make peers.

Say, 'Come! I will recite what your Lord has forbidden you, that ye may not associate aught with Him, and (may show) kindness to your parents, and not kill your children through poverty;—we will provide for you and them;—and draw not nigh to flagrant sins, either apparent or concealed, and kill not the soul, which God hath forbidden save by right[1]; that is what God ordains you, haply ye may understand.'

And draw not nigh unto the wealth of the orphan, save so as to better it, until he reaches full age; and give weight and measure with justice. We do not compel the soul save what it can compass; and when ye pronounce, then be just, though it be in the case of a relative.

And God's compact fulfil ye; that is what He

[1] That is, commit no homicide unless it be by legal execution or the slaying of infidels in war.

ordained you, haply ye may be mindful. Verily, this is my right way; follow it then, and follow not various paths, to separate yourselves from His way; that is what He has ordained you, haply ye may fear!

[155] Then we gave Moses the Book, complete for him who acts aright, and a decision and a guidance and a mercy; haply in the meeting of their Lord they will believe.

This is the Book which we have sent down; it is a blessing; follow it then and fear; haply ye may obtain mercy. Lest ye say, 'The Book was only sent down to two sects before us; verily, we, for what they read, care naught.' Or, lest ye should say, 'Had we had a book revealed to us we should surely have been more guided than they;' but there is come to them a manifest sign from their Lord, and a guidance and a mercy; who then is more unjust than he who calls God's signs lies, and turns from them? we will reward those who turn from our signs with an evil punishment for that they turned away.

What do they expect but that the angels should come for them, or that thy Lord should come, or that some signs[1] of thy Lord should come? On the day when some signs do come, its faith shall profit no soul which did not believe before, unless it has earned some good by its faith. Say, 'Wait ye expectant, then we wait expectant too.'

[160] Verily, those who divided their religion and became sects, thou hast not to do with them, their

[1] Signs of the approach of the day of judgment.

matter is in God's hands, He will yet inform them of that which they have done.

He who brings a good work shall have ten like it; but he who brings a bad work shall be recompensed only with the like thereof, for they shall not be wronged.

Say, 'As for me, my Lord has guided me to the right way, a right religion,—the faith of Abraham the 'Hanîf, for he was not of the idolaters.'

Say, 'Verily, my prayers and my devotion and my life and my death belong to God, the Lord of the worlds. He has no partner; that is what I am bidden; for I am first of those who are resigned.'

Say, 'Other than God shall I crave for a Lord when He is Lord of all?' but no soul shall earn aught save against itself[1]; nor shall one bearing a burden bear the burden of another; and then unto your Lord is your return, and He will inform you concerning that whereon ye do dispute.

[165] He it is who made you vicegerents, and raised some of you above others in degree, to try you by that which he has brought you;—verily, thy Lord is swift to punish, but, verily, He is forgiving and merciful.

[1] Not receive the recompense of other than persons' evil actions.

THE CHAPTER OF AL AARÂF[1].

(VII. Mecca.)

In the name of the merciful and compassionate God.

A. L. M. S. A book revealed to thee,—so let there be no straitness in thy breast, that thou mayest warn thereby,—and a reminder to the believers.

Follow what has been revealed to you from your Lord, and follow not beside Him patrons; little is it that ye mind.

Yet how many a town have we destroyed, and our violence came upon it by night, or while they slept at noon; and their cry, when our violence came upon them, was only to say, 'Verily, we were unjust!'
[5] But we will of a surety question those to whom the prophets were sent, and we will narrate to them with knowledge, for we were not absent. The balance on that day is true, and whosesoever scales are heavy, they are prosperous; but whosesoever scales are light, they it is who lose themselves, for that they did act unjustly by our signs.

We have established you in the earth, and we have made for you therein livelihoods; little is it that
ye thank; [10] and we created you, then we fashioned you, then we said unto the angels, 'Adore Adam,' and they adored, save Iblîs, who was not of those who did adore.

Said He, 'What hinders thee from adoring when

[1] The name of the bridge between heaven and hell described in this chapter.

I order thee?' he said, 'I am better than he; Thou hast created me from fire, and him Thou hast created out of clay.'

Said He, 'Then go down therefrom; what ails thee that thou shouldst be big with pride therein? go forth! verily, thou art of the little ones.'

He said, 'Respite me until the day when they shall be raised.' He said, 'Verily, thou art of the respited;' [15] said he, 'For that Thou hast led me into error, I will lie in wait for them in Thy straight path; then I will surely come to them, from before them and from behind them; and most of them Thou shalt not find thankful.' He said, 'Go forth therefrom, despised, expelled; whoso follows thee, I will surely fill hell with you altogether. But, O Adam, dwell thou and thy wife in Paradise and eat from whence ye will, but draw not nigh unto this tree or ye will be of the unjust.'

But Satan whispered to them to display to them what was kept back from them of their shame, and he said, 'Your Lord has only forbidden you this tree lest ye should be twain angels, or should become of the immortals;' [20] and he swore to them both, 'Verily, I am unto you a sincere adviser;' and he beguiled them by deceit, and when they twain tasted of the tree, their shame was shown them, and they began to stitch upon themselves the leaves of the garden. And their Lord called unto them, 'Did I not forbid you from that tree there, and say to you, Verily, Satan is to you an open foe?' They said, 'O our Lord! we have wronged ourselves—and if Thou dost not forgive us and have mercy on us, we shall surely be of those who are lost!' He said, 'Go ye down, one of you to the other a foe; but for you in the earth there is an abode, and a provision for a season.' He said, 'Therein shall ye live and therein shall ye die, from it shall ye be brought forth.'

[25] O sons of Adam! we have sent down to you garments wherewith to cover your shame, and plumage[1]; but the garment of piety, that is better. That is one of the signs of God, haply ye may remember.

O sons of Adam! let not Satan infatuate you as he drove your parents out of Paradise, stripping from them their garments, and showing them their shame; verily, he sees you—he and his tribe, from whence ye cannot see them. Verily, we have made the devils patrons of those who do not believe, and when they commit an abomination they say, 'We found our fathers at this, and God bade us do it.'

Say, 'God bids you not to do abomination; do ye say against God that which ye do not know?'

Say, 'My Lord bids only justice:—set steadfastly your faces at every mosque and pray to Him, being sincere in your religion. As He brought you forth in the beginning, shall ye return. A sect He guides, and for a sect of them was error due; verily, they did take the devils for their patrons instead of God, and they did count that they were guided.'

O sons of Adam! take your ornaments to every mosque[2]; and eat and drink, but do not be extravagant, for He loves not the extravagant.

[30] Say, 'Who has prohibited the ornaments of God which He brought forth for His servants, and the good things of His providing?' say, 'On the day of

[1] I. e. fine dresses.

[2] That is, wear your best apparel in the mosque.

judgment they shall only be for those who believed when in the life of this world[1].' Thus do we detail the signs unto a people that do know.

Say, 'My Lord has only prohibited abominable deeds, the apparent thereof and the concealed thereof, and sin, and greed for that which is not right, and associating with God what He has sent down no power for, and saying against God that which ye do not know.'

Every nation has its appointed time, and when their appointed time comes they cannot keep it back an hour, nor can they bring it on.

O sons of Adam! verily, there will come to you apostles from amongst you, narrating unto you my signs; then whoso fears God and does what is right, there is no fear for them, nor shall they grieve. But those who say my signs are lies, and who are too big with pride for them, these are the fellows of the Fire, they shall dwell therein for aye!

[35] Who is more unjust than he who devises against God a lie, or says His signs are lies? These, their portion of the Book shall reach them[2], until when our messengers come to take their souls away, and say, 'Where is what ye used to call upon instead of God?' they say, 'They have strayed away from us;' and they shall bear witness against themselves that they have been misbelievers.

He will say, 'Enter ye—amongst the nations who

[1] Whereas now idolaters share in the good things of this world; but on the day of judgment those only shall enjoy them who were believers here.

[2] That is, they shall have whatever portion of good or evil is written for them in the book of their fate.

have passed away before you, both of ginns[1] and men —into the fire;' whenever a nation enters therein, it curses its mate[2]; until, when they have all reached it, the last of them will say unto the first, 'O our Lord! these it was who led us astray, give them double torment of the fire!' He will say, 'To each of you double! but ye do not know.' And the first of them will say unto the last, 'Ye have no preference over us, so taste ye the torment for that which ye have earned!'

Verily, those who say our signs are lies and are too big with pride for them; for these the doors of heaven shall not be opened, and they shall not enter into Paradise until a camel shall pass into a needle's eye.

It is thus that we reward the sinners; for them is a couch of hell-fire, with an awning above them! thus do we reward the unjust!

[40] But those who believe and do what is right— we will not oblige a soul more than its capacity —they are the fellows of Paradise, they shall dwell therein for aye.

We will strip away what ill feeling is in their breasts—there shall flow beneath them rivers, and they shall say, 'Praise belongs to God who guided us to this! for we should not have been guided had not God guided us!—the apostles of our Lord did come to us with truth!' And it shall be cried out to them, 'This is Paradise which ye have as an inheritance for that which ye have done!' And the fellows of Paradise will call out to the fellows of the Fire, 'We have now found that what our Lord promised us is true; have ye found that what your

[1] See p. 127, note 2. [2] Literally, his sister.

Lord promised you is true?' They will say, 'Yea!' And a crier from amongst them will cry out, 'The curse of God is on the unjust who turn from the way of God and crave to make it crooked, while in the hereafter they do disbelieve!'

And betwixt the two there is a veil, and on al Aarâf are men who know each by marks; and they shall cry out to the fellows of Paradise, 'Peace be upon you!' they cannot enter it although they so desire.
[45] But when their sight is turned towards the fellows of the Fire, they say, 'O our Lord! place us not with the unjust people.' And the fellows on al Aarâf will cry out to the men whom they know by their marks, and say, 'Of no avail to you were your collections, and what ye were so big with pride about; are these those ye swore that God would not extend mercy to? Enter ye Paradise; there is no fear for you, nor shall ye be grieved.'

But the fellows of the Fire shall cry out to the fellows of Paradise, 'Pour out upon us water, or something of what God has provided you with[1].' They will say, 'God has prohibited them both to those who misbelieve; who took their religion for a sport and a play; whom the life of the world beguiled.'—To-day do we forget them as they forgot the meeting of this day, and for that they did deny our signs!

[50] Now we have brought them a book explaining it in knowledge, a guidance and a mercy to a people who believe.

Do they wait now for aught but its interpretation?—on the day when its interpretation shall come,

[1] The fruits of Paradise.

those who forgot it before will say, There did come to us the apostles of our Lord in truth, have we intercessors to intercede for us? or, could we return, we would do otherwise than we did.' They have lost themselves, and that which they devised has strayed away from them.

Verily, your Lord is God who created the heavens and the earth in six days; then He made for the Throne[1]. He covers night with the day—it pursues it incessantly—and the sun and the moon and the stars are subject to His bidding. Aye!—His is the creation and the bidding,—blessed be God the Lord of the worlds!

Call on your Lord humbly and secretly, verily, He loves not the transgressors. And do not evil in the earth after it has been righted; and call upon Him with fear and earnestness; verily, the mercy of God is nigh unto those who do well.

[55] He it is who sends forth the winds as heralds before His mercy; until when they lift the heavy cloud which we drive to a dead land, and send down thereon water, and bring forth therewith every kind of fruit;—thus do we bring forth the dead; haply ye may remember.

And the good land brings forth its vegetation by the permission of its Lord; and that which is vile brings forth naught but scarcity. Thus do we turn about our signs for a people who are grateful.

We did send Noah unto his people, and he said, 'O my people! serve God, ye have no god but Him; verily, I fear for you the torment of the mighty day.' Said the chiefs of his people, 'Verily,

[1] The highest heaven is so called.

we do surely see you in obvious error.' Said he, 'O my people! there is no error in me; but I am an apostle from the Lord of the worlds. [60] I preach to you the messages of my Lord, and I give you sincere advice; and I know from God what ye know not. What! do ye wonder that there came to you a reminder from your Lord by a man from amongst yourselves, to warn you, and that ye may fear? but haply ye may receive mercy.'

But they called him a liar, and we rescued him and those who were with him in the ark; and we drowned those who said our signs were lies, verily, they were a blind people.

And unto 'Âd[1] (we sent) their brother Hûd[2], who said, 'O my people! serve God, ye have no god save Him; what! will ye not then fear?' Said the chiefs of those who misbelieved amongst his people, 'Verily, we see thee in folly, and, verily, we certainly think thou art of the liars.' [65] He said, 'O my people! there is no folly in me; but I am an apostle from the Lord of the worlds; I preach to you the messages of your Lord; and, verily, I am to you a faithful adviser. What! do ye then wonder that there comes to you a reminder from your Lord by a man from amongst yourselves, to warn you? remember when He made you vicegerents after Noah's people and increased you in length of stature; remember, then, the benefits of God,—

[1] An extinct tribe of the ancient Arabs.

[2] Hûd and Thamûd, both mentioned in the works of Ptolemy, were two tribes of the ancient Arabs, extinct in Mohammed's time, whose disappearance had been attributed, by popular tradition, to divine vengeance.

haply ye may prosper!' They said, 'Hast thou come to us that we may worship God alone, and leave what our fathers used to worship? then bring us what thou dost threaten us with, if thou art of those who tell the truth!' He said, 'There shall fall upon you from your Lord horror and wrath; do ye wrangle with me about names, which ye and your fathers have named yourselves, for which God sent down no power; wait then expectant, and I with you will wait expectant too! [70] But we rescued him and those with him, by mercy from ourselves, and we cut off the hindermost parts of those who said our signs were lies and who were not believers.'

Unto Thamûd (we sent) their brother Zâli'h, who said, 'O my people! worship God; ye have no god but Him: there has come to you a manifest sign from your Lord. This she-camel of God's is a sign for you; leave her then to eat in the land of God, and touch her not with evil, or there will overtake you grievous woe. And remember how he made you vicegerents after 'Âd and stablished you in the earth, so that ye took for yourselves castles on its plains and hewed out mountains into houses[1]; and remember the benefits of God, and waste not the land, despoiling it.' Said the chiefs of those who were big with pride from amongst his people to those who were weak,—to those amongst them who believed, 'Do ye know that Zâli'h is sent from his Lord?' They said, 'We do believe in that with which he is sent.' Said those who were big with pride, 'Verily, in what ye do believe we disbelieve.'

[1] Referring to the numerous excavated rock-dwellings in Idumaea.

[75] Then they did hamstring the camel, and rebelled against the bidding of their Lord and said, 'O Zâli'h! bring us what thou didst threaten us with, if thou art of those who are sent.' Then the earthquake took them, and in the morning they lay prone in their dwellings; and he turned away from them and said, 'O my people! I did preach to you the message of my Lord, and I gave you good advice! but ye love not sincere advisers[1].'

[1] All that has been hitherto written about the legend Zâli'h and his camel is pure conjecture; the native commentators add nothing but a few marvellous details to the story as given in the Qur'ân, and the European annotators can only suggest possible identifications for Zâli'h himself, such as the Schelah of Gen. xi. 13. My own view of the matter is of course an hypothesis too, but it has at least some circumstantial evidence in its favour; it is embodied in the following extract from my 'Desert of the Exodus,' p. 50: 'Near El Watíyeh is situated the tomb of Nebi Sáleh, a wretched little building, but accounted by the Bedawin one of the most sacred spots on the Peninsula (of Sinai). Hither they resort in great numbers at certain seasons of the year to perform ceremonies and sacrificial rites. Who and what was Nebi Sáleh, "the Prophet Sáleh," or, as his name implies, "the Righteous Prophet"? A great saint with the Bedawin, perhaps the ancestor of the Sawáliheh tribe, who are named after him; but this explanation is vague and unsatisfactory, and in the absence of any certain information on the subject I will venture to propound a theory. I must premise that near the summit of Jebel Musa is a peculiar mark in the stone which has a strong resemblance to the imprint of a camel's foot. It is regarded by the Bedawin with great veneration, and the girls, when tending their flocks on the mountains, often milk their goats into it as a sure means of obtaining increase and prosperity. This mark is called Athar Nágat en Nebí, "the footprint of the Prophet's She-camel." It is generally taken for granted that the Prophet in question is Mohammed, but to my mind there are several circumstances which seem to connect the Nebi Sáleh of the tomb with the prophet of the legend. A Bedawin's notions of the separate identity of Moses, Elias, and Sáleh are of the vaguest

And Lot, when he said to his people, 'Do ye approach an abomination which no one in all the world ever anticipated you in? verily, ye approach men with lust rather than women—nay, ye are a people who exceed.' [80] But his people's answer only was to say, 'Turn them out of your village, verily, they are a people who pretend to purity.' But we saved him and his people, except his wife, who was of those who lingered; and we rained down upon them a rain;—see then how was the end of the sinners!

And unto Midian did we send their brother

---

kind, and if asked to which of his national saints the camel belonged you will find that he has never even thought of the question at all. There is no point in attributing the mysterious footprint to the camel of Mohammed, for the celebrated "night journey" to heaven, the Prophet's only recorded aeronautic trip, was performed on Borák, a creature with the feet of a mule. But Mohammed has a legend in the Qur'ân of a certain "Nebi Sáleh," who was sent as a prophet to the people of Thamûd, and whose divine mission was attested by the production of a she-camel from the rock. The author of "El Islám" certainly did visit the Sinaitic mountains, and may in all probability have taken the story from the national traditions of the Peninsula. The origin and history of Nebi Sáleh is quite unknown to the present Bedawin inhabitants, but they nevertheless regard him with more national veneration than even Moses himself. I should therefore conclude that the Nebi Sáleh of the tomb in Wády es Sheikh, the prophet of the camel's footprint, and the Sáleh of the Qur'ân are identical, and that the "people of Thamûd" are the Saracen inhabitants of Sinai, who preceded the Mohammedan invasion. Who then was Nebi Sáleh? Looking at the veneration in which his memory is held, and at the character of the miracle attributed to him--the rock smitten with a rod, and a live camel, the greatest of Bedawin blessings, miraculously produced therefrom—with the subsequent rebellion of the people for whom the Prophet worked the sign, I fancy we may recognise in the tradition a distorted reminiscence of the Israelitish lawgiver himself.'

Sho'hâib [1], who said, 'O my people! serve God, ye
have no god save Him. There has come to you
a manifest sign from your Lord; then give good
weight and measure, and be not niggardly of your
gifts to men, and do not evil in the earth after it has
been righted. That is better for you if ye are
believers; and sit not down in every path, threaten-
ing and turning from the path of God those who
believe in Him, and craving to make it crooked.
Remember when ye were few and He multiplied
you; and see what was the end of the evildoers! [85]
And if there be a party of you who believe in what
I am sent with, and a party who believe not, then
wait patiently until God judges between us, for He
is the best of judges.' Said the crowd of those who
were big with pride amongst His people, 'We will
of a surety turn thee out, O Sho'hâib! and those who
believe with thee, from our village; or else thou
shalt return unto our faith.' Said he, 'What even
if we be averse therefrom? We shall have devised
a lie against God if we return unto your faith, after
God has saved us from it; and what should ail us
that we should return thereto, unless that God our
Lord should please? our Lord embraces everything
in His knowledge;—on God do we rely. O our
Lord! open between us and between our people in
truth, for Thou art the best of those who open [2].'
And the chiefs of those who disbelieved amongst

---

[1] The Jethro of the Bible.

[2] That is, 'give us a chance,' the idiom is still current in modern parlance. A shopkeeper, for instance, who has not sold anything all day, or who refuses a bargain, always says yefta'h'allah, 'never mind! God will give me a chance of selling it.'

his people said, 'If ye follow Sho'hâib, verily, ye shall be the losers;' then there took them the earthquake, and in the morning they lay in their dwellings prone. [90] Those who called Sho'hâib a liar, (were) as though they had not dwelt therein!—Those who called Sho'hâib a liar, they were the losers then! And he turned away from them and said, 'O my people! I preached to you the messages of my Lord, and I gave you good advice; how should I be vexed for a people who do misbelieve?'

We have not sent unto a city any prophet except we overtook the people thereof with trouble and distress, that haply they might humble themselves; and then did we give them, in exchange for evil, good, until they increased and said, 'Distress and joy both touched our fathers;' then we overtook them suddenly ere they could perceive.—Had the people of the town but believed and feared, we would have opened up for them blessings from the heavens and from the earth; but they said it was a lie, so we overtook them for that which they had earned.

[95] Were the people of these cities then secure that our violence would not come on them by night, while they slept? were the people of these cities secure that our violence would not come on them in the morning whilst they played? were they secure from the craft of God? none feel secure from the craft of God except a people that shall lose.

Is it not shown to those who inherit the earth after its (former) people, that, did we please, we would smite[1] them in their sins, and would set a stamp upon their hearts, and then they should not hear?

[1] The word is used of an arrow that hits a mark, and hence of any sudden calamity that falls on a man.

These cities, we do relate to thee their stories. There came to them our apostles with manifest signs; but they did not at all believe in what they called a lie before.—Thus doth God set a stamp upon the hearts of those who misbelieve.

[100] Nor did we find in most of them a covenant; but we did find most of them workers of abomination.

Then we raised up after them Moses with our signs to Pharaoh and his chiefs; but they dealt unjustly therewith, and see what was the end of the evildoers!

Moses said, 'O Pharaoh! verily, I am an apostle from the Lord of the worlds; it is not right for me to speak against God aught but the truth. I have come to you with a manifest sign from my Lord; send then the children of Israel with me.' Said he, 'If thou hast come with a sign, then bring it, if thou art of those who speak the truth.' Then he threw
his rod down, and lo! it was an obvious snake; [105]
and he drew out his hand, and lo! it was white to the beholders. Said the chiefs of Pharaoh's people, 'Verily, this is surely a knowing magician; he desires to turn you out of your land;—what is it then ye bid?' They said, 'Give him and his brother some hope; and send into the cities to collect and bring you
every knowing magician.' [110] And the magician
came to Pharaoh and said, 'Is there indeed a reward for us if we are conquerors?' He said, 'Yea! and ye shall be of those who draw nigh unto me.' They said, 'O Moses! wilt thou cast down (thy rod) or shall we be (first) to throw?' Said he, 'Throw down;' and when they threw down, they did enchant the people's eyes, and made them dread, and brought a

mighty magic. But we inspired Moses (saying), 'Throw down thy rod, and it will gulp down that which they devise;' [115] and the truth stood fast, and vain was that which they had done; and they were conquered there, and turned back feeling small! and the magicians threw themselves down adoring. Said they, 'We believe in the Lord of the worlds, the Lord of Moses and Aaron!' [120] Said Pharaoh, 'Do ye believe in him ere I give you leave? This is craft which ye have devised in the land, to turn its people out therefrom, but soon shall ye know! I will cut off your hands and your feet from opposite sides, then I will crucify you altogether!' They said, 'Verily, we unto our Lord return! nor dost thou take vengeance on us, save for that we believe in the signs of our Lord, when they come to us.

'O our Lord! pour out upon us patience, and take us to Thyself resigned [1].' And the chiefs of Pharaoh's people said, 'Will ye leave Moses and his people to do evil in the land, and to leave thee and thy gods?' Said he, 'We will have their sons slain and their women we will let live, for, verily, we are triumphant over them.'

[125] Said Moses unto his people, 'Ask for aid from God and be patient; verily, the earth is God's! He gives it for an inheritance to whom He pleases of His servants, and the future is for those who fear.' They said, 'We have been hurt before thou didst come to us, and since thou hast come to us.' Said he, 'It may be that your Lord will destroy your foe, and will make you succeed him in the earth; and He will see how ye act.'

---

[1] Or, cause us to die Moslems.

We had overtaken Pharaoh's people with the years (of dearth) and scarcity of fruits, that haply they might remember; but when there came to them a good thing they said, 'This is ours;' and if there befel them an evil, they took the augury from Moses and those with him;—is not their augury only in God's hands?—but most of them know not.

And they said, 'Whatever thou dost bring us as a sign to enchant us therewith, yet will we not believe in thee.'

[130] Then we sent upon them the flood and the locusts and the lice and the frogs and the blood,—signs detailed; but they were big with pride and were a people who did sin.

And when there fell upon them the plague, they said, 'O Moses! call upon thy Lord for us, as He has covenanted with thee; verily, if thou dost remove the plague from us, we will believe in thee; and we will assuredly send with thee the children of Israel.' But when we removed from them the plague until the appointed time which they should reach, lo! then they broke their promise. But we took vengeance on them, and we drowned them in the sea, for that they said our signs were lies and were careless thereof. And we gave as an inheritance unto the people who had been weak, the eastern quarters of the earth and the western quarters thereof, which we had blest; and the good word of thy Lord was fulfilled on the children of Israel, for that they were patient; and we destroyed that which Pharaoh and his people had made and that which they had piled[1]. And with the children of Israel

[1] The word y'arishûn is properly used of making wooden huts,

we passed across the sea; and they came unto a people devoted to their idols, and said, 'O Moses! make for us a god as they have gods.' Said he, 'Verily, ye are ignorant people.'
[135] Verily, these —destroyed shall be that which they are given to; and vain is that which they have done.

He said, 'Other than God then do ye crave for a god, when He has preferred you above the worlds?'

And when we saved you from Pharaoh's people who wrought you evil woe, killing your sons, and letting your women live; and in that was a mighty trial from your Lord.

And we appointed for Moses thirty nights, and completed them with ten (more), so that the time appointed by his Lord was completed to forty nights. And Moses said unto his brother Aaron, 'Be thou my vicegerent amongst my people, and do what is right, and follow not the path of the evildoers.'

And when Moses came to our appointment, and his Lord spake unto him, he said, 'O my Lord! show me, —that I may look on thee!' He said, 'Thou canst not see me; but look upon the mountain, and if it remain steady in its place, thou shalt see me;' but when his Lord appeared unto the mountain He made it dust, and Moses fell down in a swoon!

[140] And when he came to himself, he said, 'Celebrated be thy praise! I turn repentant unto Thee, and I am the first of those who are resigned.'

He said, 'O Moses! verily, I have chosen thee over the people with my messages and my words, take then what I have brought thee, and be of those

but is here applied to any structures, especially the massive temples and other piles of Egyptian buildings.

who thank.' And we wrote for him upon tablets an admonition concerning everything, and a detailing of everything: 'Take them then with firmness, and bid thy people take them for what is best thereof. I will show you the abode of those who work abominations; I will turn from my signs those who are big with pride in the earth without right; and if they see every sign they shall not believe therein, and if they see the path of rectitude they shall not take it for a path; but if they see the path of error they shall take it for a path;—that is because they have said our signs are lies and have been careless of them.'

[145] But those who say our signs and the meeting of the last day are lies,—vain are their works: shall they be rewarded save for that which they have done?

And Moses' people after him took to themselves of their ornaments a corporeal calf that lowed[1]; did they not see that it could not speak with them, nor could it guide them in the path? They took it and they were unjust; but when they bit their hands with fruitless rage and saw that they had gone astray, they said, 'Verily, if our Lord have not compassion on us and forgive us we shall surely be of those who lose!'

And when Moses returned unto his people angry and grieved, he said, 'Evil is it that ye have done after me! Would ye hasten on the bidding of your Lord?' and he threw down the tablets and took his brother by the head to drag him towards him, but he said, 'O son of my mother! verily, the people

---

[1] This is also a Talmudic legend.

weakened me and well-nigh killed me; make not then mine enemies glad about me, and put me not with the unjust people.'
[150] He said, 'O Lord! pardon me and my brother, and let us enter into Thy mercy; for Thou art the most merciful of the merciful. Verily, these have taken to themselves a calf; there shall reach them wrath from their Lord, and abasement in the life of this world; for thus do we reward those who forge a lie. But those who have done bad works, and then turn again after them and believe,—verily, thy Lord, after that, is forgiving and merciful.'

And when Moses' wrath calmed down he took the tables, in the inscription of which was guidance and mercy for those who dread their Lord.

And Moses chose from his people seventy men for our appointment; and when the earthquake took them he said, 'O my Lord! hadst Thou willed, Thou hadst destroyed them before and me. Wilt Thou destroy us for what the fools amongst us have done? This is naught but Thy trial, wherewith Thou dost lead astray whom Thou pleasest and guidest whom Thou pleasest; Thou art our patron! forgive us and have mercy on us, for Thou art the best of those who do forgive!

[155] 'And write down for us in this world good, and in the future too; verily, we are guided unto Thee.' He said, 'My punishment—with it I fall on whom I will; and my mercy embraceth everything; and I will write it down for those who fear, and who give alms, and those who in our signs believe,—who follow the Apostle—the illiterate prophet [1], whom

[1] Or, the apostle of the Gentiles.

they find written down with them in the law and the gospel, bidding them what is reasonable and forbidding them what is wrong, and making lawful for them what is good, and making unlawful evil things; and setting down for them their burdens and the yokes which were upon them;—to those who believe in him and aid him and help him and follow the law which has been sent down with him—they shall be the prosperous.'

Say, 'O ye folk! verily, I am the Apostle of God unto you all,'—of Him whose is the kingdom of the heavens and the earth, there is no god but He! He quickens and He kills! believe then in God and His Apostle, the illiterate prophet,—who believes in God and in His words—then follow him that haply ye may be guided.

Amongst Moses' people is a nation guided in truth, and thereby act they justly.

[160] And we cut them up into twelve tribes, each a nation; and we revealed unto Moses, when his people asked him for drink, 'Strike with thy staff the rock!' and there gushed forth from it twelve springs, each folk knew their drinking place. And we overshadowed them with the cloud; and sent down upon them the manna and the quails, 'Eat of the good things we have provided you with!'—Yet they did not wrong us, but it was themselves they wronged.

And when it was said unto them, 'Dwell in this city and eat therefrom as ye will, and say 'hi*tt*atun and enter the gate adoring; so will we pardon you your sins;—we will increase those who do well.' But those amongst them who did wrong changed it for another word than which was said to them; and we sent upon them a plague from heaven for that they were unjust.

Ask them too about the city which stood by the sea, when they transgressed upon the Sabbath; when their fish came to them on the Sabbath day sailing straight up to them; but on the days when they kept not the Sabbath, they came not to them, thus did we try them for the abominations that they wrought[1].

And when a nation from amongst them said, 'Why do ye warn a people whom God would destroy, or punish with severe torment?' they said, 'As an excuse to your Lord, that haply they may fear.' [165] But when they forgot what they had been reminded of, we saved those who forbade evil, but we overtook those who did wrong with punishment;—evil was the abomination that they did, but when they rebelled against what they were forbidden, we said to them, 'Become ye apes, despised and spurned!' and then thy Lord proclaimed that He would surely send against them till the resurrection day, those who should wreak them evil torment; verily, thy Lord is quick at following up, but, verily, He is forgiving, merciful.

We cut them up in the earth into nations. Of them are the righteous, and of them are the reverse of that; we have tried them with good things and with bad things; haply they may return.

But there succeeded them successors who inherited the Book! They take the goods of this lower world and say, 'It will be forgiven us.' But if the like goods came to them they would take them too! Was there not taken from them a covenant by

[1] Cf. Chapter II, 61.

the Book, that they should not say against God aught but the truth? Yet they study therein! But the abode of the future life is better for those who fear—do ye not then understand? But those who hold fast by the Book and are steadfast in prayer—verily, we will not waste the hire of those who do right.

[170] And when we shook the mountain over them, as though it were a shadow, and they thought it would fall upon them (saying), 'Take ye what we have given you with firmness, and remember what is therein; haply ye may fear.'

And when thy Lord took from the children of Adam out of their loins their seed, and made them bear witness against themselves, 'Am I not your Lord?' They said, 'Yea! we do bear witness'—lest ye should say on the day of resurrection, 'Verily, for this we did not care;' or say, 'Verily, our fathers associated others with God before us, and we were but their seed after them: wilt Thou then destroy us for what vaindoers did?'—Thus do we detail the signs; haply they may return.

Read to them the declaration of him to whom we brought our signs, and who stepped away therefrom, and Satan followed him, and he was of those who were beguiled[1]. [175] Had we pleased we would have exalted him thereby, but he crouched upon the earth and followed his lust, and his likeness was as the likeness of a dog, whom if thou shouldst attack

---

[1] Said to refer to Balaam, but also to several pretenders of prophecy amongst the Arabians. By some it is referred to 'Omâiyyat ibn Abi Zalt, or to a certain Jewish Rabbi, who had prophesied the coming of a prophet about Mohammed's time, but would not acknowledge the latter as such.

he hangs out his tongue, or if thou should leave him, hangs out his tongue too. That is the likeness of the people who say our signs are lies. Tell them then these tales—haply they may reflect.

Evil is the likeness of a people who say our signs are lies; themselves it is they wrong!

We have created for hell many of the *g*inn and of mankind; they have hearts and they discern not therewith; they have eyes and they see not therewith; they have ears and they hear not therewith; they are like cattle, nay, they go more astray! these it is who care not.

But God's are the good names; call on Him then thereby, and leave those who pervert His names[1]; they shall be rewarded for that which they have done.

[180] And of those whom we have created is a nation who are guided in truth and thereby act with equity; but they who say our signs are lies, we will bring them down by degrees from whence they know not. I will let them range;—verily, my stratagem is efficacious!

Do they not then reflect that their companion[2] is not possessed[3]? he is but an obvious warner! Do they not behold the kingdoms of the heavens and of the earth, and what things God has created, and (see that), it may be, their time is already drawing nigh? in what relation then will they believe? [185] He

[1] The word yul'hidûna is used in the later Arabic for any form of atheism. The expression in the text means the perversion, as Mohammed called it, of the name Allâh in the names of the other gods, such as Allât, the feminine form of the same word.

[2] Mohammed.

[3] Literally, under the influence of the *g*inn.

whom God leads astray there is no guide for him! He leaves them in their rebellion, blindly wandering on.

They will ask you about the Hour, for what time it is fixed?—say, 'The knowledge thereof is only with my Lord; none shall manifest it at its time but He; it is heavy in the heavens and the earth, it will not come to you save on a sudden.'

They will ask as though thou wert privy to it, say, 'The knowledge thereof is only with God,'—but most folk do not know.

Say, 'I cannot control profit or harm for myself, save what God will. If I knew the unseen I should surely have much that is good, nor would evil touch me; I am but a warner and a herald of good tidings unto a people who believe.'

He it is who created you from one soul, and made therefrom its mate to dwell therewith; and when he covered her she bore a light burden and went about therewith; but when it grew heavy they called on God, Lord of them both, 'Surely if thou givest us a rightly-shaped child we shall of a surety be of those who thank.' [190] And when He gave them both a rightly-shaped child they joined partners with Him for that which He had given them, but exalted be God above that which they associate with Him [1]. Will they associate with Him those who cannot create aught,

---

[1] This story is said to refer to Adam and Eve; the act of idolatry mentioned being the naming of their first son, at the instigation of Satan, 'Abd el 'Hareth, 'servant of 'Hareth,' instead of 'servant of God,' 'Hareth being Satan's name among the angels. The legend arose probably from a misunderstanding of the title given to Cain in the Bible, 'Obed Adâma, 'a tiller of the ground,' which would read word for word in Arabic 'Abd el 'Hareth.

but are themselves created, which have no power to help them, and cannot even help themselves?

But if ye call them unto guidance they will not follow you. It is the same to them if Thou dost call them or if Thou dost hold thy tongue.

Those whom ye call on other than God are servants like yourselves. Call on them then, and let them answer you, if so be ye tell the truth! Have they feet to walk with? or have they hands to hold with? or have they eyes to see with? or have they ears to hear with? Call upon your partners; then plot against me, and do not wait.

[195] Verily, my patron is God, who hath sent down the Book, and He is the patron of the righteous. But those whom ye call on beside Him cannot help you, nor can they even help themselves. But if ye call them unto the guidance they will not hear, thou mayest see them looking towards thee, yet they do not see. Take to pardon, and order what is kind, and shun the ignorant; and if an incitement from the devil incites you, then seek refuge in God: verily, He both hears and knows.

[200] Verily, those who fear God, if a wraith from the devil touch, mention Him, and lo! they see[1].

And their brethren he shall increase in error, then they shall not desist.

Shouldst Thou not bring them a sign[2] they say, 'Hast Thou not yet made choice of one?' Say, 'I only follow what is inspired to me by my Lord.

---

[1] I. e. if an evil suggestion occurs to them, they mention God's name and immediately see the folly and wickedness thereof.

[2] That is, a verse in the Qur'ân.

These are perceptions from my Lord, and a guidance and a mercy to a people who believe.'

And when the Qur'ân is read, then listen thereto and keep silence; haply ye may obtain mercy.

And remember thy Lord within thyself humbly and with fear, not openly in words, in the morning and in the evening; and be not of those who do not care. [205] Verily, they who are with my Lord are not too big with pride for His service, but they do celebrate His praise, and Him they do adore.

The Chapter of the Spoils.

(VIII. Medînah.)

In the name of the merciful and compassionate God.

They will ask thee about the spoils. Say, 'The spoils are God's and the Apostle's; fear God and settle it amongst yourselves; obey God and the Apostle if ye do believe.'

Verily, the believers are those who, when God's name is mentioned, their hearts sink with fear; and when His signs are rehearsed to them they increase them in faith; and on their Lord do they rely; who are steadfast in prayer, and of what we have bestowed upon them give in alms; these are in truth believers; to them are degrees with their Lord, and forgiveness, and a generous provision.

[5] As thy Lord caused thee to go forth from thy house[1] with the truth, although a sect of the believers were averse therefrom. They wrangled with thee about the truth after it was made plain, as

[1] At Medînah.

though they were being driven on to death and looked thereon; and when God promised you that one of the two troops should be yours, and ye would fain have had those who had no arms. God wished to prove the truth true by His words, and to cut off the hindermost parts of those who misbelieve—to prove the truth true, and to make vain the vain, although the sinners are averse[1].

When ye asked for succour from your Lord, and He answered you, 'I will assist you with a thousand angels, with others in reserve.'

[10] God made it only glad tidings to quiet your hearts therewith; for victory is only from God! verily, God is mighty and wise.

When drowsiness covered you as a security from Him, and He sent down upon you from the heavens water to purify you withal, and to take away from you the plague of Satan, and to tie up your hearts and to make firm your footsteps[2].

When your Lord inspired the angels—'Verily, I am with you; make ye firm then those who believe; I will cast dread into the hearts of those who misbelieve,—strike off their necks then, and strike off from them every finger tip.'

---

[1] The occasion alluded to was one when Mohammed had made preparations for attacking an unarmed caravan on its way from Syria to Mecca, when Abu Sufiân, who was in charge of it, sent to Mecca and obtained an escort of nearly a thousand men; many of Mohammed's followers wished to attack the caravan only, but the prophet and his immediate followers were for throwing themselves on the escort.

[2] The Muslims were fewer in number than the enemy, and the latter had command of the water, at both of which circumstances their hearts sank. In the night, however, rain fell, refreshed them and supplied their wants.

That is, because they went into opposition against God and His Apostle; for he who goes into opposition against God and His Apostle—verily, God is keen to punish.

There, taste it! since for the misbelievers is the torment of the Fire.

[15] O ye who believe! when ye meet those who misbelieve in swarms, turn not to them your hinder parts; for he who turns to them that day his hinder parts, save turning to fight or rallying to a troop, brings down upon himself wrath from God, and his resort is hell, and an ill journey shall it be!

Ye did not slay them, but it was God who slew them; nor didst thou shoot when thou didst shoot, but God did shoot [1], to try the believers from Himself with a goodly trial; verily, God both hears and knows. There! verily, God weakens the stratagem of the misbelievers.

If ye wish [2] the matter to be decided, a decision has now come to you; but if ye desist, it is better for you; and if ye turn back we will turn too, and your troop shall avail nothing, great in number though it be, since God is with the believers!

[20] O ye who believe! obey God and His Apostle, and turn not from Him while ye hear, and be not like those who say, 'We hear,' and yet they hear not.

Verily, the worst of beasts in God's sight are the deaf, the dumb who do not understand. Had God

---

[1] Alluding to the alleged miracle of the gravel thrown into the eyes of the Qurâis at the battle of Bedr, to which the Muslim victory was due.

[2] An address to the Meccans who, when threatened with an attack from Mohammed, took sanctuary in the Kaabah, and prayed to God that if they were right He would help them, but that if Mohammed was in the right He would help him.

known any good in them, He would have made them hear; but had He made them hear, they would have turned back and have swerved aside.

O ye who believe! answer God and His Apostle when He calls you to that which quickens you; and know that God steps in between man and his heart; and that to Him ye shall be gathered. [25] And fear temptation, which will not light especially on those of you who have done wrong; but know that God is keen to punish.

Remember when ye were few in number and weak in the land, fearing lest people should snatch you away; then He sheltered you and aided you with victory, and provided you with good things; haply ye may give thanks.

O ye who believe! be not treacherous to God and His Apostle; nor be treacherous to your engagement while ye know!

Know that your wealth and your children are but a temptation, and that God—with Him is mighty hire!

O ye who believe! if ye fear God He will make for you a discrimination[1], and will cover for you your offences, and will forgive you; for God is Lord of mighty grace.

[30] And when those who misbelieve were crafty with thee to detain thee a prisoner, or kill thee, or drive thee forth; they were crafty, but God was crafty too, for God is best of crafty ones!

But when our verses were rehearsed to them they said, 'We have already heard.—If we pleased we could speak like this; verily, this is nothing but tales of those of yore.'

[1] Here used in the sense of victory.

When they said, 'O God! if this be truth, and from Thee, then rain upon us stones from heaven or bring us grievous woe!'

But God would not torment them while thou art amongst them; nor was God going to torment them while they asked Him to forgive. But what ails them that God should not torment them while they turn folk away from the Holy Mosque, though they are not the guardians thereof—its guardians are only the pious?—but most of them know not.

[35] Their prayer at the House was naught but whistling and clapping hands!—taste then the torment for that ye misbelieved!

Verily, those who misbelieve expend their wealth to turn folk from the path of God; but they shall spend it, and then it shall be for them sighing, and then they shall be overcome! Those who misbelieve, into hell shall they be gathered!—that God may distinguish the vile from the good, and may put the vile, some on the top of the other, and heap all up together, and put it into hell!—These are those who lose!

Say to those who misbelieve, if they desist they will be forgiven what is past; but if they return,—the course of those of former days has passed away[1].

[40] Fight them then that there should be no sedition, and that the religion may be wholly God's; but if they desist, then God on what they do doth look. But if they turn their backs, then know that God is your Lord; a good Lord is He, and a good help; and know that whenever ye seize anything as

[1] That is, they have the doom of former people as a warning and an example.

a spoil, to God belongs a fifth thereof, and to His Apostle, and to kindred and orphans, and the poor and the wayfarer; if ye believe in God and what we have revealed unto our servants on the day of the discrimination,—the day when the two parties met; and God is mighty over all. When ye were on the near side of the valley, and they were on the far side, and the camels were below you; had ye made an appointment then[1] ye would have failed to keep your appointment—but it was that God might accomplish a thing that was as good as done! that he who was to perish might perish with a manifest sign; and that he who was to live might live with a manifest sign; for, verily, God hears and knows!

[45] When God showed thee them in thy dream as though they were but few; but had He shown thee them as though they were many, ye would have been timid, and ye would have quarrelled about the matter; —but God preserved you; verily, He knows the nature of men's breasts!

And when He showed them to you, as ye encountered them, as few in your eyes; and made you seem few in their eyes; that God might accomplish a thing that was as good as done; for unto God do things return!

O ye who believe! when ye encounter a troop, then stand firm and remember God; and haply ye may prosper! and fear God and His Apostle, and do not quarrel or be timid, so that your turn of luck go from you; but be ye patient, verily, God is with the patient. And be not like those who went forth from their homes with insolence, and for appearance sake

[1] That is, had ye agreed to attack them.

before men, and to turn folks off God's way; for all they do God comprehends.

[50] And when Satan made their works appear seemly to them, and said, 'There is none amongst mankind to conquer you to-day, for, verily, I am your neighbour!' and when the two troops came in sight of each other, he turned upon his heels and said, 'Verily, I am clear of you! verily, I see what you see not [1]! verily, I fear God, for God is keen to punish!'

And when the hypocrites and those in whose hearts was sickness said, 'Their religion hath beguiled these men [2], but he who relies upon God, verily, God is mighty and wise.'

Couldst thou see when the angels take away the souls of those who misbelieve; they smite them on their faces and hinder parts.—'Taste ye the torment of burning! that is for what your hands have sent on before; and for that God is no unjust one towards his servants.'

As was the wont of Pharaoh's people and those before them! they disbelieved in the signs of God, and God overtook them in their sins; verily, God is strong and keen to punish.

[55] That is because God is not one to change a favour He has favoured a people with, until they change what they have in themselves, and for that God both hears and knows.

As was the wont of Pharaoh's people and those before them! they said our signs were lies, and we destroyed them in their sins, and drowned

[1] The angels who were fighting on the Muslim side.
[2] I. e. beguiled them into attacking a force superior in numbers.

Pharaoh's people; and all of them were evildoers.

Verily, the worst of beasts in God's eyes are those who misbelieve and will not believe; with whom if thou dost make a league, they break their league each time, for they fear not God; but shouldst thou ever catch them in war, then make those who come after them run by their example[1], haply they may remember then.

[60] And shouldst thou ever fear from any people treachery, then throw it back to them in like manner; verily, God loves not the treacherous. Deem not that those who misbelieve can win; verily, they cannot make (God) powerless!

Prepare ye against them what force and companies of horse ye can, to make the enemies of God, and your enemies, and others beside them, in dread thereof. Ye do not know them, but God knows them! and whatever ye expend in God's way He will repay you; and ye shall not be wronged. But if they incline to peace, incline thou to it too, and rely upon God; verily, He both hears and knows.

But if they wish to betray thee, then God is enough for thee! He it is who supports thee with His help and with the believers; and reconciles their hearts! Didst thou expend all that is in the earth thou couldst not reconcile their hearts, but God reconciled them, verily, He is mighty and wise!

[65] O thou prophet! God is sufficient for thee, with those of the believers who follow thee! O thou

[1] That is, make them an example to all future opponents by the severity of thy dealing with them.

prophet! urge on the believers to fight. If there be of you twenty patient men, they shall conquer two hundred; if there be of you a hundred, they shall conquer a thousand of those who misbelieve, because they are a people who did not discern.—Now has God made it light for you; He knows that there is a weakness amongst you: but if there be amongst you but a patient hundred, they will conquer two hundred; and if there be of you a thousand, they will conquer two thousand, by the permission of God,—for God is with the patient!

It has not been for any prophet to take captives until he hath slaughtered in the land! Ye wish to have the goods of this world, but God wishes for the next, for God is mighty, wise! Were it not for a book from God that had gone before, there would have touched you, for that which ye took, a mighty punishment[1].

Eat of what spoils ye have taken, what is lawful and good; and fear God, verily, God is forgiving and merciful.

[70] O thou prophet! say to such of the captives as are in your hands, 'If God knows of any good in your hearts, he will give you better than that which is taken from you, and will forgive you; for God is forgiving and merciful.'

But if they desire to betray thee,—they have betrayed God before! but He hath given you power over them; for God is knowing, wise!

Verily, those who believe and have fled and

[1] Mohammed here blames them for having accepted ransom from the captives which they took at the Battle of Bedr; but acknowledges that previously revealed passages of the Qur'ân did in the strict letter allow of such ransom being taken.

fought strenuously with their wealth and persons in God's way, and those who have given refuge[1] and help, these shall be next of kin to each other[2]. But those who believe, but have not fled, ye have naught to do with their claims of kindred, until they flee as well. But if they ask you for aid for religion's sake, then help is due from you, except against a people between whom and you there is an alliance; for God on what ye do doth look.

And those who misbelieve, some of them are next of kin to others—unless ye act the same there will be sedition in the land, and great corruption.

[75] Those who believe and have fled and fought strenuously in God's cause, and those who have given a refuge and a help, those it is who believe; to them is forgiveness and generous provision due. And those who have believed afterwards and have fled and fought strenuously with you; these too are of you, but blood relations are nearer in kin by the Book of God. Verily, God all things doth know.

The Chapter of Repentance or Immunity.

(IX. Medînah.)

An immunity from God and His Apostle to those idolaters with whom ye have made a league[3].

---

[1] To the prophet.

[2] The Ansârs and Muhâgerîn, that is, those who lent aid to, and those who fled with Mohammed were at first regarded as next of kin and heirs to each other's property to the exclusion of blood relationship, until the above passage was abrogated by the last words of this chapter.

[3] This chapter is without the initial formula 'In the name of God,' &c. The Caliph Othman said that the omission arose from

Roam ye at large in the land for four months, but know that ye cannot make God helpless, and that God disgraces the misbelievers.

A proclamation from God and His Apostle to the people on the day of the greater pilgrimage, that God is clear of the idolaters as is His Apostle! If then ye repent it is better for you; but if ye turn your backs, then know that ye cannot make God helpless. Give to those who misbelieve glad tidings of grievous woe!—Except to those of the idolaters with whom ye have made a league, and who then have not failed you at all, and have not backed up any one against you. Fulfil for them then your covenant until the time agreed upon with them; verily, God loves those who fear.

[5] But when the sacred months are passed away, kill the idolaters wherever ye may find them; and take them, and besiege them, and lie in wait for them in every place of observation; but if they repent, and are steadfast in prayer, and give alms, then let them go their way; verily, God is forgiving and merciful.

And if any one of the idolaters ask thee for aid, then aid him, in order that he may hear the word of God; then let him reach his place of safety,—that is, because they are a folk who do not know.

How can there be for the idolaters a treaty with God and with His Apostle, save those with whom ye have made a league at the Sacred Mosque!

---

its having been revealed shortly before Mohammed's death, who left no instructions on the subject. But some commentators assert that it arises from its having originally formed part of the previous chapter.

Then while they stand by you, stand ye by them; verily, God loves those who fear.

How!—if they prevail against you, they will not observe either ties of blood or ties of clientship; they please you with their mouths, but their hearts refuse; and most of them do work abomination. They barter God's signs for a little price, and they turn folk from His way; verily, they—evil is that which they have done.

[10] They will not observe in a believer ties of kindred nor ties of clientship; but they it is are the transgressors.

But if they repent and are steadfast in prayer and give alms, then they are your brethren in religion—we detail the signs unto a people that do know.

But if they break faith with you after their treaty, and taunt your religion, then fight the leaders of misbelief; verily, they have no faith, haply they may desist.

Will ye not fight a people who broke their oaths, and intended to expel the Apostle? They began with you at first, are ye afraid of them? God is more deserving that ye should fear Him! If ye be believers, kill them! God will torment them by your hands, and disgrace them, and aid you against them, and heal the breasts of a people who believe; [15] and will remove rage from their hearts; for God turns unto Him whomsoever He pleases, and God is knowing, wise!

Did ye reckon that ye would be left, when God knows not as yet those of you who fought strenuously, and who did not take other than God and His Apostle, and the believers for an intimate friend?

for God is well aware of what ye do. It is not for idolaters to repair to the mosques of God, bearing witness against themselves to unbelief; they it is whose works are vain, and in the Fire shall they dwell for aye!

He only shall repair to the mosques of God who believes in God and the last day, and is steadfast in prayer, and gives the alms, and fears only God; —it may be that these will be of those who are guided.

Have ye made out the giving drink to the pilgrims and the repairing to the Sacred Mosque[1] to be like being one who believes in God and in the last day, and is strenuous in the way of God? —they are not equal in God's sight, and God guides not an unjust people.

[20] Those who believe and who have fled and been strenuous in the way of God, with their wealth and with their persons, are highest in rank with God, and these it is who are happy. Their Lord gives them glad tidings of mercy from Himself, and good-will; and gardens shall they have therein and lasting pleasure, to dwell therein for aye! Verily, God, with Him is mighty here.

O ye who believe! take not your fathers and your brothers for patrons if they love misbelief rather than faith; for whosoever amongst you takes them for patrons these are the unjust.

Say, 'If your fathers, and your sons, and your brethren, and your wives, and your clansmen, and

[1] Abu 'l 'Abbâs, Mohammed's uncle, when taken prisoner and reproached with his unbelief, appealed to his having performed these duties as entitling him to as much consideration as if he had professed Islâm.

the wealth which ye have gained, and the merchandise which ye fear may be slack, and the dwellings which ye love are dearer to you than God and His Apostle, and than fighting strenuously in His way,—then wait awhile, until God brings His bidding, for God guides not a people who work abomination!'

[25] God has helped you in many a place, and on the day of 'Honein[1] when ye were so pleased with your numbers; but it did not serve you at all, and the road grew too strait for you, where it had been broad; and then ye turned your backs retreating; then God sent down His shechina[2] upon His Apostle and upon the believers; and sent down armies which ye could not see, and punished those who misbelieved; for that is the reward of the misbelievers, then God turns after that to whom He will, for God is forgiving and merciful!

O ye who believe! it is only the idolaters who are unclean; they shall not then approach the Sacred Mosque after this year. But if ye fear want[3] then God will enrich you from His grace if He will; verily, God is knowing, wise!

Fight those who believe not in God and in the last day, and who forbid not what God and His Apostle have forbidden, and who do not practice

---

[1] 'Honein is the name of a valley about three miles to the north-east of Mecca, where, in the eighth year of the Flight, a battle took place between Mohammed and his followers with an army of twelve thousand men, and two tribes of idolatrous Arabs. Too confident in their numbers the Moslems at first received a check, but were rallied by Mohammed and his immediate followers and kindred.

[2] See p. 38, note 2.

[3] That is, from the stoppage of traffic and merchandise.

the religion of truth from amongst those to whom the Book has been brought, until they pay the tribute by their hands and be as little ones.

[30] The Jews say Ezra is the son of God; and the Christians say that the Messiah is the son of God; that is what they say with their mouths, imitating the sayings of those who misbelieved before.—God fight them! how they lie[1]!

They take their doctors and their monks for lords[2] rather than God, and the Messiah the son of Mary; but they are bidden to worship but one God, there is no god but He; celebrated be His praise, from what they join with Him!

They desire to put out the light of God with their mouths, but God will not have it but that we should perfect His light, averse although the misbelievers be!

He it is who sent His Apostle with guidance and the religion of truth, to make it prevail over every other religion, averse although idolaters may be!

O ye who believe! verily, many of the doctors and the monks devour the wealth of men openly, and turn folk from God's way; but those who store up gold and silver and expend it not in God's way,

---

[1] The Moslem tradition is that Ezra, after being dead 100 years, was raised to life, and dictated from memory the whole of the Jewish Scriptures which had been lost during the captivity, and that the Jews said he could not have done this unless he had been the son of God. There is no Jewish tradition whatever in support of this accusation of Mohammed's, which probably was entirely due to his own invention or to misinformation. Bâi*dh*âvî, the well-known commentator, says that it must have been true because the Jews themselves, to whom the passage was read, did not deny it.

[2] Alluding to the word rabbi, which in Arabic is applied to God alone.

—give them glad tidings of grievous woe! [35] On the day when it shall be heated in the fire of hell, and their brows shall be branded therewith, and their sides and their backs!—'This is what ye stored up for yourselves, taste then what ye stored up!'

Verily, the number of months with God is twelve months in God's Book, on the day when He created the heavens and the earth; of these are four that are sacred; that is the subsisting religion. Then do not wrong yourselves therein, but fight the idolaters one and all, as they fight you one and all, and know that God is with those who fear.

Verily, putting off is but an increase in misbelief[1] to lead astray therewith those who misbelieve. They make it lawful one year, but they make it unlawful another year, that they may come to an understanding as to the number which God has made sacred, and make lawful what God has prohibited. Seemly to them are their evil works, but God guides not a misbelieving people.

O ye who believe! what ailed you when ye were told to march forth in God's way, that ye sank down heavily upon the earth? were ye content with the life of this world instead of the next? but the provision of this world's life is but a little to the next. Unless ye march forth He will punish you with grievous woe, and will put in your stead a people other than you! ye cannot hurt Him at all, for God is mighty over all!

---

[1] The pagan Arabs used to put off the observance of a sacred month when it was inconvenient to them and observe another instead; this Mohammed deprecates.

[40] Unless ye help him[1]—and God did help him, when those who misbelieved drove him forth the second of two[2]. When they twain were in the cave; when he said to his comrade, 'Grieve not, verily, God is with us;' and God sent down His shechina upon him, and aided him with hosts ye could not see, and made the word of those who misbelieved inferior, and the word of God superior; for God is mighty and wise. March ye then, light and heavy, and fight strenuously with your wealth and persons in God's way; that is better for you if ye did but know!

Were there goods nigh at hand, and a moderate journey, they would have followed you; but the distance was too far for them; they will swear by God, 'If we could, we would have gone forth with you.' They destroy themselves, but God knows that they lie!

God forgive thee; why didst thou give them leave (to stay) until it was made manifest to thee who spake the truth—until thou mightest know the liars?

Those who believe in God and in the last day will not beg off from fighting strenuously with their wealth and their persons; but God knows those who fear.

[45] It is only those who believe not in God and in the last day who beg off from thee, and those whose hearts are in doubt, and in their doubt do hesitate.

Had they wished to go forth, they would have prepared for it a preparation; but God was averse

[1] The prophet.

[2] That is, with only one companion, namely Abubekr.

from their starting off, and made them halt, and they were told to sit with those who sit. Had they gone forth with you they would but have made you more trouble, and they would have hurried about amongst you craving a sedition; amongst you are some who would have listened to them; but God knows those who are unjust! They used to crave sedition before and upset thy affairs; until the truth came, and God's bidding was made manifest, averse although they were.

Of them are some who say, 'Permit me[1], and do not try me!' Have they not fallen into the trial already, but hell shall encompass the misbelievers.

[50] If good befall thee it seems ill to them; but if a calamity befall thee they say, 'We had taken care for our affair before;' and they turn their backs and they are glad.

Say, 'Nought shall befall us save what God has written down for us; He is our Lord, and upon God believers do rely!'

Say, 'Do ye await for us aught but one of the two best things[2]?' we too await for you that God will inflict on you torment from Himself, or by our hands. Wait then; and we with you are waiting too!

Say, 'Expend ye in alms, whether ye will or no, it shall not be accepted from you; verily, ye are a people who do work abomination.'

But nought hinders their alms-giving from being accepted save that they misbelieve in God and His Apostle, and perform not prayer save lazily, and expend not in alms save reluctantly.

---

[1] That is, excuse me from the fighting in the cause of religion.
[2] I.e. victory or martyrdom.

[55] Let not their wealth please you nor their children, God only wishes to torment them therewith in the life of this world, and that their souls may pass away while still they misbelieve.

They swear by God that, verily, they are of you; but they are not of you, and they are a people who do stand aside in fear. Could they but have found a refuge, or some caves, or a place in which to creep, they would have turned round in haste thereto.

Of them are some who defame thee, with respect to alms; though if they are given a part thereof, they are content; and if they are not given a part thereof, then are they in a rage. Would that they were content with what God and His Apostle had brought them, and would say, 'God is enough for us! God will bring us of His grace, and so will His Apostle; verily, unto God is our desire!'

[60] Alms are only for the poor and needy, and those who work for them [1], and those whose hearts are reconciled [2], and those in captivity, and those in debt, and those who are on God's path, and for the wayfarer;—an ordinance this from God, for God is knowing, wise.

And of them are some who are by the ears [3] with the prophet, and say, 'He is all ear.' Say, 'An ear of good for you!' he believes in God, and believes in those who do believe, and is a mercy unto such of you as believe; but those who are by the ears with the Apostle of God, for them is grievous woe!

---

[1] I.e. in collecting or distributing them.

[2] Reconciled, that is, to Islâm.

[3] That is, reproach or quarrel with the prophet; I have used the old fashion English expression in order to preserve the pun upon the word ear which exists in the original.

They swear by God to please you; but God and His Apostle are more worthy for them to please if they be believers. Do they not know that whoso setteth himself against God and His Apostle, for him is the fire of hell, to dwell therein for aye? and that is mighty shame!

[65] The hypocrites are cautious lest there be revealed against them a sûrah[1] to inform them of what is in their hearts; say, 'Mock ye! verily, God will bring forth that of which ye are so cautious!' But if thou shouldst ask them, they will say, 'We did but discuss and jest;' say, 'Was it at God and His signs, and His Apostle, that ye mocked?'

Make no excuse! Ye have misbelieved after your faith; if we forgive one sect of you, we will torment another sect, for that they sinned!

The hypocrites, men and women, some of them follow others, bidding what is wrong and forbidding what is right, and they clench their hands[2]. They forget God and He forgets them! Verily, the hypocrites, they are the doers of abomination!

God has promised unto the hypocrites, men and women, and unto the misbelievers, hell-fire, to dwell therein for aye; it is enough for them! God shall curse them, and theirs shall be enduring woe.

[70] Ye are like those who were before you. They were stronger than you and more abundant in wealth and children; they enjoyed their portion then, and ye enjoy your portion, as they enjoyed their portion before you; and ye discuss as they

[1] Chapter of the Qur'ân.

[2] I. e. are niggardly and refuse to give alms.

discussed. Their works are vain in this world and the next, and they it is who lose.

Did there not come to them the declaration of those who were before them? of the people of Noah and 'Âd and Thamûd, and of the people of Abraham, and the people of Midian? and of the overturned (cities)[1]? Their apostles came to them with manifest signs; for God would not wrong them, but it was themselves they wronged.

And the believers, men and women, are some the patrons of others; they bid what is reasonable, and forbid what is wrong, and are steadfast in prayer, and give alms, and obey God and His Apostle. On these will God have mercy; verily, God is mighty, wise!

God has promised to believers, men and women, gardens beneath which rivers flow, to dwell therein for aye; and goodly places in the garden of Eden. But good-will from God is the greatest of all! that is the mighty happiness!

O thou prophet! strive strenuously against the misbelievers and the hypocrites, and be stern against them; for their resort is hell, and an ill journey shall it be.

[75] They swear by God they did not speak it, but they did speak the word of misbelief; and they disbelieved after they had embraced Islâm, and they designed what they could not attain; and they only disapproved it because God and His Apostle had enriched them of His grace[2]. If they turn again 'tis

---

[1] Sodom and Gomorrah.

[2] A plot had been set afoot at Medînah to kill Mohammed, and was only abandoned because of the increased trade and prosperity which Mohammed's residence then brought.

better for them; but if they turn their backs, God will torment them with mighty woe in this world and in the next, nor shall they have upon the earth a patron or protector.

And of them are some who make a treaty with God, that 'If He bring us of His grace, we will give alms and we will surely be among the righteous.' But when He gave them of His grace they were niggardly thereof, and turned their backs and swerved aside. So He caused hypocrisy to pursue them in their hearts unto the day when they shall meet Him,—for that they did fail God in what they promised Him, and for that they were liars!

Do they not know that God knows their secrets and their whisperings, and that God knows the unseen things?

[80] Those who defame such of the believers as willingly give their alms, and such as can find nothing to give but their exertions, and who mock at them,—God will mock at them, and for them is grievous woe!

Ask forgiveness for them or ask not forgiveness for them! if they shouldst ask forgiveness for them seventy times, yet would not God forgive them; that is because they disbelieved in God and His Apostle, for God guides not a people who work abomination.

Those who were left behind[1] rejoiced in staying behind the Apostle of God, and were averse from fighting strenuously with their wealth and their persons in God's way, and said, 'March not forth in the heat.' Say, 'The fire of hell is hotter still,

[1] At the battle of Tabûk.

if ye could but discern!' Let them then laugh little, and let them weep much, as a recompense for that which they have earned!

But if God bring thee back to a sect of them, and they ask thee then for leave to sally forth; say, 'Ye shall by no means ever sally forth with me, nor shall ye ever fight a foe with me! verily, ye were content to sit at home the first time, sit ye then now with those who stay behind.'

[85] Pray not for any one of them who dies, and stand not by his tomb; verily, they disbelieved in God and His Apostle and died workers of abomination!

Let not their wealth and their children please you, God only wishes to torment them therewith in this world, and that their souls may pass away the while they misbelieve.

Whenever a sûrah is sent down to them, 'Believe ye in God, and fight strenuously together with His Apostle,' those of them who have the means will ask thee for leave to stay at home and say, 'Let us be amongst those who stay behind.' They are content to be with those who are left behind. A stamp is set upon their hearts that they should not discern.

But the Apostle and those who believe with him are strenuous with their wealth and with their persons; these shall have good things, and these it is shall prosper.

[90] God has prepared for them gardens beneath which rivers flow, to dwell therein for aye; that is the mighty happiness!

There came certain desert Arabs that they might be excused; and those stayed behind who had called

God and His Apostle liars. There shall befall those of them who misbelieved, a mighty woe. For the weak, and the sick, and those who cannot find wherewith to expend in alms there is no hindrance, so they be only sincere towards God and His Apostle. There is no way against those who do well; for God is forgiving and merciful. Nor against those to whom, when they came to thee that thou shouldst mount them, thou didst say, 'I cannot find wherewith to mount you,' turned their backs while their eyes poured forth with tears, for grief that they could not find wherewith to expend. Only is there a way against those who ask thee for leave to stay at home while they are rich; content to be with those who are left behind; on whose hearts God has set a stamp, so that they should not know.

[95] They make excuses to you when ye return to them: say, 'Make no excuse, we believe you not; God has informed us concerning you. God sees your works and His Apostle too!' Then shall ye be brought back unto Him who knows the unseen and the seen; and He shall inform you of that which ye have done.

They will adjure you by God when ye have come back to them, to turn aside from them; turn ye aside then from them; verily, they are a plague, and their resort is hell! a recompense for that which they have earned!

They will adjure you to be pleased with them; but if ye are pleased with them, God will not be pleased with a people who work abomination.

The Arabs of the desert are keener in misbelief and hypocrisy, and are more likely not to know the bounds which God has sent down to His Apostle; but God is knowing and wise.

And of the Arabs of the desert are some who take what they expend to be a forced loan, and they wait a turn of fortune against you; against them shall a turn of evil fortune be; for God both hears and knows.

[100] And of the Arabs of the desert are some who believe in God and the last day, and who take what they expend in alms to be a means of approach to God and to the Apostle's prayers,—is it not a means of approach for them? God will make them enter into His mercy; verily, God is forgiving and merciful.

As for the foremost in the race, the first of those who fled[1], and the helpers[2], and those who followed them in their kindness, God is well pleased with them, and they are well pleased with Him; He has prepared for them gardens beneath which rivers flow, to dwell therein for aye; that is the mighty happiness.

And of those who are round about you of the Arabs of the desert, some are hypocrites, and of the people of Medînah, some are stubborn in hypocrisy; thou dost not know them—we know them; we will torment them twice over; then shall they be sent off into mighty woe.

And others have confessed their sins,—that they have mixed with a righteous action another evil action;—haply it may be God will turn again to them; verily, God is forgiving and merciful.

---

[1] The Muhâgerîn, or those who fled with Mohammed from Mecca.

[2] The Ansârs who helped him while at Medînah.

Take from their wealth alms to cleanse and purify them thereby; and pray for them; verily, thy prayer is a repose for them; for God both hears and knows.

[105] Do they not know that God accepts repentance from His servants, and takes alms; and that God is He who is easily turned and merciful.

And say, 'Act ye;' and God and His Apostle and the believers shall see your acts, and ye shall be brought back to Him who knows the seen and the unseen, and He shall inform you of that which ye have done.

And others are in hopes of God's bidding; whether He will torment them, or whether He turn again towards them; for God is knowing, wise.

And there are those who have taken to a mosque for mischief, and for misbelief, and to make a breach amongst the believers, and for an ambush for him who made war against God and His Apostle before; they surely swear, 'We only wished for what was good;' but God bears witness that they are liars.

Never stand up therein!—there is a mosque founded on piety from the first day[1]: it is more right that thou shouldst stand therein;—therein are men who love to be clean; for God doth love the clean.

[110] Is he who has laid his foundation upon the

---

[1] The Mosque of Qubâ', about two miles from Medînah, the foundation stone of which was laid by Mohammed four days before he entered Medînah on his flight from Mecca, was the first place of public prayer in Islâm. The Beni *Gh*anm had built another mosque to rival this, at the instigation of Abu 'Hâmir, a monk who was opposed to Mohammed, and wished the prophet to consecrate it.

fear of God and of His good-will better, or he who has laid his foundation upon a crumbling wall of sand, which crumbles away with him into the fire of hell?—but God guides not a people who do wrong.

The building which they[1] have built will not cease to be a source of doubt in their hearts until their hearts are cut asunder[2]; but God is knowing, wise.

Verily, God hath bought of the believers their persons and their wealth, for the paradise they are to have; they shall fight in the way of God, and they shall slay and be slain: promised in truth, in the law and the gospel and the Qur'ân;—and who is more faithful to His covenant than God?

Be ye glad then in the covenant which ye have made with Him, for that is the mighty happiness! Those who repent, those who worship, those who praise, those who fast, those who bow down, those who adore, those who bid what is right and forbid what is wrong, and those who keep the bounds of God,—glad tidings to those who believe!

[115] It is not for the prophet and those who believe to ask forgiveness for the idolaters, even though they be their kindred, after it has been made manifest to them that they are the fellows of hell.

Nor was Abraham's asking pardon for his father aught else but through a promise he had promised him; but when it was made manifest to him that he was an enemy to God, he cleansed himself of him; verily, Abraham was pitiful and clement.

---

[1] The Beni *Gh*anm.

[2] I. e. they will feel compunctions about it till the day of their death.

Nor will God lead astray a people after He has guided them until that is made manifest to them which they have to fear; verily, God all things doth know.

Verily, God's is the kingdom of the heavens and the earth! He quickens and He kills! Nor have ye beside God a patron or protector.

God has now turned towards the prophet and those who fled with him, and towards the helpers who followed him in the hour of difficulty, after that the hearts of a part of them had well-nigh gone amiss.

Then He turned unto them; verily to them He is kind and merciful:—unto the three[1] who were left behind, so that the earth with all its ample space was too strait for them, and their souls were straitened for them, and they thought that there was no refuge for them from God save unto Him.

Then He turned again towards them that they might also turn; verily, God, He is easily turned and merciful!

[120] O ye who believe! fear God and be with those who speak the truth.

It was not for the people of Medînah, and those around about them of the Arabs of the desert, to stay behind the Apostle of God and not to prefer their souls to his: that is because neither thirst, nor toil, nor heat, nor hunger befel them on God's way. Nor do they stop to anger the misbelievers, nor do they get any (harm) from the enemy without

[1] Three of the Ansârs who refused to accompany Mohammed to Tabûk.

a good work being written down to them; verily, God wastes not the hire of those who do well.

Nor do they expend in alms a small or great expense, nor do they cross a wady[1] without it being written down to them; that God may reward them with better than that which they have done.

The believers should not march forth altogether; and if a troop of every division of them march not forth, it is only that they may study their religion and warn their people when they return to them, that haply they may beware.

O ye who believe! fight those who are near to you of the misbelievers, and let them find in you sternness; and know that God is with those who fear.

[125] And whenever a sûrah is sent down, there are some of them who say, 'Which of you has this increased in faith?' But as for those who believe, it does increase them in faith, and they shall rejoice: but as for those in whose hearts is sickness, it only adds a plague to their plague, and they die misbelievers.

Do they not see that they are tried in every year once or twice? Yet they do not turn again, nor do they mind!

And whenever a sûrah is sent down, some of them look at the others—'Does any one see you?'—Then they turn away! God has turned their hearts, for that they are a people who do not discern.

There has come to you an apostle from amongst

---

[1] A wady is the bed of a torrent, which in Arabia is generally dry, but occasionally after a storm is filled with the torrent.

yourselves; hard for him to bear is it that ye commit iniquity; he is anxious over you after the believers, pitiful, compassionate.

[130] But if they turn their backs, then say, 'God is enough for me! there is no god but He! upon Him do I rely, for He is Lord of the mighty throne!'

THE CHAPTER OF JONAH, (PEACE BE ON HIM!)

(X. Mecca.)

IN the name of the merciful and compassionate God.

A. L. R. Those are the signs of the wise Book! was it a wonder to the folk[1] that we inspired a man from amongst themselves, 'Warn thou the folk; and give glad tidings to those who believe, that for them there is an advance of sincerity[2] gone before them with their Lord?' The misbelievers say, 'Verily, this is an obvious sorcerer!'

Verily, your Lord is God, who created the heavens and the earth in six days; then He made for the throne, to govern the affair; there is no intercessor, except after His permission. That is God for you—your Lord! Then worship Him—do ye not mind?

To Him is your return all of you—God's promise in truth; verily, He produces the creature, then He makes it return again, that He may recompense

---

[1] Of Mecca.

[2] I.e. a reward awaiting them for their sincerity.

those who believe and do what is right with justice; but those who misbelieve, for them is a drink of boiling water, and grievous woe, for that they did misbelieve.

[5] He it is who made the sun for a brightness, and the moon for a light, and decreed for it mansions, that ye may know the number of the years and the reckoning.—God only created that in truth. He details the signs unto a people who do know.

Verily, in the alternation of night and day, and in what God has created of the heavens and the earth, are signs unto a people who do fear.

Verily, those who hope not for our meeting, and are content with the life of this world, and are comforted thereby, and those who are neglectful of our signs,—these, their resort is fire for that which they have earned!

Verily, those who believe and do what is right, their Lord guides them by their faith; beneath them shall rivers flow in the gardens of pleasure.

[10] Their cry therein shall be, 'Celebrated be Thy praises, O God!' and their salutation therein shall be, 'Peace!' and the end of their cry shall be, 'Praise (belongs) to God, the Lord of the worlds!'

And if God should hasten on the bad to men as they would hasten on the good, their appointed time would surely be fulfilled. But we will let those who hope not for our meeting go on in their rebellion, blindly wandering on.

When distress touches man, he calls us to his side, whether sitting or standing; but when we have removed from him his distress, he passes on as though he had not called on us in a distress that touched him. Thus unto the extravagant is made seemly that which they have done.

We have already destroyed generations before you when they did wrong, and there came to them their apostles with manifest signs, but they would not believe. Thus do we reward the sinful people.

[15] Then we made you their successors in the earth after them, that we may see how ye will act.

But when our evident signs are recited to them, those who hope not for our meeting say, 'Bring a Qur'ân other than this; or change it.' Say, 'It is not for me to change it of my own accord; I do not follow aught but what I am inspired with; verily, I fear, if I rebel against my Lord, the torment of a mighty day!'

Say, 'Had God pleased, I should not have recited it to you, nor taught you therewith. I have tarried a lifetime amongst you before it;—have ye not then any sense?'

Who is more unjust than he who forges against God a lie, or says His signs are lies? verily, the sinners shall not prosper.

They worship beside God what can neither harm them nor profit them, and they say, 'These are our intercessors with God!' Say, 'Will ye inform God of aught in the heavens or the earth, that He knows not of?' Celebrated be His praise! and exalted be He, above what they associate with Him!

[20] People were but one nation once, then they disagreed; and had it not been for thy Lord's word already passed, there would have been decided between them that concerning which they disagreed.

They say, 'Why is not a sign sent down upon him from his Lord?' Say, 'The unseen is only God's; but wait ye for a while, verily, I with you am one of those who wait!'

When we have let men taste of mercy after distress which has touched them, lo! they use a stratagem against our signs! Say, 'God is quicker at stratagem.' Verily, our messengers[1] write down what stratagem ye use.

He it is who makes you travel in the land and sea, until when ye are in the ships—and these carry them[2] afloat with a favouring wind, and they rejoice therein, there comes to them a violent wind, and there comes to them the wave from every place, and they think that they are encompassed about; then they call on God, sincere in religion towards Him, 'If thou dost save from this we will surely be of those who thank.' But when He has saved them, lo! they are wilful in the earth unjustly;—O ye folk! your wilfulness against yourselves is but a provision of this world's life; then unto us is your return, and we will inform you of that which ye have done!

[25] Verily, the likeness of this world's life is like water which we send down from the sky, and the plants of the earth, from which men and cattle eat, are mingled therewith; until when the earth puts on its gilding and is adorned, the people thereof think that they have power over it. Our order comes to it by night or day, and we make it as it

[1] The recording angels.

[2] An instance of the frequent abrupt changes of persons with which the Qur'ân abounds.

were mown down—as though it had not yesterday been rich!—Thus do we detail the signs unto a people who reflect.

God calls unto the abode of peace, and guides whom He will into the right path.

To those who do what is good, goodness and increase! nor shall blackness or abasement cover their faces! these are the fellows of Paradise, they shall dwell therein for aye.

But, as for those who have earned ill, the reward of evil is the like thereof; abasement shall cover them! they shall have none to defend them against God;—as though their faces were veiled with the deep darkness of the night; these are the fellows of the Fire, and they shall dwell therein for aye.

And on the day we gather them all together then we will say to those who associated other gods (with us), 'To your places, ye and your associates!' and we will part them; and their associates will say, 'It was not us ye worshipped.—[30] But God is witness enough between us and you, that we were heedless of your worshipping us.' There shall every soul prove what it has sent on before; and they shall be returned unto God, their God, their true sovereign, and that which they devised shall stray away from them.

Say, 'Who provides you from the heaven and the earth? who has dominion over hearing and sight? and who brings forth the living from the dead, and brings forth the dead from the living? and who governs the affair?' And they will say, 'God.' Say, 'Do ye not then fear?'

That is God, your true Lord! and what is there

after the truth but error? how then can ye turn away?

Thus is the word of thy Lord verified against those who commit abomination; verily, they will not believe. Say, 'Is there any of your associates who can produce a creature and then turn it back again?' Say, 'God produces a creature, then turns it back again; how then can ye lie?' [35] Say, 'Is there any of your associates who guides unto the truth?' Say, 'God guides unto the truth.' Is then He who guides unto the truth more worthy to be followed, or he that guides not except he be himself guided? What ails you then, how ye judge?

But most of them follow only suspicion; verily, suspicion does not avail against the truth at all; verily, God knows what they do.

This Qur'ân could not have been devised by any beside God; but it verifies that which was before it, and details the Book—there is no doubt therein—from the Lord of the worlds.

Do they say, 'He[1] hath devised it?' say then, 'Bring a sûrah like it,—and call, if ye can, on other than God, if ye do tell the truth!'

[40] Yet they call that a lie, the knowledge of which they cannot compass, while its interpretation has not yet come to them; so did those before them charge with lying, and see what was the end of the unjust!

Of them are some who believe therein; and of them are some who do not believe therein; but thy Lord knows best who are corrupters.

---

[1] I. e. Mohammed.

But if they call thee liar, say, 'I have my work, and ye have your work; ye are clear of what I work, and I am clear of what ye work.'

There are some of them who listen to thee—canst thou make the deaf to hear, although they have no sense? And of them are some who look at thee—canst thou guide the blind, although they cannot see?

[45] Verily, God wrongs not man at all, but men do wrong themselves.

And on the day when we will gather them together it will be as though they had not tarried save an hour of the day, they shall know each other. Lost are those who called the meeting with God a lie, and were not guided!

Either we will show thee something of that with which we threatened them, or we will take thee to ourself, for unto us is their return; then is God a witness to what they do.

Every nation has its apostle; and when their apostle comes to them, it is decided between them with justice, and they are not wronged.

But they say, 'When is this threat (to come), if ye tell the truth?'

[50] Say, 'I have no power over myself for harm or for profit, save what God will. Every nation has its appointed time; when their appointed time comes to them they cannot delay it for an hour or bring it on.'

Say, 'Let us see now when the torment comes to you, by night or day, what will the sinners fain bring on thereof? And when it has fallen—will ye believe in it now!—And yet ye wish to bring it on! Then shall it be said to those who have done wrong, Taste ye the torment of eternity! shall ye be recompensed except for that which ye have earned?' They will ask thee to inform them whether it be true. Say, 'Aye, by my Lord! verily, it is the truth, nor can ye weaken him.'

[55] And if every soul that hath done wrong had whatever is in the earth, it would give it as a ransom. They will utter their repentance when they see the torment; and it shall be decided between them with justice, nor shall they be wronged.

Is not indeed what is in the heavens and what is in the earth God's? is not indeed the promise of God true? Though most of them know not. He quickens and He kills, and unto Him are ye returned!

O ye folk! there has come to you a warning from your Lord, and a balm for what is in your breasts, and a guidance and a mercy to believers.

Say, 'By the grace of God and by His mercy,—and in that let them rejoice! It is better than that which they collect!'

[60] Let us see now what God has sent down to you of provision! and yet ye have made of it unlawful and lawful. Say, 'Does God permit you, or against God do ye forge lies?'

What will those who forge lies against God think on the resurrection day? Verily, God is Lord of grace towards men, but most of them do not give thanks!

Nor shalt thou be in any affair, nor shalt thou recite concerning it a Qur'ân [1]—nor shall ye do a work, without our being witness against you, when

[1] A portion of the Qur'ân. The word means reading.

ye are engaged therein: nor does the weight of an atom escape thy Lord in earth or in heaven; nor is there less than that or greater, but it is in the perspicuous Book.

Are not, verily, the friends of God those on whom there is no fear, neither shall they be grieved?—They who believed and who did fear—[65] for them are good tidings in the life of this world, and in the future too; there is no changing the words of God! That is the mighty happiness!

Let not their speech grieve thee; verily, power is wholly God's! He both hears and knows.

Is not, verily, whoever is in the heavens and whoever is in the earth God's? What then do they follow who call on associates other than God?

Verily, they follow nothing but suspicion, and verily, they are telling naught but lies.

He it is who made for you the night, that ye might rest therein, and the day to see therein; verily, in that are signs unto a people who can hear.

They say, 'God has taken to Himself a son.' Celebrated be His praises! He is the rich one! His is whatever is in the heavens, and whatever is in the earth. Ye have no authority for this! will ye say against God, that which ye do not know?

[70] Say, 'Verily, those who forge against God a lie shall not prosper!'

A provision in this world—then unto us is their return! then we will make them taste keen torment for that they misbelieved.

Recite to them the story of Noah, when he said to his people, 'O my people! if my stay with you be grievous to you, and my reminding you of the signs of God, yet upon God do I rely! Collect then your affairs and your associates[1]; nor let your affair (be ordered) for you in the dark; then decide respecting me, and do not wait; and if ye turn your backs, I ask you not for hire; my hire is only due from God, and I am bidden to be of those resigned.' But they called him a liar; and we saved him, and those with him, in the ark; and we made these[2] successors, and drowned those who had said our signs were lies; see then how was the end of those who had been warned!

[75] Then we raised up after him apostles unto their people, and they came to them with manifest signs; but they would not believe in what they had called a lie before. Thus do we set a stamp upon the hearts of the transgressors.

Then we raised up after them Moses and Aaron, unto Pharaoh and his chiefs with our signs; but they were too big with pride, and were a sinful people; and when the truth came to them from us they said, verily, 'This is obvious sorcery.'

Moses said, 'Will ye say of the truth when it comes to you, Is this sorcery? But sorcerers shall not prosper.'

They said, 'Hast thou come to turn us away from what we found our fathers at, that there may be for you twain grandeur in the earth? but we will not believe you.'

[80] And Pharaoh said, 'Bring me every knowing sorcerer;' and when the sorcerers came, Moses said to them, 'Throw down what ye have to throw!' and when they threw down, Moses said, 'What ye have brought is sorcery! verily, God will make

---

[1] Your idols.

[2] Noah's people.

it vain; verily, God rights not the work of evildoers!'

But God verifies the truth by His words, although the sinners are averse therefrom.

But none believed in Moses, save a race of his own people, through fear of Pharaoh and his chiefs; lest he should afflict them, for verily, Pharaoh was lofty in the earth, and verily, he was extravagant.

And Moses said, 'O my people! if ye did believe in God, then on Him rely, if ye be resigned.'
[85] They said, 'Upon God do we rely. O our Lord! make us not a cause of trial for a people who do wrong, but save us by Thy mercy from the people who misbelieve!'

And we inspired Moses and his brother thus, 'Establish, ye twain, houses for your people in Egypt; and make ye your houses a qiblah[1]; and be ye steadfast in prayer, and give glad tidings to those who believe.'

Moses said, 'O our Lord! verily, Thou hast brought to Pharaoh and his chiefs ornaments and wealth in the life of this world; O our Lord! that they may err from Thy way! O our Lord! confound their wealth and harden their hearts that they may not believe until they see grievous woe!' He said, 'Your prayer is answered; be upright then, ye two, and follow not the path of those who do not know!'

[90] And we brought the children of Israel across the sea; and Pharaoh and his hosts followed them eager and hostile, until when drowning overtook him, he said, 'I believe that there is no god but

[1] I.e. adapt them by their position and construction to become places in which prayer may be performed.

He in whom the children of Israel believe, and I am of those who are resigned!'—'Now[1]! but thou didst rebel aforetime, and wert of those who do evil; but to-day we will save thee in thy body, that thou mayest be to those who come after thee a sign, for verily, many men are careless of our signs[2]!'

And we established the people of Israel with a sure establishment, and we provided them with good things; nor did they disagree until there came to them the knowledge. Verily, thy Lord shall decide between them on the resurrection day concerning that whereon they did dispute.

And if thou art in doubt of that which we have sent down unto thee, ask those who read the Book before thee; verily, the truth is come to thee from thy Lord, be not then of those who are in doubt. And be not of those who say the signs of God are lies, or thou wilt be of those who lose! [95] Verily, those against whom God's word is pronounced will not believe, even though there come to them every sign, until they see the grievous woe. Were it not so, a city would have believed and its faith would have profited it. But (none did) except the people of Jonas; when they believed we removed from them the torment of disgrace in this world, and we gave them provision for a while. But had thy Lord pleased, all who are in the earth would have believed altogether; as for thee, wilt thou force men to become believers?

---

[1] This is supposed to be the taunting reply of the angel Gabriel.

[2] Compare Exodus xiv. 30. The Mohammedan legend is that as some of the children of Israel doubted whether Pharaoh was really drowned, the angel Gabriel caused the naked corpse to swim that they might see it.

[100] It is not for any person to believe save by the permission of God; He puts horror on those who have no sense.

Say, 'Behold what is in the heavens and in the earth! but signs and warners avail not a people who do not believe. Do they await aught but the like of the days of those who passed away before them?' Say, 'Wait ye then! verily, I am with you one of those who wait.' Then we will save our apostles and those who believe; thus is it due from us to save believers.

Say, 'O ye folk! if ye are in doubt concerning my religion, I will not worship those ye worship other than God; but I worship God, who takes you to Himself, and I am bidden to be of the believers!'
[105] And, 'Make steadfast thy face to the religion as a 'Hanîf[1]; and be not of the idolaters; and call not besides God on what can neither profit thee nor harm thee; for if thou dost, verily, thou art then of the unjust!'

And should God touch thee with harm, there is none to remove it save He; and if He wish thee well, there is none to repel His grace; He makes it fall on whom He will of His servants; for He is pardoning and merciful!

Say, 'O ye people! there has come to you the truth from your Lord, and he who is guided, his guidance is only for his soul; and he who errs, errs only against it; and I am not a guardian over you.'

Follow what is revealed to thee, and be patient until God judges, for He is the best of judges.

---

[1] See p. 19, note 1.

The Chapter of Hûd.

(XI. Mecca.)

A. L. R. A book whose signs are confirmed and then detailed, from the wise one, the aware: that ye worship not other than God,—verily, I am to you from Him a warner and a herald of glad tidings; and that ye seek pardon from your Lord, then turn again to Him! He will cause you to enjoy a good provision to a named and appointed time, and will give His grace to every one deserving grace; but if ye turn your backs, I fear for you the torment of a great day.

Unto God is your return, and He is mighty over all.

[5] Do they not, verily, fold up their breasts, that they may hide from Him? But when they cover themselves with their garments, does He not know what they conceal and what they display? verily, He knows the nature of men's breasts!

There is no beast that walks upon the earth but its provision is from God. He knows its settlement and its resting-place; all is in the perspicuous Book.

He it is who created the heavens and the earth in six days, and His throne was upon the water[1] that He might try you, which of you did best.

[10] But shouldst thou say, 'Ye will be raised up after death,' those who misbelieve will surely say, 'This is naught but obvious sorcery;' and if we keep back from them the torment to a stated generation,

---

[1] That is, before the creation; see Genesis i. 2.

they will surely say, 'What hinders it?'—Aye! on the day it comes to them there is no turning it away from them, but that shall close in on them at which they mocked.

And if we make man taste of mercy from us and then strip it off from him, verily, he is despairing, ungrateful; and if we make him taste of comfort after distress has touched him, he will surely say, 'The evils have gone away from me;' verily, then he is joyful and boasting. Save those who are patient and do right; these—for them is pardon and a mighty hire!

[15] Haply thou art leaving part of what is revealed to thee and thy breast is straitened thereby, lest they should say, 'Why is not a treasure sent down to him? or why did not an angel come with him?—thou art only a warner, and God is guardian over all.'

Or they will say, 'He hath devised it;' say, 'Bring ten sûrahs like it devised; and call upon whom ye can beside God, if ye do tell the truth!' And if they do not answer, then know that it is revealed by the knowledge of God, and that there is no god but He—are ye then resigned?

Whosoever shall wish for the life of this world and its ornaments, we will pay them their works therein, and they shall not be cheated. These are those for whom there is nothing in the hereafter save the Fire; and void is what they made therein, and vain what they were doing!

[20] Is he (like them) who stands upon a manifest sign from his Lord, which is a witness from Him, and recites it, with the book of Moses before him for a model and a mercy? These believe in it; and

whosoever of the crews[1] disbelieves in him, the Fire is his promise.

Be not thou in doubt about it; verily, it is truth from thy Lord, though most men do not believe.

Who is more unjust than he who forges against God a lie? they shall be set before their Lord, and the witnesses shall say, 'These it is who lied against their Lord.' Aye! God's curse is on the unjust who turn men away from the path, and crave to make it crooked, and in the hereafter disbelieve! They cannot make Him helpless in the earth, nor have they other than God for patrons. Doubled for them is the torment. They could not hear, nor did they see! Those it is who lose themselves; and that which they did devise has strayed away from them. No doubt but that in the hereafter these are those who lose!

[25] Verily, those who believe and do what is right, and humble themselves to their Lord, they are the fellows of Paradise; they shall dwell therein for aye. The two parties' likeness is as the blind and the deaf, and the seeing and the hearing; shall they two be equal in likeness? will ye not mind?

We did send Noah unto his people, 'Verily, I am to you an obvious warner; that ye should not worship any save God. Verily, I fear for you the torment of the grievous day. But the chiefs of those who misbelieved amongst his people said, 'We only see in thee a mortal like ourselves; nor do we see that any follow thee except the reprobates amongst us by a rash judgment; nor do we see that you have any preference over us; nay more,

---

[1] That is, of the idolater.

we think you liars!' [30] He said, 'O my people!
let us see! if I stand upon a manifest sign from my
Lord, and there come to me mercy from him, and ye
are blinded to it; shall we force you to it while
ye are averse therefrom?

'O my people! I do not ask you for wealth in return for it; my hire is only from God; nor do I repulse those who believe; verily, they shall meet their Lord. But I see you, a people who are ignorant. O my people! who will help me against God, were I to repulse you? do ye not then mind? I do not say that I have the treasures of God; nor do I know the unseen; nor do I say, "Verily, I am an angel;" nor do I say of those whom your eyes despise, "God will never give them any good!"—God knows best what is in their souls—verily, then should I be of the unjust.'

They said, 'O Noah! thou hast wrangled with
us, and hast multiplied wranglings with us; bring us
then what thou hast threatened us with, if thou art
of those who tell the truth.' [35] Said he, 'God will
only bring it on you if He pleases, nor can ye make
Him helpless; nor will my advice profit you, should I wish to advise you, if God wish to lead you into error. He is your Lord, and unto Him shall ye be returned.'

Do they say, 'He has devised it[1]?' Say, 'If I have devised it, then on me be my sin. But I am clear of that wherein ye sin.'

And Noah was inspired, 'None shall surely believe amongst thy people but those who have believed already; take not then ill that which they

[1] The Qur'ân.

do. And make the ark under our eyes, and at our inspiration; and plead not with me for those who have done wrong; verily, they shall be drowned.'

[40] So he made the ark, and every time the chiefs of his people passed by him they jested at him. Said he, 'If ye jest at us, verily, we shall jest at you even as ye are jesting, and ye shall surely know.

'He to whom a torment comes, it shall shame him, and there shall light upon him lasting torment.'

Until at length when our order came, and the oven boiled[1], we said, 'Load therein of every kind two, and likewise thy family,—save those on whom the sentence has already been passed—likewise those who believe;' but there believed not with him save a few. And he said, 'Ride ye therein; in the name of God is its course, and its mooring. Verily, my Lord is forgiving and merciful.'

And it floated on with them mid waves like mountains; and Noah cried to his son who had gone aside, 'O my boy! ride with us and be not with the misbelievers.' [45] Said he, 'I will betake me to a mountain that shall save me from the water.' Said he, 'There is none to save to-day from the command of God, except for him on whom He may have mercy.' And the wave came between them, and he was amongst the drowned[2].

And it was said, 'O earth! swallow down thy

---

[1] Tannûr (oven) signifies also a reservoir of water. Its use in this passage has, however, given rise to some ridiculous superstitions amongst the Mohammedans as to the origin of the deluge.

[2] This story and the further allusion to Noah's son in the next page were probably suggested by Genesis ix. 20–25.

water!' and, 'O heaven! hold!' and the water abated; and the affair was decided, and it[1] settled on *G*ûdî[2], and it was said, 'Away with the people who are evildoers!'

And Noah went unto his Lord and said, 'My Lord, verily, my son is of my people, and, verily, Thy promise is true, and Thou art the justest of judges.' He said, 'O Noah! he is not of thy people; verily, it is a work that is not right. Then, ask me not for that of which thou knowest naught. Verily, I admonish thee that thou shouldst not be of the ignorant.' He said, 'My Lord, verily, I seek refuge in Thee from asking Thee for aught of which I know nothing; and, unless Thou dost forgive me and have mercy on me, I shall be of those who lose.'

[50] It was said, 'O Noah! descend in safety from us, and blessings upon thee and upon (some) nations of those who are with thee[3]; but (some) nations we will allow to enjoy prosperity and then there shall touch them from us grievous woe.' These are stories of the unseen which we reveal to thee; thou didst not know them, thou nor thy people before this. Be patient, then; verily, the issue is for those who fear.

And unto 'Âd (we sent) their brother Hûd; he said, 'O my people! serve God; ye have no god but Him. Ye do but devise a lie. O my people! I do not ask you for hire in return; my hire is

[1] The ark.

[2] *G*ûdî is a corruption apparently for Mount Giordi, the Gordyæi of the Greeks, situated between Armenia and Mesopotamia.

[3] I. e. upon some of the nations who are to form the posterity of thyself and the members of thy family saved with thee.

only from Him who created me: have ye then no sense?

'O my people! ask pardon of your Lord; then turn to Him; He will send the skies down on you in torrents; [55] and He will add strength to your strength: do not then turn back sinners.'

They said, 'O Hûd! thou hast not come to us with a manifest sign; nor will we leave our gods at thy word; nor will we believe in thee. We can only say that some of our gods have attacked thee with evil.' Said he, 'Verily, I call God to witness, and do ye bear witness too, that I am free from that which ye associate beside Him.

'Plot then against me altogether, and give me no delay. Verily, I rely upon God, my Lord and your Lord. There is no beast that walks, but He taketh it by its forelock. Verily, my Lord is on the right way!

[60] 'But if ye turn your backs,—then I have conveyed to you what I was sent to you with; and my Lord will make another people your successors. Ye cannot harm Him at all; verily, my Lord is guardian over all!'

And when our order came we saved Hûd, and those who believed with him, by mercy from us; and we saved them from harsh torment. That (tribe of) 'Âd denied the signs of their Lord, and rebelled against His apostles, and followed the bidding of every headstrong tyrant. They were followed in this world by a curse, and on the resurrection day—'Did not 'Âd disbelieve their Lord? Aye! away with 'Âd the people of Hûd!'

And unto Thamûd (we sent) their brother Zâli'h; said he, 'O my people! worship God; ye have no god but Him. He it is that produced you from the earth, and made you live therein! Then ask pardon of Him; then turn again to Him: verily, my Lord is nigh and answers!'

[65] They said, 'O Zâli'h! thou wert amongst us one we hoped in before this: dost thou forbid us to worship what our fathers worshipped? verily, we are in hesitating doubt as to that to which thou callest us.'

He said, 'O my people! let us see; if I stand upon a manifest sign from my Lord, and there come from Him mercy, who will help me against God if I rebel against Him? Ye will add only to my loss.

O my people! this she-camel[1] of God is a sign for you; leave her, then, to feed in God's earth, and touch her not with evil, or there will catch you torment that is nigh.' But they did hamstring her, and he said, 'Enjoy yourselves in your houses for three days;—that is the promise that shall not be belied.'

And when our order came we saved Zâli'h, and those who believed with him, by our mercy, from disgrace upon that day. Verily, thy Lord He is powerful and mighty.

[70] And the noise caught those who had done wrong; and on the morrow they were lying corpses in their houses, as though they had never dwelt therein. Did not Thamûd indeed disbelieve in their Lord? Aye! away with Thamûd!

Our messengers did come to Abraham with glad tidings; they said, 'Peace!' He said, 'Peace be

[1] See note, p. 107.

it!' nor did he delay to bring the roasted calf. But when he saw that their hands reached not thereto, he could not understand them, and harboured fear of them. They said, 'Fear not. Verily, we are sent unto the people of Lot.' And his wife was standing by, laughing; and we gave her the glad tidings of Isaac, and of Jacob after Isaac. [75] Said she, 'Alas for me! shall I bear a son when I am an old woman, and this husband of mine an old man? Verily, this is a wonderful thing!' They said, 'Dost thou wonder at the bidding of God? God's mercy and blessings upon you, ye people of the house! Verily, He is to be praised and glorified.'

And when his terror left Abraham, and the glad tidings came to him, he wrangled with us about the people of Lot; verily, Abraham was clement, pitiful, relenting.

'O Abraham! avoid this; verily, the bidding of thy Lord has come; verily, there is coming to them torment that cannot be put off.'

[80] And when our messengers came to Lot, he was grieved for them; but his arm was straitened for them[1], and he said, 'This is a troublesome day!' And his people came to him, rushing at him, for before that they used to work evil. He said, 'O my people! here are my daughters, they are purer for you; then, fear God, and do not disgrace me through my guests;—is there not among you one right-thinking man?'

They said, 'Thou knowest that we have no claim on thy daughters; verily, thou knowest what we want!' He said, 'Had I but power over you; or

[1] I.e. he was powerless to help them.

could I but resort to some strong column[1]....!' (The angels) said, 'O Lot! verily, we are the messengers of thy Lord, they shall certainly not reach thee; then travel with thy people in the darkness of the night, and let none of you look round except thy wife: verily, there shall befall her what befalls them. Verily, their appointment is for the morning! and is not the morning nigh?'

And when our bidding came, we made their high parts their low parts[2]. And we rained down upon them stones and baked clay[3] one after another, marked[4], from thy Lord, and these are not so far from the unjust[5]!

[85] And unto Midian (we sent) their brother Sho'hâib[6]. He said, 'O my people! serve God; ye have no god but Him, and give not short measure and weight. Verily, I see you well off; but, verily, I fear for you the torments of an encompassing day. O my people! give measure and weight fairly, and defraud not men of their things; and wreak not wrong in the earth, corrupting it. God's residue[7]

---

[1] I.e. some support, such as a powerful clan or chieftain.

[2] That is, overturned the cities of the plain.

[3] The Abyssinians, who had invaded Mecca some years before, are mentioned in the Chapter of the Elephant (CV) as being destroyed in a similar manner by flocks of birds, who threw down such missiles upon them.

[4] The legend is that they each contained the name of the person for whom they were destined; so the old saying, 'every bullet has its billet.'

[5] I.e. the same punishment is likely to overtake other wrongdoers, the threat being especially directed against the unbelieving inhabitants of Mecca.

[6] See Chapter VII.

[7] A little which God leaves you after paying every one his due.

is better for you if ye be believers. But I am not a guardian over you.'

They said, 'O Sho'hâib! Do thy prayers bid thee that we should forsake what our fathers served, or that we should not do as we please with our wealth? Thou art, forsooth, the clement and straightforward one!'

[90] He said, 'O my people! Do ye see? If I stand upon a manifest sign from my Lord, and He provides me from Himself with a goodly provision, and I consent not with you to that which I forbid you, I only wish to better you so far as I can,—nor comes my grace through any one but God; on Him do I rely, and unto Him I turn. O my people! let not a breach with me make you so sin that there befall you the like of that which befel the people of Noah, or the people of Hûd, or the people of Zâli'h—nor are the people of Lot so far from you! Ask pardon, then, from your Lord, then turn to Him; verily, my Lord is merciful, loving!'

They said, 'O Sho'hâib! we do not understand much of what thou sayest, and we see that thou art weak amongst us; and were it not for thy family we would stone thee, nor couldst thou be powerful over us.'

He said, 'O my people! are my family more esteemed by you than God? or have you taken Him as something to cast behind your backs? Verily, my Lord, whate'er ye do, doth comprehend. [95] O my people! act according to your power; verily, I too will act, and ye at length shall know! To whomsoever torment comes it shall disgrace him, and him who is a liar. Watch then; verily, I with you am watching too!'

And when our bidding came we saved Sho'hâib, and those who believed with him, by our mercy; and the noise caught those who had done wrong, and on the morrow they were in their houses prone, as though they had not dwelt therein. Aye! 'Away with Midian!' as it was, 'Away with Thamûd!'

And we sent Moses with our signs and with obvious power unto Pharaoh and his chiefs; but they followed Pharaoh's bidding, and Pharaoh's bidding was not straightforward.

[100] He shall approach his people on the resurrection day, and take them down to water[1] at the Fire,—an evil watering-place to water at!

In this (world) were they followed by a curse; and on the resurrection day evil shall be the aid they are aided with!

That is one of the stories of the cities which we recite to thee—some of them are standing now and some mown down!

We did not wrong them, but they wronged themselves. Their gods availed them naught, on which they called instead of God, when once the bidding of thy Lord had come; nor did they add save to their downfall!

Thus is thy Lord's overtaking when He overtakes the cities that have done wrong; verily, His overtaking is grievous, keen.

[105] Verily, in that is a sign to him who fears the torment of the last day;—that is a day unto which men shall be gathered;—that is a witnessed day!

---

[1] The word used is that always applied by desert Arabs to going to a spring for water.

We will not delay it, save unto a numbered and appointed time. The day when it shall come no soul shall speak save by His permission, and amongst them (shall be) the wretched and the glad.

And as for those who are wretched—why, in the Fire! there shall they groan and sob! to dwell therein for aye, so long as the heavens and the earth endure; save what thy Lord will. Verily, thy Lord is one who works His will.

[110] And as for those who are glad—why, in Paradise! to dwell therein for aye, so long as the heavens and the earth endure; save what thy Lord will [1],—a ceaseless boon!

Be not then in doubt concerning what these men do serve;—they only serve as their fathers served before; and we will give them their portion undiminished.

We gave Moses the Book before, and then they disagreed concerning it, and, had it not been for a word that had been passed by thy Lord, it would have been decided between them; but, verily, they are (still) in hesitating doubt concerning it.

But, verily, every one thy Lord will surely repay for their works; verily, He of what they do is well aware!

Do thou then be upright, as thou art bidden, and whosoever turns repentantly with thee; and transgress ye not:—verily, He on what ye do doth look.

[115] Lean not unto those who do wrong, lest the Fire touch you, for ye have no patrons but God; and, moreover, ye shall not be helped!

---

[1] I.e. unless He please to increase their happiness.

And be thou steadfast in prayer at the two ends of the day, and the (former and latter) parts of the night. Verily, good works remove evil works;—that is a reminder to the mindful! And be thou patient, for God wastes not the hire of those who do good.

And were there among the generations before you any endowed with a remnant (of piety) forbidding evildoing in the earth, save a few of those whom we saved; but the evildoers followed what they enjoyed, and were sinners.

Thy Lord would not have destroyed the cities unjustly while the people of them were welldoers.

[120] Had thy Lord pleased, He would have made men one nation; but they will not cease to differ, save those thy Lord has had mercy on. For this has He created them, and the word of thy Lord is fulfilled, 'I will surely fill hell with *g*inns and mankind altogether.'

And all that we relate to thee of the stories of the apostles is what will stablish thy heart: and herein has the truth come to thee, and an admonition and a reminder to the believers.

Say to those who believe not, 'Act according to your power, verily, we are acting too! And wait ye, verily, we are waiting too!'

God's are the unseen things of the heavens and of the earth; and unto Him the affair doth all return. Then serve Him and rely on Him; for thy Lord is not heedless of that which ye do.

The Chapter of Joseph, (peace be on him!)

(XII. Mecca.)

In the name of the merciful and compassionate God.

A. L. R. Those are the signs of the perspicuous Book. Verily, we have revealed it, an Arabic Qur'ân; haply ye may understand.

We tell thee the best of stories, in inspiring thee with this Qur'ân, though thou wert before it among the heedless.

When Joseph said to his father, 'O my sire! verily, I saw eleven stars, and the sun, and the moon,—I saw them adoring me!'

[5] He said, 'O my boy! tell not thy vision to thy brethren, for they will plot a plot against thee; verily, the devil is to man an open foe.'

Thus does thy Lord choose thee, and teach thee the interpretation of sayings, and fulfil His favour upon thee, and upon Jacob's people, as He fulfilled it upon thy two forefathers before thee, Abraham and Isaac,—verily, thy Lord is knowing, wise!

In Joseph and his brethren were signs to those who enquire!

When they said, 'Surely, Joseph and his brother are dearer to our father than we, a band[1] although we be; verily, our father is in obvious error.

'Slay Joseph, or cast him in some land; that your father's face may be free for you, and ye may be, after he is gone, a people who do right.'

[10] A speaker from amongst them spake, 'Slay

---

[1] The word means a band of between twenty and forty persons.

not Joseph, but throw him into the bottom of the pit; some of the travellers may pick him up, if so ye do.'

Said they, 'O our father! what ails thee that thou wilt not trust us with Joseph while we are unto him sincere? Send him with us to-morrow to revel and to play, and, verily, we over him will keep good guard.'

Said he, 'Verily, it grieves me that ye should go off with him, for I fear lest the wolf devour him while ye of him do take no heed.'

Said they, 'Why, if the wolf should devour him while we are (such) a band, verily, we then should deserve to lose!'

[15] And when they had gone off with him and agreed to put him in the depths of the pit, and we inspired him, 'Thou shalt surely inform them of this affair of theirs and they shall not perceive[1].'

And they came to their father at eve and weeping said, 'O our father! verily, we went forth to race and left Joseph by our goods, and the wolf devoured him,—but thou wilt not believe us, truth tellers though we be.'

And they brought his shirt with lying blood upon it. Said he, 'Nay, but your souls have induced you to do this; but patience is fair! and God is He whom I ask for aid against that which ye describe.'

And travellers came and sent their water-drawer; and he let down his bucket. Said he, 'O glad tidings! this is a youth.' And they kept him secret, as a chattel; but God knew what they were doing.

---

[1] This is a prophetic intimation to Joseph of his future interview with his brethren in Egypt.

[20] And they sold him for a mean price,—drachmæ counted out,—and they parted with him cheaply.

And the man from Egypt who had bought him said to his wife, 'Honour his abiding here; it may be he will be of use to us, or we may adopt him as a son.'

Thus did we stablish Joseph in the land; and we did surely teach him the interpretation of sayings; for God can overcome His affairs, though most men do not know.

And when he had reached his strength[1] we brought him judgment and knowledge, for thus do we reward those who do good.

And she in whose house he was desired him for his person; and she locked the doors and said, 'Come along with thee!' Said he, 'Refuge in God! verily, my Lord has made good my abiding here; verily, the wrong-doers shall not prosper.'

And she was anxious for him, and he would have been anxious for her, had it not been that he saw the demonstration[2] of his Lord; thus did we turn evil and fornication from him; verily, he was of our sincere servants.

[25] And they raced to the door and she rent his shirt from behind; and they met her master at the door. Said she, 'What is the recompense of him who wishes evil for thy family, but that imprisonment or a grievous torment?'

Said he, 'She desired me for my person.' And

---

[1] The age of puberty.

[2] The angel Gabriel in the form of his father appeared with a warning gesture, according to the Muslim commentators.

a witness from among her family bore witness: 'If his shirt be rent from in front, then she speaks the truth and he is of the liars; but if his shirt be rent from behind, then she lies and he is of the truth tellers.'

And when he saw his shirt rent from behind he said, 'This is one of your tricks; verily, your tricks are mighty! Joseph! turn aside from this. And do thou, woman, ask pardon for thy fault; verily, thou wert of the sinners.'

[30] And women in the city said, 'The wife of the prince desires her young man for his person; he has infatuated her with love: verily, we see her in obvious error.' And when she heard of their craftiness, she sent to them and prepared for them a banquet, and gave each of them a knife; and she said, 'Come forth to them!' And when they saw him they said, 'Great God!' and cut their hands[1] and said, 'God forbid! This is no mortal, this is nothing but an honourable angel.' Said she, 'This is he concerning whom ye blamed me. I did desire him for his person, but he was too continent. But if he do not what I bid him he shall surely be imprisoned and shall surely be among the small!' Said he, 'My Lord! Prison is dearer to me than what they call on me to do; and unless Thou turn from me their craftiness I shall feel a passion for them and shall be among the ignorant!' And his Lord answered him and turned from him their craftiness; verily, He both hears and knows!

[35] Then it appeared good to them, even after they had seen the signs[2], to imprison him until a time.

---

[1] In their sudden emotion at his beauty. [2] Of his innocence.

And there entered the prison with him two young men. Said one of them, 'Verily, I see myself[1] pressing wine.' And the other said, 'Verily, I see myself bearing on my head loaves from which the birds do eat; inform us of the interpretation thereof; verily, we see that thou art of those who do good.'

He said, 'There shall not come to you any food with which ye are provided, but I will inform you both of its interpretation before it comes to you. That is (some) of what my Lord has taught me; verily, I have left the faith of a people who do not believe in God, while in the future too they disbelieve. And I have followed the faith of my fathers, Abraham and Isaac and Jacob; we could not associate aught with God; that is from God's grace upon us and upon men: but most men give not thanks. O ye twain fellow-prisoners! Are manifold lords better, or God, the one, the dominant? [40] What ye worship beside Him are naught but names which ye have named, ye and your fathers, for which God has sent down no authority. Judgment is only God's; He bids you worship only Him. That is the standard of religion,—but most men do not know. O ye twain fellow-prisoners! as for one of you, he shall pour out wine for his lord: and as for the other, he shall be crucified, and the birds shall eat of his head. The matter is decreed whereon ye asked me for a decision!'

And he said to him whom he thought would escape of those two, 'Remember me with thy lord!' But Satan made him[2] forget the remembrance of his lord, so he tarried in prison a few years.

---

[1] In a dream.

[2] The application of the pronoun is vague in the text of this

Then said the king, 'Verily, I see seven fat kine which seven lean kine devoured; and seven green ears of corn and others dry. O ye chiefs! Explain to me my vision, if a vision ye can expound!'

Said they, 'Confused dreams, and naught of the exposition of such dreams know we!'

[45] Then he who had escaped of those twain said,—remembering after a while,—'Verily, I will inform you of the interpretation thereof, so send me.'

'Joseph! O thou truth teller! explain to us the seven fat kine which seven lean devoured; and the seven green ears of corn and others dry. Haply I may go back to the men, haply they then may know!'

He said, 'Ye shall sow for seven years, as is your wont; but what ye reap, let it remain in the ear, except a little whereof ye shall eat. Then there shall come after that seven severe (years) which shall devour what ye have put by before for them, save a little of what ye shall preserve. Then there will come after that a year in which men shall have rain and in which they shall press[1].'

[50] Then said the king, 'Bring him to me.'

And when the messenger came to him, he said, 'Go back to thy lord, and ask him, "What meant the women who cut their hands? Verily, my lord knows their craftiness!"'

He said, 'What was your design when ye desired Joseph for his person?' They said, 'God

passage, which is variously interpreted, either that Satan made the butler forget to mention Joseph to his lord Pharaoh, or that Satan made Joseph forget for the moment his Lord God, and place his trust on the man rather than on Him.

[1] I.e. press wine and oil.

forbid! we know no bad of him.' Said the wife of the prince, 'Now does the truth appear! I desired him for his person and, verily, he is of those who tell the truth.'

'That' (said Joseph) 'was that he might know that I did not betray him in his absence, and that God guides not the craft of those who do betray! Yet I do not clear myself, for the soul is very urgent to evil, save what my Lord has had mercy on; verily, my Lord is forgiving and merciful!'

And the king said, 'Bring him to me. I will take him specially for myself.' And when he had spoken with him he said, 'Verily, to-day thou art with us in a permanent place of trust.'

[55] He said, 'Place me over the treasures of the land; verily, I will be a knowing keeper.'

Thus did we stablish Joseph in the land that he might settle in what part thereof he pleased—we overtake with our mercy whom we will, nor do we waste the hire of those who do good; and surely the hire of the future life is better for those who believe and who have feared.

And his brethren came to Joseph, and they entered in unto him and he knew them, but they recognised not him.

And when he had equipped them with their equipment he said, 'Bring me a brother that ye have from your father; do ye not see that I give good measure, and that I am the best of entertainers? [60] But if ye bring him not to me, no measure shall ye have with me, nor shall ye come nigh me.'

They said, 'We will desire him of our father, and we will surely do it.'

Then he said to his young men, 'Put their chattels[1] in their packs, haply they may know it when they are come back to their family; haply they may return.'

And when they returned to their father, they said, 'O our father! Measure is withheld from us; so send with us our brother that we may get measure, and, verily, him we will keep!'

He said, 'Shall I entrust you with him, save as I entrusted you with his brother before? but God is the best of keepers, and He is the most merciful of the merciful.'

[65] And when they opened their goods they found their chattels restored to them. Said they, 'O our father! What more can we crave? Here are our chattels restored to us, and we shall guard our brother, and shall have an additional measure beside that—a small measure[2].'

He said, 'I will by no means send him with you until you give me a compact from God that ye will surely bring him to me, unless ye be encompassed[3].'

So when they had given him their compact he said, 'God over what ye say has charge.'

And he said, 'O my sons! enter not by one gate, but enter by several gates; but I cannot avail you aught against God. Judgment is only God's; upon Him do I rely, and on Him do the reliant rely.'

[1] The goods which they had brought to barter, or the money they had paid for the corn.

[2] Commentators differ as to whether this means that what they had brought was insufficient, or whether the additional measure was a small quantity for Pharaoh to bestow, or whether Jacob utters the words meaning that it is not enough to induce him to part with his son.

[3] By some unavoidable hindrance.

And when they had entered as their father bade them, it availed them nothing against God, save for a want in Jacob's soul which it fulfilled; for, verily, he was possessed of knowledge, for that we had taught him;—but most men do not know.

And when they entered in unto Joseph, he took his brother to stay with him, and said, 'Verily, I am thy brother—then take not ill that which they have been doing.'

[70] And when he had equipped them with their equipment he placed the drinking cup in his brother's pack; then a crier cried out, 'O ye caravan! verily, ye are thieves!'

They said, approaching them, 'What is it that ye miss?'

Said they, 'We miss the goblet of the king, and whoso brings it shall have a camel-load, and I am guarantee thereof.'

They said, 'By God! Ye knew we came not to do evil in the land, and that we were not thieves.'

They said, 'And what shall be the recompense thereof if ye be liars?'

[75] They said, 'The recompense thereof is he in whose pack it is found—he shall be the recompense thereof; thus do we recompense the unjust.'

And he began with their sacks before the sacks of his brother; then he drew it forth from his brother's sack. Thus did we devise a stratagem for Joseph. He could not take his brother by the king's religion[1] except God pleased;—we raise the degrees of

[1] I.e. by the law of Egypt it was not lawful for Joseph to take his brother for a bondsman as a punishment for theft.

whomsoever we please, and over every possessor of knowledge is one who knows.

They said, 'If he has stolen, a brother of his has stolen before him.'

But Joseph kept it secret in his soul and disclosed it not to them. Said he, 'Ye are in a bad case, and God knows best about what ye describe.'

They said, 'O prince! Verily, he has a father, a very old man; take then one of us instead of him; verily, we can see that thou art of those who do good.'

Said he, '(I seek) refuge in God from taking any save him with whom we found our property; verily, we should then be certainly unjust.'

[80] And when they despaired of him they retired to consult privately. Said the eldest of them, 'Do ye not know that your father has taken a compact from God against you? Aforetime ye exceeded in the matter of Joseph—I will surely not quit the land until my father give me leave, or God judge for me, for He is the best of judges.

'Return ye to your father and say, "O our father! verily, thy son has committed theft, and we bore testimony to naught but what we knew; for of the unforeseen we were not keepers!"

'Ask then in the city where we were, and of the caravan in which we approached it, for, verily, we tell the truth.'

Said he, 'Nay, your souls have induced you to do this thing. But patience is fair. It may be that God will give me them all together;—verily, He is knowing, wise.'

And he turned away from them and said, 'O my

lament for Joseph!' and his eyes grew white with grief, for he repressed (his woe).

[85] They said, 'By God! thou wilt not cease to remember Joseph till thou art at the point of death, or art of those who perish!'

Said he, 'I only complain of my emotion and my grief to God, for I know that from God which ye know nothing of.

'O my sons! go and enquire concerning Joseph and his brother, and despair not of God's comfort; for, verily, none need despair of God's comfort save a misbelieving people!'

And when they entered in unto him they said, 'O prince! distress has touched both us and our families, and we have brought trifling chattels. So give us full measure and bestow upon us in charity; verily, God rewards the charitable.'

He said, 'Do ye know what ye did with Joseph and his brother, while ye were ignorant?'

[90] They said, 'Art thou then indeed Joseph?' He said, 'I am Joseph, and this is my brother; God has been gracious towards us. Verily, whoso fears God and is patient,—verily, God wastes not the hire of those who do good!'

They said, 'By God! God has chosen thee over us; and we indeed were sinners.'

He said, 'No reproach against you to-day! God will pardon you, for He is the most merciful of the merciful. Take this my shirt, and throw it over the face of my father, he will become able to see; and bring me your families all together.'

And when the caravan departed, their father said, 'Verily, I find the smell of Joseph, unless ye think I dote!'

[95] They said, 'By God! thou art in thy old error.' And when the herald of glad tidings came he threw it on his face, and he was restored to sight.

Said he, 'Did I not tell you that I know from God that of which ye know not?'

They said, 'O our father! ask pardon for us of our sins;—verily, we were sinners!'

He said, 'I will ask pardon for you from my Lord; verily, He is the pardoning and merciful.'

[100] And when they entered in unto Joseph, he took his father to stay with him, and said, 'Enter ye into Egypt, if it please God, safe.' And he raised his father upon the throne, and they fell down before him adoring.

And he said, 'O my sire! This is the interpretation of my vision aforetime; my Lord has made it come true, and He has been good to me, in bringing me forth out of prison, and bringing you from the desert, after Satan had made a breach between me and my brethren;—verily, my Lord is kind to whomsoever He will;—verily, He is the knowing, the wise!

'O my Lord! thou hast given me dominion, and hast taught me the interpretation of sayings; O originator of the heavens and the earth! Thou art my patron in this world and the next; take me to Thyself resigned, and let me reach the righteous!'

That is one of the stories of the unseen which we inspire thee with, though thou wert not with them when they agreed in their affair, when they were so crafty.—And yet most men, though thou shouldst be urgent, will not believe.

Thou dost not ask them for it a hire; it is naught but a reminder to the world.

[105] How many a sign in the heavens and the earth do they pass by and turn away therefrom!

Nor do most of them believe in God without associating (other gods) with Him.

Are they safe, then, from overwhelming vengeance coming on them from the torment of God? or from the Hour coming upon them suddenly while they do not perceive?

Say, 'This is my way; I call now unto God on clear proof, I and those who follow me; and celebrated be God's praises, for I am not of the idolaters.'

Nor did we ever send before thee any save men whom we inspired, of the people of the cities. Have they not journeyed on in the earth, and beheld how was the end of those before them? But the abode of the future is surely better for those who believe;—what! have they then no sense?

[110] Until when the apostles despaired and they thought that they were proved liars, our help came to them, and whosoever we pleased was saved; but our violence is not averted from the sinful people.

Their stories were a lesson to those endowed with minds. It was not a tale forged, but a verification of what was before it, and a detailing of everything, and a guide and a mercy to a people who believe.

The Chapter of Thunder.

(XIII. Mecca.)

In the name of the merciful and compassionate God.

A. L. M. R. Those are the signs of the Book, and that which is sent down to thee from thy Lord is the truth; but most people will not believe. God it is who has raised the heavens without columns that ye can see; then He made for the throne, and subjected the sun and the moon; each one runs on to a stated and appointed time; He governs the affair, details the signs;—haply of the meeting with your Lord ye will be sure.

And He it is who has stretched out the earth and placed therein firm mountains and rivers, and of every fruit has He placed therein two kinds. He makes the night cover the day;—verily, in that are signs unto a people who reflect.

And on the earth are neighbouring portions, and gardens of grapes and corn and palms growing together (from one root) and not growing together; they are watered with one water, yet we distinguish one over the other as food;—verily, in that are signs unto a people who have sense.

[5] And if thou shouldst wonder, wondrous is their speech: 'What! when we have become dust, shall we really then be created anew?'

These are they who disbelieve in their Lord, and these are they with fetters round their necks, and these are the fellows of the Fire; they shall dwell therein for aye!

They will wish thee to hasten on the evil rather

than the good; examples have passed away before them: but thy Lord is possessor of forgiveness unto men, notwithstanding their injustice; but, verily, thy Lord is keen to punish.

Those who misbelieve say, 'Unless a sign be sent down upon him from his Lord . . . .'—Thou art only a warner, and every people has its guide.

God knows what each female bears, and what the wombs fall short of or add; for dimensions of everything are with Him.

[10] He who knows the unseen and the visible,—the great, the lofty one.

Alike among you is he who keeps secret his speech and he who displays it; and he who hides by night and he who stalks abroad by day. Each of them has pursuers[1] before him and behind him, to keep guard over him at the command of God; verily, God changes not what a people has until they change it for themselves And when God wishes evil to a people there is no averting it, nor have they a protector beside Him.

He it is who shows you the lightning for fear and hope[2]; and He brings up the heavy clouds.

And the thunder celebrates His praise, and the angels too for fear of Him; and He sends the thunder-clap and overtakes therewith whom He will;—yet they wrangle about God! But He is strong in might.

[15] On Him is the call of truth, and those who call on others than Him shall not be answered at all,

---

[1] Guardian angels.

[2] I.e. hope of rain; lightning is always hailed with joy by the Arabs as a precursor of rain.

save as one who stretches out his hand to the water that it may reach his mouth, but it reaches it not! The call of the misbelievers is only in error.

And God do those who are in the heavens and the earth adore, whether they will or no! as do their shadows also morn and eve.

Say, 'Who is Lord of the heavens and the earth?' say, 'God;' say, 'Do ye take beside God patrons who cannot control profit or harm for themselves?' say, 'Shall the blind and the seeing be held equal? or shall the darkness and the light be held equal? or have they made associates with God who can create as He creates, so that the creation seem familiar to them?' say, 'God is the creator of everything, and He is the one, the dominant.'

He sends down from the sky water, and the water-courses flow according to their bulk, and the torrent bears along the floating scum: and from what they set fire to, craving ornaments or utensils, comes a scum like that;—thus does God hit the truth and the falsehood;—and as for the scum it is thrown off, and as for what profits man it stays on the earth. Thus does God strike out parables!

For those who respond to their Lord is good; but those who respond not to Him, had they all that is in the earth and the like thereof as well, they would give it for a ransom; these shall have an evil reckoning up! and their resort is hell,—an evil couch shall it be!

Is he who knows that naught but the truth is sent down upon thee from thy Lord like him who is blind? Only those possessed of minds will remember!

[20] Those who fulfil God's covenant and break not the compact, and those who attain what God has bidden to be attained, and dread their Lord and fear the evil reckoning up; and those who are patient, craving their Lord's face, and are steadfast in prayer, and expend in alms of what we have bestowed upon them secretly and openly, and ward off evil with good,—these shall have the recompense of the abode, gardens of Eden, into which they shall enter with the righteous amongst their fathers and their wives and their seed; and the angels shall enter in unto them from every gate:—'Peace be upon you! for that ye were patient; and goodly is the recompense of the abode.'

[25] And those who break God's covenant after compacting for it, and who cut asunder what God hath bidden to be joined, and who do evil in the earth, these—upon them is the curse of God, and for them is an evil abode.

God extends his bounty freely to whomsoever He will, or He metes it out; and they rejoice in the life of this world, but the life of this world is naught but a (temporary) provision compared with the next.

Those who misbelieve say, 'Unless a sign is sent down upon him from his Lord . . . .' Say, 'God leads whom He will astray, but guides unto Him those who turn again.

'Those who believe and whose hearts are comforted by the mention of God,—aye! by the mention of God shall their hearts be comforted, who believe and do what is right. Good cheer for them and an excellent resort.'

Thus have we sent thee to a nation before

which other nations have passed away, to recite to them that which we have inspired thee with; yet they misbelieve in the merciful! Say, 'He is my Lord; there is no god but He; upon Him do I rely, and unto Him is my repentance.'

[30] And though it were a Qur'ân by which the mountains were moved, or by which the earth were cut up, or the dead made to speak[1]—nay, God's is the command altogether! Did not those who believed know[2] that if God had pleased He would have guided men altogether?

And a striking calamity shall not cease to overtake those who misbelieve for what they have wrought, or to alight close by their dwellings; until God's promise comes—verily, God fails not in His promise.

Before thee have apostles been mocked at; and those who misbelieved have I allowed to range at large; and then it caught them up! How then was my punishment?

Shall He who is standing over every soul (to note) what it has earned——? And they join partners with God! Say, 'Name them; can ye inform Him of what He does not know in the earth? or is it for name's sake only (that ye call upon them)?

'Nay, then, stratagem is made seemly to those who misbelieve, and they turn folks from the path of God! But whomsoever God doth lead astray, no guide has he.'

---

[1] They would not believe.

[2] The word used in the original, yâi'as, means 'despair,' but in the patois of the Na'*h*a'h tribe signifies 'know,' and is so interpreted by the native commentators on this passage.

For them is torment in this world's life; but surely the torment of the next is more wretched still—nor have they against God a keeper.

[35] The likeness of the Paradise which those who fear God are promised, beneath it rivers flow, its food is enduring, and likewise its shade! That is the recompense of those who fear; but the recompense of misbelievers is the Fire!

And those to whom we brought the Book rejoice in that which we have sent down to thee; but of the confederates are some who deny a part thereof.

Say, 'I am only bidden to serve God and not to associate any with Him; on Him I call and to Him is my recourse.'

Thus have we sent it down, an Arabic judgment, but hadst thou followed their lusts, after the knowledge that has come to thee, thou hadst not had against God a patron or a keeper.

And we sent apostles before thee, and we made for them wives and seed; and no apostle could bring a sign save by God's permission;—for every period there is a book.

God blots out what He will, or He confirms; and with Him is the Mother of the Book[1].

[40] Either we will let thee see a part of what we threaten them with, or we will take thee to Ourself; but thy duty is only to deliver thy message, and ours to reckon up.

Did they not see that we come to the land and diminish the borders thereof[2]? God judges, and there is none to reverse His judgment, and He is swift at reckoning up!

---

[1] See p. 2, note 2.

[2] Alluding to the conquests of Islâm.

And those who were before them were crafty too; but God's is the craft altogether! He knows what every soul earns; and the misbelievers shall know whose is the recompense of the abode.

And those who misbelieve say, 'Thou art not sent!' Say, 'God is witness enough between me and you; and so is he who has the knowledge of the Book!'

The Chapter of Abraham, (peace be on him!)

(XIV. Mecca.)

In the name of the merciful and compassionate God.

A. L. M. A book which we have sent down to thee, to bring men forth from darkness into light, by permission of their Lord, unto the way of the mighty and praiseworthy one.

God is He whose is whatsoever is in the heavens and whatsoever is in the earth. Alas for the misbelievers, for their torment is keen! Who love this world's life better than the next, and turn folks from the path of God, and crave to make it crooked; these are in remote error.

We have not sent any apostle save with the language of his people, that he might explain to them. But God leads whom He will astray, and guides whom He will; and He is the mighty, the wise.

[5] We did send Moses with our signs, 'Bring forth thy people from the darkness into the light,

and remind them of the days[1] of God!' verily, in that are signs to every patient, grateful one.

When Moses said to his people, 'Remember the favours of God towards you, when He saved you from Pharaoh's people, who sought to wreak you evil woe, slaughtering your sons and letting your women live;' in that was a great trial for you from your Lord. When your Lord proclaimed, 'If ye give thanks I will surely give you increase; but if ye misbelieve, verily, my torment is severe!' And Moses said, 'If ye misbelieve, ye and those who are on the earth altogether—then, verily, God is rich, and to be praised!'

Has not the story come to you of those who were before you, of the people of Noah, and 'Âd, and Thamûd, [10] and those who came after them? none knows them save God. Apostles came unto them with manifest signs; but they thrust their hands into their mouths[2] and said, 'Verily, we disbelieve in that which ye are sent with, and we are in hesitating doubt concerning that to which ye call us!' Their apostles said, 'Is there doubt about God, the originator of the heavens and the earth? He calls you to pardon you for your sins, and to respite you until an appointed time.'

They said, 'Ye are but mortals like ourselves; ye wish to turn us from what our fathers used to serve. Bring us, then, obvious authority!'

Their apostles said unto them, 'We are only

---

[1] This may, according to the Arab idiom, mean either 'battles' in which God had given victory to the believers; or simply 'days' on which God has shown them favour.

[2] Easterns, when annoyed, always bite their hands; see Chapter III, verse 115.

mortals like yourselves; but God is gracious unto whomsoever He will of His servants, and it is not for us to bring you an authority, save by His permission; but upon God do the believers rely!'
[15] What ails us that we should not rely on God when He has guided us in our paths? we will be surely patient in your hurting us; for upon God rely those who do rely.

And those who misbelieved said to their apostles, 'We will drive you forth from our land; or else ye shall return to our faith!' And their Lord inspired them, 'We will surely destroy the unjust; and we will make you to dwell in the land after them. That is for him who fears my place and fears my threat!'

Then they asked for an issue; and disappointed was every rebel tyrant! Behind such a one is hell, and he shall be given to drink liquid pus[1]!
[20] He shall try to swallow it, but cannot gulp it down; and death shall come upon him from every place, and yet he shall not die; and behind him shall be rigorous woe!

The likeness of those who disbelieve on their Lord,—their works are as ashes whereon the wind blows fiercely on a stormy day. They have no power at all over that which they have earned.—That is the remote error!

Dost not thou see that God created the heavens and the earth in truth? If He please He can take

[1] Sale and Rodwell have softened down this filthy expression, one rendering it 'filthy water' and the other 'tainted water;' the Arabic, however, will not bear this rendering. The first word meaning 'water' or 'liquid,' and the second, in apposition with it, 'pus,' or purulent matter oozing from a corpse or a sore.

you off and bring a new creation; nor is that hard for God!

They all come out to God; and the weak say to those who were big with pride, 'We were followers of yours, can ye now avail us aught against God's torment?'

[25] They say, 'If God had guided us we would have guided you. It is the same to us if we are agonized or if we are penitent, we have no escape.'

And Satan says, when the affair is decided, 'Verily, God promised you a promise of truth; but I promised you and failed you; for I had no authority over you. I only called you, and ye did answer me; then blame me not, but blame yourselves; I cannot help you, nor can you help me. I disbelieved in your associating me (with God) before; verily, the wrong-doers, for them is grievous woe!'

But I will cause those who believe and do aright to enter gardens beneath which rivers flow, to dwell therein for aye by the permission of their Lord; their salutation therein is 'Peace!'

Dost thou not see how God strikes out a parable? A good word is like a good tree whose root is firm, and whose branches are in the sky; [30] it gives its fruit at every season by the permission of its Lord—but God strikes out parables for men that haply they may be mindful.

And the likeness of a bad word is as a bad tree, which is felled from above the earth, and has no staying place.

God answers those who believe with the sure word in this world's life and in the next; but

God leads the wrong-doers astray; for God does what He will.

Dost not thou see those who have changed God's favours for misbelief, and have made their people to alight at the abode of perdition?—in hell they shall broil, and an ill resting-place shall it be!

[35] And they made peers for God, to lead men astray from His path. Say, 'Enjoy yourselves, for, verily, your journey is to the Fire.'

Say to my servants who believe, that they be steadfast in prayer and expend in alms of what we have bestowed upon them in secret and in public, before there comes the day when there shall be no buying and no friendship.

God it is who created the heavens and the earth; and sent down from the sky water, and brought forth therewith fruits as a provision for you; and subjected to you the ships, to float therein upon the sea at His bidding; and subjected for you the rivers; and subjected for you the sun and the moon, constant both; and subjected for you the night and the day; and brought you of everything ye asked Him: but if ye try to number God's favours, ye cannot count them;—verily, man is very unjust and ungrateful.

And when Abraham said, 'My Lord, make this land[1] safe, and turn me and my sons away from serving idols!

'My Lord, verily, they have led many men astray; but he who follows me, verily, he is of me; but he who rebels against me,—verily, thou art pardoning, merciful!

[1] Mecca and its neighbourhood.

[40] 'O our Lord! verily, I have made some of my seed dwell in a valley without corn, by thy Sacred House[1]. O our Lord! let them be steadfast in prayer and make the hearts of men yearn towards them, and provide them with fruits, haply they may give thanks.

'O our Lord! verily, Thou knowest what we hide and what we publish; for naught is hid from God in the earth or in the sky. Praise to God who hath bestowed on me, notwithstanding my old age, Ishmael and Isaac!—verily, my Lord surely hears prayer.

'O my Lord! make me steadfast in prayer, and of my seed likewise! O our Lord! and accept my prayer! O our Lord! pardon me and my parents and the believers on the reckoning day!'

So think not God careless of what the unjust do; He only respites them until the day on which all eyes shall stare!

Hurrying on, raising up their heads, with their looks not turned back to them[2], and their hearts void; and warn men of the day when the torment shall come!

[45] And those who have done wrong shall say, 'O our Lord! respite us until an appointed time nigh at hand, and we will respond to Thy call, and follow the apostles!'—'What! did ye not swear before, ye should have no decline?'

And ye dwelt in the dwellings of those who had wronged themselves; and it was made plain to you how we did with them; and we struck out parables

---

[1] The Kaabah at Mecca.

[2] I.e. with their looks fixed straight in front of them through terror.

for you: but they plotted their stratagems, but with God is a stratagem for them, although at their stratagem the mountains should give way.

Think then not indeed that God fails in his promise to his apostles;—verily, God is mighty, the Lord of vengeance; on the day when the earth shall be changed for another earth, and the heavens too; and (all) shall go forth unto God, the one, the dominant.

[50] Thou shalt see the sinners on that day bound together in fetters; with shirts of pitch, and fire covering their faces;—that God may reward each soul according to what it has earned; verily, God is swift at reckoning up!

This is a message to be delivered to men that they may be warned thereby, and know that only He is God,—one,—and that those who have minds may remember.

The Chapter of El '*Hagr*[1].

(XV. Mecca.)

In the name of the merciful and compassionate God!

A. L. R. Those are the signs[2] of the Book and of a perspicuous Qur'ân.

Many a time will those who disbelieve fain they had been resigned[3].

---

[1] El '*Hagr*, literally, 'the rock:' the Petra of Strabo, and the traditional habitation of 'the people of Thamûd.'

[2] Verses.

[3] See note 1, p. 15.

Leave them to eat and enjoy themselves and let hope beguile them, but they at length shall know!

We never destroyed a city without it had its noted doom.

[5] No nation can hasten on its appointed time, nor put it off.

But they say, 'O thou to whom the Reminder has been sent down! verily, thou art possessed. Why dost thou not bring us the angels if thou dost tell the truth?'

We sent not down the angels save by right; nor even then would these be respited.

Verily, we have sent down the Reminder, and, verily, we will guard it.

[10] And we sent before thee among the sects of those of yore. But there never came an apostle to them but they mocked at him. Such conduct also will we put into the hearts of the sinners. They will not believe therein, but the course of those of yore is run. But had we opened to them a door of the sky and they had mounted up into it all the while; [15] then also had they said, 'Our eye-sight is only intoxicated; nay, we are an enchanted people!'

And we have placed in the sky the signs of the zodiac, and have made them seemly to the beholders; and we have guarded them from every pelted devil[1]; save from such as steal a hearing, and there follows him an obvious shooting-star.

And the earth we have stretched out and have thrown on it firm mountains, and have caused to

[1] See note 2, pp. 50, 51.

grow upon it of everything a measured quantity.
[20] And we have made for you means of livelihood
therein, and for those for whom ye have not to
provide.

Nor is there aught but the treasuries of it are with us, and we do not send it down save in a noted quantity.

And we send forth the impregnating winds[1], and we send down water from the sky, and we give it to you to drink, nor is it ye who store it up.

And we, verily, we quicken and kill; and we are of (all things) heirs.

And we already know the foremost of you, and we know the laggards too!

[25] And, verily, it is your Lord who will gather you; verily, He is wise and knowing.

And we did create man from crackling clay of black mud wrought in form.

And the *g*inns had we created before of smokeless fire.

And when thy Lord said to the angels, 'Verily, I am creating a mortal from crackling clay of black mud wrought into shape;

[30] 'And when I have fashioned it, and breathed into it of my spirit, then fall ye down before it adoring.'

And the angels adored all of them together, save Iblîs, who refused to be among those who adored.

He said, 'O Iblîs! what ails thee that thou art not among those who adore?'

---

[1] I. e. the winds that bring the rain-clouds and fertilise the earth.

Said he, 'I would not adore a mortal whom Thou hast created from crackling clay of black mud wrought into form.'

He said, 'Then get thee forth therefrom, and, verily, thou art to be pelted! [35] And, verily, the curse is upon thee until the day of judgment.'

Said he, 'O my Lord! respite me until the day when they shall be raised.' He said, 'Then, verily, thou art of the respited until the day of the noted time.'

He said, 'O my Lord! for that Thou hast seduced me I will surely make it seem seemly for them on earth, and I will surely seduce them all together; [40] save such of Thy servants amongst them as are sincere.' Said He, 'This is a right way against me. Verily, my servants thou hast no authority over, save over those who follow thee of such as are seduced: and, verily, hell is promised to them all together. It has seven doors; at every door is there a separate party of them.'

[45] Verily, those who fear God shall dwell amidst gardens and springs: 'Enter ye therein with peace in safety!' And we will strip off whatever ill-feeling is in their breasts; as brethren on couches face to face[1].

No toil shall touch them therein, nor shall they be brought forth therefrom.

Inform my servants that I am the pardoning, the merciful; [50] and that my woe is the grievous woe.

And inform them concerning Abraham's guests

[1] Because to turn their backs on each other would appear contemptuous.

when they entered in unto him and said, 'Peace!' he said, 'Verily, we are afraid of you.' They said, 'Be not afraid! verily, we give thee glad tidings of a knowing boy.' He said, 'Do ye give me this glad tidings although old age has touched me? give me the glad tidings then!' [55] They said, 'We give the glad tidings of the truth, then be not of those who despair!' He said, 'Who would despair of the mercy of his Lord save those who err?' He said, 'What is your business, O ye messengers?' They said, 'Verily, we are sent unto a sinful people; save only Lot's family, them will we save all together, [60] except his wife; we have decreed, verily, she shall be of those who linger.'

And when the messengers came unto Lot's family, he said, 'Verily, ye are a people whom I recognise not.' They said, 'Nay, but we have come to thee with that whereof they[1] did doubt. And we have brought thee the truth, and, verily, we speak the truth! [65] Travel then with thy family in the deep darkness of the night, and follow thou their rear; and let not any one of you turn round to look; but go on to where ye are bidden.'

And we decided for him this affair because the uttermost one of these people should be cut off on the morrow.

Then the people of the city came, glad at the tidings. Said he, 'Verily, these are my guests, therefore disgrace me not; but fear God, and put me not to shame.'

[70] They said, 'Have we not forbidden thee[2] everybody in the world?' He said, 'Here are

[1] I. e. thy people.

[2] I. e. to protect.

my daughters, if do it ye must.'—By thy life[1]! verily, they were surely in their intoxication blindly wandering on!—

And the noise caught them at the dawn. And we made the higher parts (of the cities) their lower parts, and rained down on them stones of baked clay. [75] Verily, in that is a sign to those who mark. And, verily, the (cities) are on a path that still remains[2]. Verily, in that is a sign to the believers.

And the fellows of the Grove[3] too were unjust; and we took vengeance on them, and, verily, they both[4] are for an obvious example.

[80] And the fellows of El '*H*agr[5] called the messengers liars, and we brought them our signs, but they therefrom did turn away. And they did hew them in the mountain houses to dwell in in safety.

But the noise caught them in the morn; and that which they had earned availed them naught.

[85] We did not create the heavens and the earth and all that is between them both, save in truth. And, verily, the Hour is surely coming; then do thou pardon with a fair pardon.

Verily, thy Lord He is the creator, the knowing! We have already brought thee Seven of the Repetition[6], and the mighty Qur'ân.

---

[1] Addressed to Mohammed.

[2] On the road from the territory of the Qurâis to Syria.

[3] The Midianites, who are spoken of as dwelling in a grove, and to whom Jethro, or, as he is called in the Qur'ân, Sho'hâib, was sent as an apostle; see p. 148.

[4] I. e. both Sodom and Midian.

[5] The tribe of Thamûd, see p. 146.

[6] The Opening Chapter, which contains seven verses, and is

Let not thine eyes strain after what we have allowed a few pairs of them[1] to enjoy, nor grieve for them; but lower thy wing[2] to the believers, and say, 'Verily, I am an obvious warner.'

[90] As we sent down (punishment) on the separatists[3] who dismember the Qur'ân.

But, by thy Lord! we will question them, one and all, about what they have done.

Therefore, publish what thou art bidden, and turn aside from the idolaters.

[95] Verily, we are enough for thee against the scoffers.

Who place with God other gods; but they at length shall know! And we knew that thy breast was straitened at what they say.

Then celebrate the praises of thy Lord, and be thou of those who adore.

And serve thy Lord until the certainty shall come to thee.

The Chapter of the Bee.

(XVI. Mecca.)

In the name of the merciful and compassionate God.

God's bidding will come; seek not then to hasten it on. Celebrated be His praises from what they join with Him!

---

named the Seven of Repetition (sab'h al Mathânî), from this passage, and because it is to be repeated on so many occasions.

[1] The unbelievers.

[2] Behave with humility and gentleness.

[3] Probably referring to the Jews and Christians who are here and elsewhere accused of mutilating and altering the Scriptures.

He sends down the angels with the Spirit at His bidding upon whom He will of His servants (to say), 'Give warning that there is no god but Me; Me therefore do ye fear.' He created the heavens and the earth in truth! Exalted be He above that which they join with Him!

He created man from a clot; and yet, behold, he is an open opponent!

[5] The cattle too have we created for you; in them is warmth and profit, and from them do ye eat.

In them is there beauty for you when ye drive them home to rest, and when ye drive them forth to graze. And they bear your heavy burdens to towns which ye could not otherwise reach, except with great wretchedness of soul;—verily, your Lord is kind and merciful.

And horses too, and mules, and asses, for you to ride upon and for an ornament.—He creates also what ye know not of. God's it is to show the path; from it some turn aside: but had He pleased He would have guided you one and all.

[10] He it is who sends down water from the sky, whence ye have drink, and whence the trees grow whereby ye feed your flocks.

He makes the corn to grow, and the olives, and the palms, and the grapes, and some of every fruit;—verily, in that is a sign unto a people who reflect.

And He subjected to you the night and the day, and the sun, and the moon, and the stars are subjected to His bidding. Verily, in that are signs to a people who have sense.

And what He has produced for you in the earth varying in hue, verily, in that is a sign for a people who are mindful.

He it is who has subjected the sea, that ye may eat fresh flesh therefrom; and ye bring forth from it ornaments which ye wear,—and thou mayest see the ships cleaving through it,—and that ye may search after His grace,—and haply ye may give thanks.

[15] And He has cast firm mountains on the earth lest it move with you; and rivers and roads; haply ye may be guided.

And landmarks; and by the stars too are they guided.

Is He who creates like him who creates not?—are they then unmindful?

But if ye would number the favours of God, ye cannot count them. Verily, God is forgiving, merciful.

God knows what ye keep secret, and what ye disclose.

[20] And those on whom ye call beside God cannot create anything, for they are themselves created. Dead, not living, nor can they perceive!

When shall they be raised?

Your God is one God, and those who believe not in the hereafter their hearts are given to denial, and they are big with pride!

Without a doubt God knows what ye keep secret and what ye disclose!

[25] Verily, He does not love those big with pride!

And when it is said to them, 'What is it that your Lord has sent down?' they say, 'Old folks' tales!'

Let them bear the burden of their sins entirely on the resurrection day, and some of the burdens of those whom they led astray without knowledge.—Aye! an ill burden shall they bear.

Those who were before them devised a stratagem, but God brought their building off its foundations, and the roof fell over them, and the torment came to them, from whence they could not perceive[1].

Then on the resurrection day He will put them to shame, and say, 'Where are your associates whom ye divided into parties about?' Those to whom knowledge is brought will say, 'Verily, disgrace to-day, and evil are upon the misbelievers!'

[30] Those whom the angels took away were wronging themselves; then they offered peace: 'We have done no evil.'—'Yea! verily, God knows what ye did. Wherefore enter ye the doors of hell, to dwell therein for aye; for ill is the resort of the proud.'

And it will be said to those who fear God, 'What is it that your Lord has sent down?' They will say, 'The best,' for those who do good, good in this world; but certainly the abode of the next is best, and surely pleasant is the abode of those who fear.

Gardens of Eden which they shall enter, beneath them rivers flow; therein shall they have what they please;—thus does God reward those who fear Him.

To those whom the angels take off in a goodly state they shall say, 'Peace be upon you! enter ye into Paradise for that which ye have done.'

[35] Do they expect other than that the angels should come to take them off, or that thy Lord's bidding should come?—thus did those before them; God did not wrong them; but it was themselves they wronged.

---

[1] Said to refer to the building and overthrow of the tower of Babel.

And the evil which they had done befel them, and that environed them at which they used to mock!

And those who associated (others with God) said, 'Had God pleased we had not served aught beside Him, neither we nor our fathers; nor had we prohibited aught without Him;'—thus did those before them: but have messengers aught to do but to deliver their message plainly?

We have sent in every nation an apostle (to say), 'Serve ye God, and avoid *Tâghût*!' and amongst them are some whom God has guided, and amongst them are some for whom error is due;—go ye about then on the earth, and behold how was the end of those who called (the apostles) liars!

If thou art ever so eager for their guidance, verily, God guides not those who go astray, nor have they any helpers.

[40] They swear by their most strenuous oath, 'God will not raise up him who dies.'—Yea! a promise binding on him true!—but most men do not know. To explain to them that which they disputed about, and that those who misbelieved may know that they are liars.

We only say unto a thing we wish, 'BE,' and it is.

But those who fled for God's sake, after they were wronged, we will surely establish them in this world with good things; but the hire of the future life is greater, if ye did but know.

Those who are patient, and upon their Lord rely!

[45] And we have not sent before thee any but men whom we inspire,—ask ye those who have the Reminder[1], if ye know not yourselves,—with mani-

[1] The Pentateuch and Gospels.

fest signs and with scriptures; and we have sent down the Reminder to thee too, that thou mayest explain to men what has been sent down to them, and haply they may reflect.

Are those who were so crafty in evil sure that God will not cleave open the earth with them, or bring them torment from whence they cannot perceive, or seize them in their going to and fro? for they cannot make Him helpless.

Or that He should seize them with a gradual destruction? for, verily, your Lord is kind, merciful.

[50] Do they not regard whatever thing God has created; its shadow falls on the right or the left, adoring God and shrinking up?

Whatever is in the heavens and in the earth, beast or angel, adores God; nor are they big with pride!

They fear their Lord above them, and they do what they are bidden.

And God says, 'Take not to two gods; God is only one; me then do ye fear!'

His is what is in the heavens and in the earth; to Him is obedience due unceasingly; other than God then will ye fear?

[55] And whatever favours ye have, they are from God; then, whenever distress touches you, unto Him ye turn for succour. Yet, when He removes the distress from you, lo! a party of you join partners with their Lord.

That they may disbelieve in what we have brought them and may enjoy,—but at length they shall know!

And they set aside for what they know not a

portion of what we have bestowed upon them [1].—By God! ye shall be questioned concerning that which ye have devised.

They make for God daughters;—celebrated be His praise!—and for themselves they like them not [2].

[60] When any one of them has tidings of a female child, his face is overclouded and black, and he has to keep back his wrath.

He skulks away from the people, for the evil tidings he has heard;—is he to keep it with its disgrace, or to bury it in the dust?—aye! evil is it that they judge!

For those who disbelieve in the future life is a similitude of evil: but for God is the loftiest similitude; for He is the mighty, the wise!

If God were to punish men for their wrong-doing He would not leave upon the earth a single beast; but He respites them until a stated time; and when their time comes they cannot put it off an hour, nor can they bring it on.

They set down to God what they abhor themselves; and their tongues describe the lie that 'good is to be theirs.' Without a doubt theirs is the Fire, for, verily, they shall be sent on there!

[65] By God! we sent (messengers) to nations before thee, but Satan made their works seemly to them, for he is their patron to-day, and for them is grievous woe!

---

[1] See note 2, p. 132.

[2] The Arabs used to call the angels 'daughters of God.' They, however, objected strongly (as do the modern Bedawîn) to female offspring, and used to bury their infant daughters alive. This practice Mohammed elsewhere reprobates. See p. 132, note 3.

We have only sent down to thee the Book, that thou mayest explain to them that which they did dispute about, and as a guidance and a mercy to a people who believe.

And God sends down water from the sky, and quickens therewith the earth after its death; verily, in that is a sign to a people who can hear.

Verily, ye have in cattle a lesson; we give you to drink from that which is in their bellies, betwixt chyme and blood,—pure milk,—easy to swallow for those who drink.

And of the fruit of the palms and the grapes ye take therefrom an intoxicant and a goodly provision; verily, in that is a sign to a people who have sense!

[70] And thy Lord inspired the bee, 'Take to houses in the mountains, and in the trees, and in the hives they build.

'Then eat from every fruit, and walk in the beaten paths of thy Lord;' there cometh forth from her body a draught varying in hue[1], in which is a cure for men; verily, in that are signs unto a people who reflect.

God created you; then He will take you to Himself; but amongst you are some whom He will thrust into the most decrepit age; so that he may not know aught that once he knew. Verily, God is knowing, powerful.

And God has preferred some of you over others in providing for you; but those who have been preferred will not restore their provision to those

[1] The Arab writers mention several varieties of honey differing in colour, and some of which are used as medicine.

whom their right hands possess[1] that they may share equally therein:—is it God's favours they gainsay?

And God has made for you from amongst yourselves wives, and has made for you from your wives sons and grandchildren; and has provided you with good things;—is it in vanity that they believe, while for God's favour they are ungrateful?

[75] And they serve beside God what cannot control for them any provision from the heavens or the earth, and have no power at all.

Do not then strike out parables for God! Verily, God knows, but ye do not know.

God has struck out a parable; an owned slave, able to do nothing; and one whom we have provided with a good provision, and who expends therefrom in alms secretly and openly:—shall they be held equal?—Praise be to God, most of them do not know!

And God has struck out a parable: two men, one of them dumb, able to do nothing, a burden to his lord; wherever he directs him he comes not with success; is he to be held equal with him who bids what is just and who is on the right way?

God's are the unseen things of the heavens and the earth; nor is the matter of the Hour aught but as the twinkling of an eye, or nigher still! Verily, God is mighty over all!

[80] God brings you forth out of the wombs of your mothers knowing naught; and He makes for you hearing, and sight, and hearts,—haply ye may give thanks!

---

[1] Their slaves.

Do they not see the birds subjected in the vault of the sky?—none holds them in but God: verily, in that is a sign unto a people who believe.

God made for you in your houses a repose; and made for you, of the skins of cattle, houses[1], that ye may find them light, on the day ye move your quarters and the day when ye abide; and from their wool, and from their fur, and from their hair come furniture and chattels for a season.

And God has made for you, of what He has created, shades; and has made for you shelters in the mountains; and He has made for you shirts to keep you from the heat, and shirts[2] to keep you from each other's violence:—thus does He fulfil His favours towards you,—haply ye yet may be resigned.

But if they turn their backs,—thine is only to preach thy plain message.

[85] They recognise the favours of God, and yet they deny them, for most men are ungrateful.

And on the day when we shall send from every nation a witness; then shall those who misbelieve not be allowed (to excuse themselves), and they shall not be taken back into favour.

And when those who join their partners with God say, 'Our Lord! these be our partners on whom we used to call beside Thee.' And they shall proffer them the speech, 'Verily, ye are liars!' And they shall proffer on that day peace unto God; and that which they had devised shall stray away from them.

---

1 'Tents' are called 'houses of hair' or 'of hide' by the desert Arabs.

2 Of mail.

[90] Those who misbelieve and turn folks off God's path, we will add torment to their torment, for that they were evildoers.

And on the day when we will raise up in every nation a witness against them from among themselves, and we will bring thee as a witness against these[1]; for we have sent down to thee a book explaining clearly everything, and a guidance, and a mercy, and glad tidings to the believers.

Verily, God bids you do justice and good, and give to kindred (their due), and He forbids you to sin, and do wrong, and oppress; He admonishes you, haply ye may be mindful!

Fulfil God's covenant when ye have covenanted, and break not your oaths after asseverating them, for ye thereby make God your surety; verily, God knows what ye do.

And be not like her who unravels her yarn, fraying it out after she hath spun it close, by taking your oaths for mutual intrigue, because one nation is more numerous than another; God only tries you therewith, but He will make manifest to you on the resurrection day that whereon ye did dispute[2].

[95] But had God pleased He would have made you one nation; but He leads astray whom He will, and guides whom He will;—but ye shall be questioned as to that which ye have done.

Take not therefore your oaths for mutual intrigue, lest a foot slip after being planted firmly, and ye

[1] The Meccans.

[2] The Arabs, like most half-savage tribes, used to consider superior numerical strength as entitling them to disregard a treaty.

taste of evil for that ye turned folks off the path of God, and for you there be mighty woe!

And sell not God's covenant for a little price; with God only is what is better for you, if ye did but know.

What ye have is spent, but what God has endures; and we will recompense the patient with their hire for the best deeds they have done.

Whoso acts aright, male or female, and is a believer, we will quicken with a goodly life; and we will recompense them with their hire for the best deeds they have done.

[100] When thou dost read the Qur'ân, ask refuge with God from Satan the pelted one[1].

Verily, he has no power over those who believe and who upon their Lord rely. His power is only over those who take him for a patron, and over the idolaters.

And whenever we change one verse for another, —God knows best what He sends down. They say, 'Thou art but a forger!'—Nay, most of them do not know. Say, 'The Holy Spirit[2] brought it down from thy Lord in truth, to stablish those who believe, and for a guidance and glad tidings to those who are resigned[3].'

[105] We knew that they said, 'It is only some mortal who teaches him.'—The tongue of him they lean towards is barbarous, and this is plain Arabic[4].

Verily, those who believe not in God's signs, God will not guide them, and for them is grievous woe.

---

[1] See p. 50, note 2. [2] Gabriel. [3] See p. 15, note 1.

[4] For an account of the persons supposed to have helped Mohammed in the compilation of the Qur'ân, see Introduction.

Only they are the forgers of a lie who believe not in God's signs; and these, they are the liars.

Whoso disbelieves in God after having believed, unless it be one who is forced and whose heart is quiet in the faith,—but whoso expands his breast to misbelieve,—on them is wrath from God, and for them is mighty woe!

That is because they preferred the love of this world's life to the next;—but, verily, God guides not the unbelieving people. [110] These are they on whose hearts, and hearing, and eyesight, God has set a stamp, and these, they are the careless. Without a doubt that in the next life they will be the losers.

Then, verily, thy Lord, to those who fled[1] after they had been tried, and then fought strenuously and were patient,—verily, thy Lord after that will be forgiving and merciful.

On the day every soul will come to wrangle for itself, and every soul shall be paid what it has earned, and they shall not be wronged.

God has struck out a parable: a city[2] which was safe and quiet, its provision came to it in plenty from every place, and then it denied God's favours, and God made it feel[3] the clothing of hunger and fear, for that which they had wrought.

And there came to them an apostle from amongst themselves, but they called him a liar, and the torment seized them, while yet they were unjust.

[115] Eat, then, from what God has provided

[1] The Ansârs. [2] Any town, but Mecca in particular.

[3] Literally, 'taste.'

you with, things lawful and good, and give thanks for the favours of God, if it be Him ye serve.

He has only forbidden you that which dies of itself, and blood, and the flesh of swine, and that which is devoted to other than God; but he who is forced, neither revolting nor transgressing, it is no sin for him: verily, God is forgiving and merciful.

And say not of the lie your tongues pronounce, 'This is lawful, and this is unlawful,' forging against God a lie; verily, those who forge against God a lie shall not prosper. A little enjoyment—then for them is grievous woe!

For those who are Jews we have forbidden what we have narrated to thee before[1]; we did not wrong them, but it was themselves they wronged.

[120] Then, verily, thy Lord to those who have done evil in ignorance and then repented after that and done aright,—verily, thy Lord afterwards is forgiving and merciful.

Verily, Abraham was a high priest[2], a 'Hanîf, and was not of the idolaters: thankful for His favours; He chose him and He guided him unto the right way.

And we gave him in this world good things; and, verily, in the next he will be among the righteous.

Then we inspired thee, 'Follow the faith of Abraham, a 'Hanîf, for he was not of the idolaters.'

[125] The Sabbath was only made for those who dispute thereon; but, verily, thy Lord will judge

[1] See p. 134.

[2] Some commentators take this word ummatan as equivalent to imâman, 'antistes,' and this interpretation I have followed. Others take it in its ordinary sense of 'nation;' but the use of the other epithets seems to favour the former interpretation.

between them on the resurrection day concerning that whereon they do dispute.

Call unto the way of thy Lord with wisdom and goodly warning; and wrangle with them in the kindest way; verily, thy Lord He knows best who has erred from His way, for He knows best the guided ones.

But if ye punish, punish (only) as ye were punished; but if ye are patient, it is best for those who are patient[1].

Be thou patient then; but thy patience is only in God's hands. Do not grieve about them; and be not in a strait at their craftiness;—verily, God is with those who fear Him, and with those who do well.

[1] This passage refers to the killing of 'Hamzah, Mohammed's uncle, at the battle of O'hod, and the subsequent mutilation of his corpse by the Meccans, and is a protest against taking too severe a revenge.

TRANSLITERATION OF ORIENTAL ALPHABETS ADOPTED FOR THE TRANSLATIONS OF THE SACRED BOOKS OF THE EAST.

CONSONANTS.	MISSIONARY ALPHABET.			Sanskrit.	Zend.	Pehlevi.	Persian.	Arabic.	Hebrew.	Chinese.
	I Class.	II Class.	III Class.							
Gutturales.										
1 Tenuis	k	...	...	क	𐬐	[illegible]	ک	ك	כּ	k
2 " aspirata	kh	...	...	ख	𐬑	[illegible]	...	...	כ	kh
3 Media	g	...	...	ग	𐬔	[illegible]	گ	...	גּ	...
4 " aspirata	gh	...	...	घ	𐬖	[illegible]	...	...	ג	...
5 Gutturo-labialis	q	...	...	...	...	...	ق	ق	ק	...
6 Nasalis	ṅ (ng)	...	...	ङ	{𐬣 (ng) / 𐬧 (N)}	...	...	...	...	...
7 Spiritus asper	h	...	...	ह	𐬵 (𐬓 *hv*)	[illegible]	ه	ه	ה	h, hs
8 " lenis	'	...	...	...	...	...	ا	ا	א	...
9 " asper faucalis	ʻh	...	...	...	...	...	ح	ح	ח	...
10 " lenis faucalis	ʼh	...	...	...	...	...	ع	ع	ע	...
11 " asper fricatus	...	*ʻh*	...	...	...	...	خ	خ	ח	...
12 " lenis fricatus	...	*ʼh*	...	...	...	...	غ	غ	...	...
Gutturales modificatae (palatales, &c.)										
13 Tenuis	...	*k*	...	च	𐬗	[illegible]	چ	...	...	*k*
14 " aspirata	...	*kh*	...	छ	...	...	...	...	...	*kh*
15 Media	...	*g*	...	ज	𐬘	[illegible]	ج	ج	...	...
16 " aspirata	...	*gh*	...	झ	...	...	غ	غ	...	...
17 " Nasalis	...	*ñ*	...	ञ	...	...	...	...	...	...

CONSONANTS (*continued*).	MISSIONARY ALPHABET. I Class.	II Class.	III Class.	Sanskrit.	Zend.	Pehlevi.	Persian.	Arabic.	Hebrew.	Chinese.
18 Semivocalis	y	...	...	य	𐬌𐬌 [illegible] init.	[illegible]	ي	ي	י	y
19 Spiritus asper	...	($\acute{y}$)	...	...	...	...	...	...	...	...
20 „ lenis	...	($\grave{y}$)	...	...	...	...	...	...	...	...
21 „ asper assibilatus	...	*s*	...	श	𐬱	[illegible]	ش	ش	...	...
22 „ lenis assibilatus	...	*z*	...	...	𐬲	[illegible]	ژ	...	...	*z*
Dentales.										
23 Tenuis	t	...	...	त	𐬙	[illegible]	ت	ت	תּ	t
24 „ aspirata	th	...	...	थ	𐬚	...	...	...	ת	th
25 „ assibilata	...	...	TH	...	...	...	ث	ث	...	...
26 Media	d	...	...	द	𐬛	[illegible]	د	د	דּ	...
27 „ aspirata	dh	...	...	ध	𐬜	...	...	...	ד	...
28 „ assibilata	...	...	DH	...	...	...	ذ	ذ	...	...
29 Nasalis	n	...	...	न	𐬥	[illegible]	ن	ن	נ	n
30 Semivocalis	l	...	...	ल	...	[illegible]	ل	ل	ל	l
31 „ mollis 1	...	*l*	...	ळ	...	...	...	...	...	...
32 „ mollis 2	...	...	L	...	...	...	...	...	...	...
33 Spiritus asper 1	s	...	...	स	𐬯	[illegible]	س (ث)	س	שׁ	s
34 „ asper 2	...	...	s (ʃ)	...	...	...	...	...	ס	...
35 „ lenis	z	...	...	...	𐬰	[illegible]	ز (ذ)	ز	ז	z
36 „ asperrimus 1	...	...	z (ʒ)	...	...	...	ص	ص	צ	ʒ, ʒh
37 „ asperrimus 2	...	...	ẓ (ʒ)	...	...	...	ض	...	...	...

	I	II	III	Sanskrit	Zend	Pehlevi	Persian	Arabic	Hebrew	Chinese
Dentales modificatae (linguales, &c.)										
38 Tenuis	...	*t*	....	ट	....	...	ط	ط	ט	...
39 „ aspirata	...	*th*	....	ठ	....	...	ظ	ظ	...	...
40 Media	...	*d*	....	ड	𐬛	𐬛	...	...	...	...
41 „ aspirata	...	*dh*	....	ढ	....	...	...	ض	...	...
42 Nasalis	...	*n*	....	ण	𐬣	...	...	...	...	...
43 Semivocalis	r	...	....	र	𐬭	), ل, ا	ر	ر	ר	...
44 „ fricata	...	*r*	....	...	....	...	...	...	...	*r*
45 „ diacritica	...	...	R	...	....	...	...	...	...	...
46 Spiritus asper	sh	...	....	ष	𐬴	𐬴	...	...	...	sh
47 „ lenis	zh	...	....	...	....	...	...	...	...	...
Labiales.										
48 Tenuis	p	...	....	प	𐬞	𐬞	پ	...	פּ	p
49 „ aspirata	ph	...	....	फ	....	...	...	...	פ	ph
50 Media	b	...	....	ब	𐬠	𐬠	ب	ب	בּ	...
51 „ aspirata	bh	...	....	भ	....	...	...	...	ב	...
52 Tenuissima	...	*p*	....	...	....	...	...	...	...	...
53 Nasalis	m	...	....	म	𐬨	𐬨	م	م	מ	m
54 Semivocalis	w	...	....	...	𐬰	...	...	...	...	w
55 „ aspirata	hw	...	....	...	....	...	...	...	...	...
56 Spiritus asper	f	...	....	...	𐬟	𐬟	ف	ف	...	f
57 „ lenis	v	...	....	व	𐬬	1, 𐬬	و	و	ו.	...
58 Anusvâra	...	*m*	....	अं	𐬆 ã	...	...	...	...	...
59 Visarga	...	*h*	....	अः	....	...	...	...	...	...

VOWELS.	Missionary Alphabet. I Class.	II Class.	III Class.	Sanskrit.	Zend.	Pehlevi.	Persian.	Arabic.	Hebrew.	Chinese.
1 Neutralis	0	...	...	...	...	...	...	...	ֲ	ă
2 Laryngo-palatalis	ĕ	...	...	...	...	...	...	...	...	...
3 " labialis	ŏ	...	...	...	...	𐭠 fin.	...	...	...	...
4 Gutturalis brevis	a	...	...	अ	𐬀	𐬀 init.	َ	َ	ַ	a
5 " longa	â	(*a*)	...	आ	𐬁	𐬀	َا	َا	ָ	â
6 Palatalis brevis	i	...	...	इ	𐬌	...	ِ	ِ	ִ	i
7 " longa	î	(*i*)	...	ई	𐬍	ى	ِي	ِي	ִי	î
8 Dentalis brevis	*li*	...	...	ऌ	...	...	...	...	...	...
9 " longa	*lî*	...	...	ॡ	...	...	...	...	...	...
10 Lingualis brevis	*ri*	...	...	ऋ	...	...	...	...	...	...
11 " longa	*rî*	...	...	ॠ	...	...	...	...	...	...
12 Labialis brevis	u	...	...	उ	𐬎	...	ُ	ُ	ֻ	u
13 " longa	û	(*u*)	...	ऊ	𐬏	𐭅	ُو	ُو	וּ	û
14 Gutturo-palatalis brevis	e	...	...	...	𐬆(e) 𐬈(*e*)	...	...	...	ֶ	e
15 " longa	ê (ai)	(*e*)	...	ए	𐬉, 𐬇	ى	َيْ	َيْ	ֵ	ê
16 Diphthongus gutturo-palatalis	âi	(*ai*)	...	ऐ	...	...	َيْ	َيْ	...	âi
17 " "	ei (ĕi)	...	...	...	...	...	...	...	...	ei, êi
18 " "	oi (ŏu)	...	...	...	...	...	...	...	...	...
19 Gutturo-labialis brevis	o	...	...	...	𐬊	...	...	...	ָ	o
20 " longa	ô (au)	(*o*)	...	ओ	𐬋	𐭅	...	...	וֹ	...
21 Diphthongus gutturo-labialis	âu	(*au*)	...	औ	𐬃𐬎 (*au*)	...	َوْ	َوْ	...	âu
22 " "	eu (ĕu)	...	...	...	...	...	...	...	...	...
23 " "	ou (ŏu)	...	...	...	...	...	...	...	...	...
24 Gutturalis fracta	ä	...	...	...	...	...	...	...	...	...
25 Palatalis fracta	ï	...	...	...	...	...	...	...	...	...
26 Labialis fracta	ü	...	...	...	...	...	...	...	...	ü
27 Gutturo-labialis fracta	ö	...	...	...	...	...	...	...	...	...